Pulse of the People

AMERICAN GOVERNANCE: POLITICS, POLICY, AND PUBLIC LAW

Series Editors:
Richard Valelly, Pamela Brandwein, Marie Gottschalk, Christopher Howard

A complete list of books in the series is available from the publisher.

PULSE *of the* PEOPLE

Political Rap Music and Black Politics

Lakeyta M. Bonnette

PENN

UNIVERSITY OF PENNSYLVANIA PRESS

PHILADELPHIA

Published by
University of Pennsylvania Press
Philadelphia, Pennsylvania 19104-4112
www.upenn.edu/pennpress

Printed in the United States of America
on acid-free paper

10 9 8 7 6 5 4 3 2 1

Library of Congress Cataloging-in-Publication Data

Bonnette, Lakeyta M. (Lakeyta Monique), 1981–, author.
   Pulse of the people : political rap music and black politics / Lakeyta M. Bonnette.
      pages   cm—(American governance: politics, policy, and public law)
   Includes bibliographical references and index.
   ISBN 978-0-8122-4684-1
   1. Rap (Music)—Political aspects—United States—History—20th century. 2. Rap (Music)—Political aspects—United States—History—21st century. 3. African Americans—Politics and government—20th century. 4. African Americans—Politics and government—21st century. 5. African Americans—Political activity—History—20th century. 6. African Americans—Political activity—History—21st century. 7. African Americans—Attitudes—History—20th century. 8. African Americans—Attitudes—History—21st century. I. Title. II. Series: American governance.
   ML3918.R37B66   2015
   782.421649'1599—dc23   2014040779

This book is dedicated to my family; there is no greater group of people. Specifically, I dedicate this book to Lorenzo Bailey, Jahzari Nelson, Imani Bailey, Frances Bonnette, Barney Allen, Tiffany Bonnette-Wallington and Terence Wallington. Thank you for holding me down, for supporting me, for being patient and helping me when I most needed it. I love you all very much!

Contents

Watch for the Hook

Scholars of popular music treat it as a truism that African Americans have always turned to music to voice their discontent, their grievances, and their outrage.
—Zillman et al., "Radical Rap: Does It Further Ethnic Division?" 1–2

Y'all got me, well I got y'all, long as I know y'all listenin
I'ma always bring food for thought to the table in the kitchen
—Big Boi of Outkast, War, *Speakerboxx*

In 2006, comedian Dave Chappelle released *Dave Chappelle's Block Party*, a documentary chronicling a 2004 concert he produced in Brooklyn, New York. Featuring socially and politically conscious rap artists such as Dead Prez, Erykah Badu, The Roots, The Fugees, Lauryn Hill, Talib Kweli, Kanye West, Common, and Yasiin Bey, formerly known as Mos Def, the secret and free event was easily the rap concert of the year. It was reminiscent of the many street rap battles that existed on New York corners when Hip-Hop first came into existence. Chapelle is a vocal fan of not only Hip-Hop but political rap in particular, and his documentary features interviews with Dead Prez and Fred Hampton, Jr., son of slain Black Panther Fred Hampton Sr. During a performance by New York rap artist and half of the duo Black Star (with rapper Talib Kweli) Yasiin Bey,[1] Hampton took to the stage briefly to remind the concert goers to continue supporting and fighting for the release of political prisoners. Now rewind about forty years when Fred Hampton, Sr., also advocated "power to the people" and used music to

facilitate discussions about the importance of supporting political prisoners. Clearly, Hip-Hop has a strong relationship with political and social
issues.

As I settled in my seat to watch *Block Party* for the first time, I had no
great expectations and was only looking for entertainment and distraction
from the analytical life of a graduate student. This movie, however, had
the opposite effect: instead of surrendering to mind-numbing pleasure, I
immediately begin to think of activities I could orchestrate, support, and
participate in to advance political equality in America for African Americans. I found myself invigorated and excited even after I left the theater.
Could this euphoric, contemplative, and politically charged feeling stem
from exposure to political rap music? Yes, this film definitely primed certain
views and attitudes in me.

It was not Chappelle, his comedy, or his commentary that inspired me,
but rather the lyrics that were passionately spoken and sung. At a time when
many believed that using culture as a resistance mechanism was a dying
aspect of the rap genre, this film reasserted the importance of culture—and
specifically rap music—in Blacks' continual demand for political inclusion.
Thus, I wondered, was I the only one to leave the theater feeling as if he had
been charged with righting the political wrongs of the world? Or would
exposure to this type of music have a similar impact upon others? Does rap
music influence an individual's attitude and/or behavior? In light of my
personal transformation, I was willing to argue for the affirmative. Specifically, it is my contention that exposure to political rap not only provides
political information but also impacts specific political attitudes of those
exposed. In this book I examine how one form of "everyday talk" influences
public opinion and political behavior (Harris-Lacewell 2004).

Like the Black Arts Movement, Hip-Hop was initially seen as the cultural extension of politics in the Black community. Within the Hip-Hop
culture of break dancing, disc-jockeying, rapping, and graffiti, one could
observe the political sentiments, issues, and desires of the urban Black community. Currently, the Hip-Hop genre has expanded from its original space
of urban northern communities into a commercial worldwide subculture.
Yet, it is still effective as a cultural platform from which its artists can advocate for the involvement and resistance of those who are marginalized and
alienated in the United States and abroad. Hip-Hop is still a vehicle that
teaches the world about places in America that progress has neglected,
where mouths go hungry and the American Dream is nearly impossible.
Inhabitants of this community need not share gender or race, but rather

only be accustomed to marginalization and oppression from political and economic institutions.

Cathy Cohen details the concepts of marginalization and secondary marginalization in *Boundaries of Blackness* (1999). Marginal groups are "those who exist politically, socially or economically outside of dominant norms and institutions" (37). It can be argued that the Black community became more ostracized when increased poverty in America led to increased geographical separation in America. These poverty differences were observed most prominently in housing segregation and education (Wilson 1978; Kozol 1991). As a result of the Civil Rights Acts, which prohibited housing discrimination, many White Americans abandoned the country's inner cities and other areas where Black population was increasing. The exodus of White Americans to the suburbs was dubbed "White flight." It resulted in de facto segregation that was not only evident in communities, but also in the public school demographics, thus ensuring continued segregation and marginalization of Blacks (Wilson 1987).

Cohen goes farther by introducing secondary marginalization, particularly of gay African Americans in the Black community. She describes how the issue of HIV/AIDS was not addressed in the Black community as in White communities, especially gay White communities, because of the secondary marginalization of gay Blacks and the framing of HIV/AIDS as a "gay" disease. I argue that the secondary marginalization that was experienced by gay and lesbian African Americans is also being applied to the Hip-Hop community. Often issues and concerns of the Hip-Hop community, specifically urban youth, are ignored or dismissed until they become salient within the larger Black community. This submarginalized group has embraced and utilized rap music as a method, space, and organizing tactic not only to fight injustice but to also voice their opinions, detail their grievances, and express their outrage. As a form of resistance "oppressed people use language, dance and music to mock those in power, express rage, and produce fantasies of subversion" (Rose 1994: 99). This book examines the utilization of the cultural form of rap music as a resistance tactic that influences the support and adoption of particular Black political attitudes that can affect political behavior and issue saliency. Specifically, I am interested in the impact of rap music and its psychological role in political attitude formation.

Rap music, which represents a source of political information for a segment of the population, has the ability to affect the political attitudes and knowledge of its listeners. Tricia Rose explains that rap is a voice for the

concerns of inner city youth. She states that rap has "articulated the pleasures and problems of Black urban life in contemporary America" (Rose
1994: 2). Not only has rap recently experienced an increase in the diversity
of its audience, but it has also seen an increase in the political activities of
rap artists. In 2001 Michael Dawson demonstrated in his research "that
both exposure to rap music and the belief that it constitutes an important
resource of the Black community play substantial roles in shaping Black
political opinion both directly and indirectly" (Dawson 2001: 78).

Public opinion research covers various subtopics, including attitude formation and attitude change, the importance of ideology, and the study of
how opinions are formed, measured, and asserted. The prevailing assumption in the field is that the public does not have consistent and stable opinions or attitudes about most political issues. Essentially, many political
analysts conclude that the majority of Americans are willfully and woefully
uninformed. In contrast, other public opinion research suggests that the
masses do have organized and specific attitudes about certain public issues
as well as possess definitive attitudes about government actions and political leaders (Hurwitz and Peffley 1987; Zaller 1992; Lodge, Steenbergen, and
Brau 1995). Specifically, this book lays a foundation for the study between
political rap music and public opinion research, particularly observing the
acceptance of Black political attitudes. My research adds to the debate about
information sources, the voice of political groups, political responsiveness
and the importance of public opinion.

In order to understand attitude formation, we must examine the various models and theories of attitude adoption that have been presented in
the past. Chapter 1 begins this discussion by detailing several theories of
political attitude formation and adoption. For instance, many have supported schema theory (Hurwitz and Peffley 1987; Kuklinski et al. 1991),
bounded rationality, or the use of mental shortcuts (Lodge, McGraw, and
Stroh 1989; Sniderman et al. 1991; Lupia 1994), and the associative networks model (Park and Hastie 1986) to explain attitude formation. Chapter
1 also presents the criteria for identifying political rap music, a specific
subgenre of rap music.

In Chapter 2, I examine the history of culture as a resistance mechanism
within both the Black community and other oppressed communities. The
role of music as a means to discuss politics demonstrates precisely what
Melissa Harris-Lacewell (2004) detailed in her book, *Barbershops, Bibles,
and BET*; when observing communities of color that have a history of alienation from the political system, one must study media outlets, cultural

forms, establishments, or institutions within the community to understand how political information is disseminated, acquired, and used to form opinions. This chapter provides a history of rap music and its relationship and extension from other cultural and political vehicles in Black America.

In the succeeding chapters, I examine empirically the relationship between exposure to political rap and Black Nationalist and Black Feminist ideologies. I begin with a quick recap of statistics of rap music exposure as well as lyrical analysis of rap songs that espouse Black Nationalist and Black Feminist attitudes. These lyrical analyses demonstrate that the most important unit of analysis when addressing the relationship between culture and political attitudes is in fact the songs and not the artists. This research differs in that it does not use the artists and their particular ideological stances (if known) or categorizations to determine the type of message that is presented, but instead directly examines the lyrics. This method recognizes that a single artist can make a variety of music instead of being confined to a subgenre specified label. Chapter 3 examines the relationship between rap music, specifically political rap, and Black Nationalism, while Chapter 4 delves into the relationship between rap music and Black Feminist attitudes.

Finally, in Chapter 5, I discuss the political behavior of rap artists and those who are a part of the Hip-Hop community to demonstrate ways political attitudes asserted in music have been transformed into direct action and behavior. In this last segment of the book I detail examples of the Hip-Hop community's involvement in social movements, whether by offering monetary support or by donating time and other resources.[2] I discuss the major effects that members of the Hip-Hop community, including rappers, have had on the formation of organizations which fight for the rights of those that are marginalized in American society and alienated from the political system, specifically young, urban African Americans.[3] I discuss at length Hip-Hop's integral role in elections, including the 2008 and 2012 elections of President Obama. Hip-Hop community members have been involved in electoral politics from rap artists running for office to campaigning with politicians to quietly endorsing candidates at their shows and venues. As I will show, Hip-Hop is not a monolithic cultural genre, and it indeed has a very diverse relationship with political attitudes and participation.

Chapter 1

Behind the Music: Black Political Attitudes and Rap Music

> By searching too narrowly for signs of political consciousness and revolutionary activity among slaves and freed people, we have missed other manifestations of their group consciousness, sense of pride, and use of their culture to define themselves and comment upon their status.
> —Lawrence W. Levine, "African American Music as Resistance," in *African American Music* 2006: 587

> Uh, one thing 'bout music
> When it hit you feel no pain
> White folks say it controls your brain
> I know better than that
> That's game and we ready for that
> —M1 of Dead Prez, "Hip-Hop," *Let's Get Free*

> C'mon baby light my fire
> Everything you drop is so tired
> Music is supposed to inspire
> How come we ain't gettin no higher?
> —Lauryn Hill, "Superstar," *The Mis-Education of Lauryn Hill*

In 2005, Chicagoan rap artist Kanye West, one of Hip-Hop's most defiant and politically incorrect rappers, decided to deviate from the teleprompter before him and instead voice his opinion on live television during a fundraiser for the victims of Hurricane Katrina and the rebuilding of New Orleans. When it was his turn to speak, West publicly stated "George Bush doesn't like Black people." The shocking comment caught the co-host of the telethon, Michael Myers, and the producers by surprise. After days of watching Black people in New Orleans wade through filthy water, beg to be saved from their flooded homes, and be referred to as "refugees," West was simply stating the opinion of many Blacks. From West's and many other Black Americans' perspectives, the government could not possibly care about the displacement and agony the victims of hurricane Katrina, residents of New Orleans, experienced, based on its response. West identified former President Bush as the main culprit because he, as the nation's chief executive, represented the American government. While the lack of efficient government response to its citizens shocked the world, many African Americans viewed the Federal Emergency Management Agency's inept response as simply another link in the chain of political exclusion, lack of support and disregard experienced by a marginalized community. Even before West made his statement, the slow response had been framed as a racial and class issue. In homes, barbershops, beauty salons, churches, around water coolers, and in other gathering spots the sentiment was that if the disaster had occurred in a city where the majority of residents affected had been white and middle class, the response would have been completely different.[1]

West was following a tradition of musicians who used their popularity and celebrity status to speak for those whose voices and concerns are often not considered (Iton 2008). From Scott Joplin to Marvin Gaye to, now, Kanye West, there has been a history of African American celebrities using their notoriety to demand a seat at the political table to advocate against injustice and provide a voice for the voiceless. Billie Holiday's "Strange Fruit" about lynching of Blacks or Sam Cooke's "A Change Is Gonna Come" are examples of discussions about the government's lack of response to African Americans in a time of need. Thus, Blacks have used both overt and covert cultural measures to resist injustice and demand equality.

Many white viewers were shocked to hear West express his discontent with the government's lack of response to the catastrophe that occurred in New Orleans in the aftermath of hurricane Katrina. West's words echoed the sentiment not only on behalf of a specific racial and economic group, but also those of a generation that is often viewed as apathetic in terms of political attitudes, ideologies, and participation: the Hip-Hop generation.

It is posited that "Black music may be viewed as a symbolization of the Black experience" (Walker 1975: 2). One can gain an understanding of the various struggles and issues encountered by Blacks throughout their history in America by studying various forms of Black music during different eras. Culture—specifically Black music—historically has been a resistance mechanism that Blacks utilized to assert their visibility in arenas whose majority players deemed them invisible. Blacks have used culture to disseminate information, increase solidarity, fight against injustice, and maintain political and social movements. This is evident in the illegal demonstration by rapper Yasiin Bey, formerly known as Mos Def, outside the 2006 VMAs; he protested, again, the lack of response in New Orleans after Hurricane Katrina. Similarly, Marvin Gaye decided to discuss more political issues in his songs, including anti-Vietnam war sentiments and the refusal of Ray Charles to sing in segregated Georgia (Iton 2008; Spence 2011). Culture has allowed those who typically do not have a voice to assert their demands in political and social spheres from which they were typically ostracized. Music in the Black community has always represented a counter-public or as Spence (2011) states, a "parallel public" (9), for ideas and attitudes of this community, and has been significant to resistance struggles for African Americans (Spence 2011; Ogbar 2007; Levine 2006; Norfleet 2006; Harris-Lacewell 2004; Pough 2004a).

From its beginnings in New York, rap has been a vehicle for the young and disenfranchised. Early on it provided dispatches from America's crumbling inner cities ravaged by crack cocaine, violence, and apathy from elected officials. It has evolved into a multi-billion dollar industry, whose stars accumulate wealth that its pioneers could only have imagined. Rap is used to sell everything from Hillshire Farms meat to sneakers and cars (Ogbar 2007). Yet in 2013, the political and economic circumstances which gave rise to this music genre persist.

Political rap, a subgenre of the larger rap genre, follows the model of uniting African Americans through music by discussing issues relevant to the Black community and providing information about injustices the community members face. Michael Dawson (1999: 322) states, "rap has become an integral part of a grapevine that is constantly critiquing the state of American race relations." Summarily, the music of the Hip-Hop generation is critical for knowledge, awareness, mobilization, and action. Rap has a future as a political agent. In fact, Gwendolyn Pough (2004: 194) contends that "rap's ability to move the crowd has the possibility to do more than make them dance; it could very well be used to spark political activism." However, there is still debate over how much impact music has on the political attitudes of a listener (Henry 1990).

For example, Lester Spence (2011) argues that rap does impact Black political attitudes but not always in the direction proponents of Hip-Hop suggest. Spence argues that there is a relationship between rap consumption and support of Black Nationalist tenets as well as a heightened criticism of the American legal system. He also concludes that those who consume rap are more xenophobic. But Spence's primary argument is that rap music follows or recreates neoliberal attitudes and not specifically radical attitudes.

Cathy Cohen (2010) finds in her research that exposure to rap music also affects the political attitudes of youth. Specifically, those who are exposed to rap assert more alienation from the political system, but many youth do not think that rap music should be more political.

These analyses are excellent and represent initial examinations of the influence of rap on political attitudes. However, this research does lack a crucial element that will allow political scientists, politicians, and music artists to make a more concrete decision about how much rap music influences political attitudes and that is the differentiation of subgenres of rap music. One cannot discuss rap as if it is a homogeneous genre espousing one set of views and attitudes. Like the Black community, variations within Hip-Hop demand separate analysis. Rap, depending on the song produced and the lyrics created, can have various effects on the political attitudes and behaviors of the Black community. To accurately evaluate whether rap affects specific political ideologies, we must observe the impact of political rap separately.

Politics of Exclusion

Why should we observe culture in the Black community as a possible avenue for influencing political behaviors and attitudes? For many reasons, culture influences the political exclusion and consistent political neglect of certain segments of American society. America is seen as the place where upward mobility, even for the most downtrodden, is absolutely possible. Americans love a "rags to riches" story and revere anyone perceived to have "pulled themselves up by the bootstraps." Each year, tens of thousands of people come to the United States seeking "The American Dream"—a good job, house in the suburbs, two cars, 2.5 children, vacations once a year to a sandy locale, and complete access to the political system. It goes without saying that many people, native and immigrant, find a different reality. Historically, certain groups (Blacks, women, gays, Catholics, Germans, Irish, etc.) have been excluded from politics in the United States, often in opposition to the pluralist paradigm that everyone has equal access to the government. In fact, many have supported this claim of pluralism and full political incorporation for all U.S. citizens (Dahl 1961; Browning, Marshall, and Tabb 2003).

Both pluralist and coalition theories assert that all citizens are able to participate in the political system and be heard (Dahl 1961). Dahl contends that decision making and power are not relegated only to the economic notables, but that the democratic political system is a two-step decision-making process where officials can be held accountable to citizens. Browning, Marshall, and Tabb (2003) assert coalition theory as an alternative method to ensure political inclusion of marginalized voices. They argue that forming coalitions of minority groups with majority groups can ensure political considerations of those often not included in formal politics. Yet pluralism and coalition building are often rejected as theories of inclusion of minorities into the political system (Schnattsneider 1960; Bachrach and Baratz 1962). The pluralist theory is problematic because it does not take into account the lack of focus on issues that affect minority communities, and coalition building has been criticized as continued suppression of minority voices even among participants of political coalitions.

Hence, the political process is not as democratic and open as pluralists would contend. Pluralist theory asserts that everyone has equal opportunity to participate politically and have their issue represented in the political agenda of this country (Dahl 1961). But pluralism does not work for all communities, and those that comprise minority and lower class communities are often excluded from the traditional political world due to a lack of resources or knowledge of how to participate (Schnattsneider 1960; Bachrach and Baratz 1962).

Despite a growing Black middle class, many young people in urban areas have seen a decline in their communities rather than improvement. Older generations have ridiculed them, (e.g., Bill Cosby and Stanley Crouch) and taught them that no one cares about their voices (Cohen 2010). They are left with outlets such as rap to express their angst, anger, and disappointment at being left behind. This secondary marginalization makes it difficult to understand or identify the dominant problems of this segment of the Black community.[2]

Often, issues that resonate with the larger Black community are also issues of the Hip-Hop generation in general or Black youth in particular. Black youth have concerns about many moral issues including abortions, same-sex marriages and relationships, denigration of Black women, violence, and crime. However, according to Cohen (2010), Black youth suffer greater political alienation than youth of other races. Rarely do we analyze arenas where some of these concerns may be asserted by and about Black youth specifically.

Artists use music and culture as a means to detail the political neglect their marginalized communities experience. In contrast, marginalization gives mainstream America a reason not to listen to their voices. In fact, "members of marginal groups, even when granted the power of speech, find their voices devalued or disrespected, increasing their isolation and alienation from the public sphere" (Hancock 2004, 4). Indeed, the form of devaluation Hancock describes is prevalent in rap music as observed by the numerous attempts to censor rap as well as deem it as an illogical, turbulent, and nihilistic musical form. Two prominent examples in rap music's history demonstrate the use of censorship in the genre. The first is the banning of record sales for the Florida rap group 2 Live Crew, whose sales were banned for obscenity, and the second is the censoring and banning of Ice T.'s "Cop Killer," calling for parental advisory labels (Crenshaw 1991b; Johnson, Jackson, and Gatto 1995; Johnson, Trawalter, and Dovidio 2000; Rubin, West, and Mitchell 2001; Carpentier, Knobloch, and Zillmann 2003).

Looking more closely at the 2 Live Crew charges of obscenity, one can identify racial implications as well as the further silencing of marginalized voices. As Crenshaw (1991b) argues, 2 Live Crew's songs were not the only popular culture acts that suggested or lyrically presented lewd, lascivious, obscene, violent, or sexual acts and ideas. Yet they were the ones to face prosecution and be linked to sexual violence throughout the nation.[3] While most of their songs are not political by the criteria to be established in this book, the action taken by law enforcement and state politicians made the album and the case highly political, as it was believed to threaten freedom of expression.[4] One can observe a number of popular artists during this time (e.g., Madonna and George Michael), as well as a growing pornography industry that display a variety of sexual acts which could all have been deemed obscene. But Crenshaw (1991b) argues that what made Hip-Hop artists unique in their received charges was not specifically their lyrics or performances but a combination of all those things and fear of Black male hypersexuality that has roots in stereotypes of Black male and female sexual prowess and sexual appetite. Crenshaw argues that the prosecution of these artists was based not simply on obscenity but on White fear of the "Black Brute." Instead of criminalizing this group and rap music in general, we, as a nation should have observed the roots of sexual violence and disrespect of woman and Black women, specifically, historically in this country.

Thus, instead of allowing rap music to represent the voices of those who are oppressed, alienated, and marginalized, we group the entire genre as negative, violent, inaccurate, and a minstrelesque depiction of African Americans. While negative, stereotypical characterizations are typical images of Blacks presented in mainstream media outlets, political rap music acts as a counter-public for presenting alternative images. All rap music is not bad.

Importance of Black Counter-Publics

Safe spaces or counter-publics are important among marginalized individuals because they allow usually voiceless elements of society to assert their voices. There are numerous examples of Black people using safe places such as the church and the coded language of music to avoid retaliation from those who seek to oppress them. The church was first recognized as a safe space during the period of American slavery because it was the one place White people had no interest in monitoring (at least until the Nat Turner rebellion). In fact, it was assumed that church service during this time encouraged enslaved Africans to be content with their lot in life. Instead, church time was often used as a cover to discuss issues within the Black community that were not and could not be addressed by the plantation owners, to create laws, establish relationships, and validate each other's visibility and value, and to plan actions of rebellion and escape. The Black church has continued to represent a safe space for African Americans throughout various resistance movements in the U.S. One of the most prominent uses of the church as a safe space was during the Civil Rights

Movement. Churches were often used as meeting locations to discuss plans of resistance, spread community information of injustices, murders, kidnappings, births, and weddings, and serve as a place of motivation and worship.

While safe spaces existed, there was a racial connection that kept the spaces private and the language coded. The shared experiences of oppression and discrimination morphed into a phenomenon commonly referred to as "the Black experience," which united Blacks and created a space where they could discuss issues that specifically affected them and their political desires, opportunities, and progress.

Political scientists recognize safe spaces and the impact they have on assessing and observing accurate public opinion. For instance, studies have shown the impact appearance, dialect, and race of an interviewer may have on subject's responses (Kinder and Sanders 1996; Finkel, Gutterbock and Borg 1991; Davis 1997; Berinsky 1999). The best known qualitative demonstration of interviewer effects was observed during the Works Progress Administration (WPA) project to record slave narratives. Consistently, White interviewers heard a completely different description of life as a slave from Black interviewers. For instance, Blacks would temper their descriptions of slavery's hardships when speaking with White interviewers, but would offer the horrid details when speaking with Black interviewers. It has been demonstrated that the race of the interviewer when assessing political attitudes can lead to socially desirable responses among both Black and White subjects, who may fear sounding racist (among Whites) or unpatriotic (among Blacks) (Kinder and Sanders 1996; Finkel, Gutterbock, and Borg 1991; Davis 1997; Berinsky 1999). This phenomenon of "wearing the mask" or being politically correct may also have been a survival mechanism among American Blacks who feared being persecuted, ostracized, labeled, or murdered for expressing their true attitudes.

Similarly, Toure (Carmichael) and Hamilton also support and assert the importance of safe spaces among Blacks to ensure movements and political progress are not co-opted and destroyed before they occur. Often culture, particularly when not part of the mainstream, is utilized by oppressed groups as a safe space to discuss issues relevant to group members by asserting attitudes and issues that do not appear on the national agenda. One cultural element known as a safe space and a type of "everyday talk," a component of the Black information network is rap music (Harris-Lacewell

2004). This musical genre, because of its origins among Black and Latino youths, is a space that allows for the assertion of issues, attitudes, and feelings relevant to these communities. Therefore, rap constitutes an outlet of not only anger, joy, and satiric comedy, but also political and social attitudes of Black and Latino communities. Thus, rap music gives a submarginalized group the opportunity to assert its voice.

But these assertions and knowledge of marginalization do not demonstrate explicitly how oppressed groups' voices and attitudes continue to be eliminated from political consideration. One of the most important aspects of learning and knowing citizens' public opinion and to include these opinions in the larger political arena is to access their political attitudes and ideology. A study of Black political ideologies must begin with Black political attitudes, which are the essential elements of ideology. Attitudes lead to ideological formation.

Political Attitudes and Music

African Americans utilize informal avenues to receive the political information necessary for them to organize and create political attitudes that are often observable in public opinion and political behavior (Harris-Lacewell 2004). African Americans do not rely on mainstream media as the sole source of information but supplement it with outlets that offer a Black perspective, such as *Jet* and *Ebony* magazines, rap music, BET, and the *Tom Joyner Morning Show*. Melissa Harris-Lacewell (2004) contends that a combination of exposure to Black information sources leads to discussions that crystallize attitudes. I argue that political rap, alone, affects political attitudes by discussing relevant political issues of the Black community. Still one may ask, why rap music?

Hip-Hop has been studied in numerous fields, including marketing, psychology, communication, education, and sociology. Yet, political science has been slow to embrace and explore the art form, although many scholars suggest the political relevancy of music (Kofsky 1970; Henry 1990; Walker 1976; Dawson 1994; Henderson 1996; Walton and Smith 2000; Dawson 2001; Harris-Lacewell 2004; George 2005; Ogbar 2007; Cohen 2010; Spence 2011). With the exceptions of Errol Henderson (1996), Michael Dawson (2001), Melissa Harris-Lacewell (2004), Cathy Cohen (2010) and Lester Spence (2011) few scholars have completed research focused on rap music and its relationship with Black political attitudes. Other scholars, including Richard Iton (2008), have examined the relationship between music and politics, and Darren Davis and Christian Davenport have analyzed the effects of media, such as television and movies, on African American political attitudes (Davis and Davenport 1997).

The examination of rap music is situated in the literature of public opinion research as well as the politics of inclusion. In public opinion studies, media and culture are examined to assess influence on political information, ideologies and attitudes. Many have argued that rap music represents a "hidden transcript," a mechanism to assert public opinion and attitudes of the marginalized communities of urban Black and Latino youth. Rap music provides information, in addition to making issues salient that otherwise may not have garnered much attention outside minority communities. For example, seminal west coast gangster rap group NWA (Niggas with Attitude) accentuate the problem of police brutality in minority communities. Their infamous song "F the Police" resulted in memos from police departments and eventually the CIA. Because the song was deemed a threat to officers across the nation, more serious discussions occurred that questioned the significance, truth, and accuracy of police brutality in minority communities. Years later, rappers Jay-Z and Chamillionaire assisted in the discussions of police brutality and racial profiling with the very popular rap songs "99 Problems" and "Ridin' Dirty" respectively. Through these songs artists were able to demonstrate that issues that plagued the Black community, as publicized by NWA, and the Rodney King beating almost twenty-five years ago, were still relevant issues in urban communities today. Such issues include the current controversial New York police strategy of stop and frisk. An examination of how attitudes are formed, followed by an analysis of the influence of music on attitudes in general and on political attitudes specifically, is crucial.

Music as Media Source

There are numerous studies that discuss the relationship between media, attitude formation, and public opinion. Scholars have noted the role of media in agenda setting, priming, and framing political messages (Iyengar and Kinder 1987; Nelson and Kinder 1996). Chuck D has dubbed rap "the CNN of the inner city," a claim reasserted by Jay-Z with the lyric, "I give you the news, with a twist"[5] (Dawson 2001: 128; Spence 2011). Rap has been called a Black information source by many others (Decker 1993; Rose 1994, 2008; Henderson 1996; Harris-Lacewell 2004; Spence 2011), and it is therefore necessary that we observe the informational effects of rap music.

This research project examines the persuasive effects of rap music as a form of media on attitude formation and public opinion. Oskamp and Schultz (2005) detail that persuasive communication is the most popular way of changing and forming attitudes. In fact, they state that "all of our knowledge, beliefs, and attitudes come from others, and the great majority probably come from some mass communication medium (ranging from books to billboards to radio and television)" (202). If this is true, rap music, which is defined as "the art of verbal engagement intended to impress or *persuade* the listener" (Norfleet 2006: 355), should play a role in the formation or changing of an individual's attitude. Because Hip-Hop music is so popular, its influence on the attitude formation of individuals is important. Similarly, others have discussed the educational and socialization possibilities of rap music (Powell 1991). Particularly, Powell (245) asserts that "in addition to entertainment, rap music provides a significant form of informal education for adolescents, one that extends far beyond the confines of the classroom and into their peer group circles."

Attitude Formation

There have been many discussions about how attitudes are organized. One of the most popular is schema theory models. *Schema theory* posits that knowledge is abstracted from experience and organized hierarchically. Specifically, when a person receives information, whether new or old, it is organized according to preexisting beliefs. The new information is compared to the old, and the most accurate information, according to the individual, supersedes the other (Axelrod 1973). Four steps occur when new information is presented. Initially new information is modified if a belief is present. If no belief is present, then the attitude is accepted. Next, the information is clarified or understood by the individual, followed by organizing the attitude to fit with previous attitudes. This usually takes place by eliminating opposing views or modifying existing viewpoints in light of new information acquired. Finally, the new information is used to answer a question or provide an opinion. Hence, schema allows for the storage and organization of ideas and attitudes. Schemata or the ability to "actively process and store information and generate expectations about future events and actions" (Allen, Dawson, and Brown 1989: 422) vary depending on status, access to information sources, and ability to interpret and organize new information. Observing culture, "exposure to antisocial messages in rap music can activate and help maintain antisocial schemas and eventually manifest in measurable behavior" (Tyson 2006: 213). For instance, if you believe politicians do not care about your opinions and you listen to an artist such as Paris who asserts antigovernment messages in his lyrics, it is expected that your previous attitude would be bolstered through exposure to this type of music. Alternatively, if you do not have low efficacious attitudes about the U.S. government, it is plausible that exposure to Paris' song may change your attitude to one of low political efficacy.

William McGuire (1985) suggests in his *stage theory* that a message must go through seven stages to be considered persuasive: presentation, exposure, attention, comprehension, yielding, retention, and behavior. John Zaller (1992) contends that presentation, exposure, attention, and comprehension are all part of the reception stage; yielding is the same as acceptance; and retention and behavior comprise the sampling stage. Thus, his model has only three stages: reception, acceptance, and sampling. According to variations of McGuire's stage theory model, rap music is persuasive and should follow the path detailed by McGuire and condensed by Zaller. The key component of this chart is comprehension. Without comprehension the model would be void and there would not be any effects on behavior or attitude formation. Rap music must be comprehended by its audience in order to lead to the yielding stage. Thus, if an individual is exposed to rap but unable to comprehend the words or meanings then their attitude will not be impacted. However, with the current commodification of rap and urban terminology, many rap messages are no longer coded, covert, or hidden and fans are able to understand what the artists are conveying. Yielding should include acceptance of the beliefs followed by retention of the attitudes the music asserts. This will manifest in organization of attitudes into Black political ideologies and result in the behavior those attitudes or ideologies promote.

Figure 1 details how information should be organized when an individual receives it via exposure to a political rap song. Exposure to political rap will bring one's attention to the political issue discussed in the song. Using New York rap group Wu-Tang Clan's[6] rap song, "I Can't Go to Sleep," I

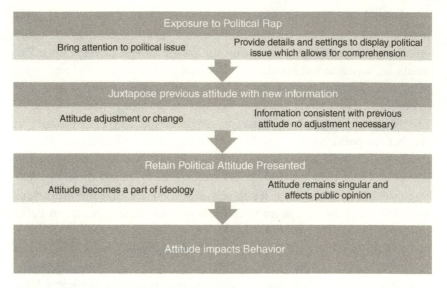

Figure 1. How music affects political attitudes and behavior.

detail how this song affects political attitudes and behaviors according to the figure. This song is interesting because it discusses a number of political and social issues. It opens with descriptions of police brutality, racial profiling, and interactions with the criminal justice system, specifically focusing on crack cocaine and possible government involvement with crack in the Black community. The second stanza deals with political assassinations and exportation of individuals known to be proponents of Blacks' civil rights. Based on the lyrics by rapper RZA (pronounced rizzah) the listener is informed about politically related assassinations. RZA raps,

> I can't go to sleep, I can't shut my eyes
> They shot the father at his mom's building seven times
> They shot Malcolm in the chest, front of his little seeds
> Jesse watched as they shot King on the balcony
> Exported Marcus Garvey cause he tried to spark us
> With the knowledge of ourselves and our forefathers
> Oh Jacqueline you heard the rifle shots crackling
> Her husband's head in her hands, you tried to put it back in
> America's watching, blood-stained ink blotches

Medgar took one to the skull for integrating college
What's the science? Somebody? This is trick knowledge
They try to keep us enslaved and still scrape for dollars

In this verse the listener is prompted to recall famous Black leaders. The first leader referenced is Clarence 13th X, who is known as the founder of the religious sect, the Nation of Gods and Earths (NG&E), and who was shot seven times and killed (Miyakawa 2005). The second leader referenced is Malcolm X (El Hajj Malik El-Shabazz), former leader and spokesperson of the Nation of Islam, who was assassinated in the Audubon Ballroom in 1965 in front of his wife and four children. Next, RZA mentions Martin Luther King, Jr., leader of the Southern Christian Leadership Conference (SCLC) and promoter of nonviolent resistance for the Civil Rights Movement (CRM) in the United States. King was assassinated at the Lorraine Motel in Memphis, Tennessee, in 1968 surrounded by civil rights leaders Jesse Jackson and Ralph Abernathy. RZA then references Black liberation leader, Jamaica native, founder of the Universal Negro Improvement Association (UNIA) and the shipping line the Black Star Line, Marcus Garvey. Unlike the other victims in this verse, Marcus Garvey was not killed but was indicted of alleged mail fraud, imprisoned, and ultimately deported back to Jamaica. Garvey was known as the creator of the Black liberation flag (a red, black, and green flag), introducing the idea that Jesus and God are Black and as having millions of followers internationally. RZA also alludes to the assassinations of thirty-fifth president of the United States and civil rights proponent John F. Kennedy, assassinated while riding in a political convoy in Dallas, Texas, and of field secretary of the National Association for the Advancement of Colored People (NAACP) Medgar Evers, assassinated in the driveway of his home. All these assassinations targeted people who were involved in the CRM in some capacity, and all assassinations were linked to government conspiracies. In these lyrics, RZA educates his listeners about these leaders and implicates the government in their untimely deaths, promoting distrust of government in issues involving the African American fight for universal freedom and inclusion. By providing minor details of each assassination, RZA brought attention to the CRM and possible government involvement in order to encourage distrust of the government.

Following Figure 1, listeners of this song will then juxtapose their previous attitudes with the new information presented in the lyrics. Those who

were not distrustful of the government have to adjust their previous attitudes based on the distrust and conspiracy allegations presented in this
stanza. Those who already had a considerable amount of distrust will not
have to adjust previously held beliefs, but the poem may solidify and
increase their distrustful attitude. Next, the attitude of government distrust
will become part of the individual's political ideology, replacing or con-
firming previously held beliefs, and affecting the political public opinion of
the individual when questioned about her or his trust in government.
Finally, this attitude will affect the listener's political behavior in a number
of other ways, including opinions of the government and both electoral and
nonelectoral participation. The listener may not participate in voting
because of lack of trust in government, but may instead be more enticed
to participate in grassroots efforts like protesting, demonstrating, and
organizing.

Still, one may question the accuracy and adherence of this model of
attitude adoption. For instance, the argument can be made that the process
can only occur if the individuals are familiar with any of the leaders referenced. I assert that most individuals are familiar with at least one of these
leaders and the conspiracy theory associated with the leader; however, if
they are not familiar, these lyrics will serve as the impetus to educational
research. For individuals not familiar with any of the leaders referenced,
their attitude change or acceptance may not happen immediately after initial exposure. For some, attitudinal influence of the song may occur after
more exposure to the song and engagement of "everyday talk" with others.
Through "everyday talk" as presented by Harris-Lacewell (2004), individuals will discuss the song, research the references, share their opinions,
and hear the views of others, all of which affect attitude adoption and
acceptance.

Thus the references in this song serve as an educational impetus for the
listeners. While some may view music and other forms of popular culture
as merely entertainment, I argue that music serves as a point of information
and can psychologically affect one's political attitudes.

Music's psychological impact is widely studied. Doctors, psychologists,
and others have alluded to the numerous psychological influences of music.
Pregnant women are told to place headphones playing classical music on
their bellies to promote intelligence and development. Music has been suggested as therapy for ICU patients (Updike 1990); as treatment for pain,
anxiety, depression; as therapy for severe mental illnesses (Chan et al. 2003;

Gold et al. 2009); to lessen animosity during wait times (e.g., "elevator" music when placed on hold by a business) (Tansik and Rothieaus 1999); as influential with brand acceptance in advertisements; for healthy parenting and child development (Nicholson et al. 2008); and psychotherapy (Nelson and Weathers 1998). There are numerous psychological effects of music including attitude formation and adoption.

Black Political Ideology

The history of ideology in American politics is long and varied and includes assorted definitions and discussions of ideology and its importance. Ideology has been defined as "a consistent integrated pattern of thoughts and beliefs explaining man's attitude towards life and existence in society and advocating a conduct and action pattern responsive to and commensurate with such thoughts and beliefs" (Lowenstein 1953: 52). Similarly, ideology is believed to be "an organization of opinions, attitudes, and values—a way of thinking about man and society. We may speak of an individual's total ideology or of his ideology with respect to different areas of social life; politics, economics, religion, minority groups and so forth" (Adorno et al. 1950: 2).

Ideology is a concept that is often discussed in politics as representing a heuristic for citizens' decision making process. It "not only shows up in people's electoral and policy decisions, it also can be evidenced in the schools where they send their children, the places where they buy their cars, and the way they style their hair" (Harris-Lacewell 2004: 18–19). Many Black political ideologies have existed over time (Dawson 2001). I am most interested in the relevance of Black Nationalist and Black Feminist ideologies in rap music. The differing economic backgrounds of those who accept each position make these ideologies interesting in juxtaposition. For instance, poor urban youth, especially males, are most accepting of Black Nationalist attitudes and least accepting of Black Feminist attitudes. These ideologies are particularly important to consider because they are the two most dominant ideologies in the Black community.

Understanding who accepts and what mediums advance certain ideologies is important because "political ideology helps to define who are one's friends and enemies [and] with whom one would form political coalitions" (Dawson 2001: 4). Not only is understanding the information presented in rap music necessary when analyzing and discussing the Black community, but, as rap music becomes more popular, it also becomes more essential to understanding the political attitudes of various populations. The study of political thought is important to understanding the role political attitudes represent "in shaping political debate and action in America" (3).

The study of Black "political ideology functions as a social narrative that explains the sources of Black inequalities, justifies action on behalf of the group, provides strategies for addressing Black inequality and provides a vision of a different future" (Harris-Lacewell 2004: 20). Finally, "which Black ideology becomes dominant . . . will greatly shape the future of both Black and American politics" (Dawson 2001: 54). African Americans use both mainstream and non-mainstream sources for attitudes and ideological formations. These non-mainstream sources have been identified as a system of Black information networks or Black information enclaves, one of which is rap music (Dawson 2001; Harris-Lacewell 2004). Rap music serves as a heuristic for African Americans by providing information that can assist them in their attitude and ideological formations. Thus two ideologies will be examined to understand the impact of rap music on an individual's political attitudes, public opinion, and ideological stance: Black Feminism and Black Nationalism. Importantly, rap's origins and historical lineage places it on the heels of the Black Arts Movement, a period when Black Nationalism and Black Feminism became increasingly popular ideologies.

Within the genre of rap music, multiple subgenres exist. Most of the research on rap music is specifically on violent or "gangsta" rap and its effect on behavior and attitude formation, while researchers rarely observe its impact on political attitudes and behavior. This work differs in that it identifies, classifies and examines a genre of rap different from "gangsta" or violent rap music: political rap. Does exposure to political rap impact political attitudes and behavior?

What Are You Listening To? Identifying Political Rap

The term "rap" refers to an expansive genre that includes such subgenres as message/conscious rap, trap rap, snap rap, gospel rap, gangster rap, party rap, and southern rap. Political rap is rap music that provides political information by detailing political strategies, injustices, and grievances. Unfortunately, gangster rap, with its hard hitting bass, misogynistic, and violent lyrics, is often mistakenly held as standard bearer of the genre. Rap covers a broad spectrum and its artists may transcend two or more sub-genres. For instance, some rappers may release songs that are both political and "gangster," such as artist Plies, who discusses social and political issues in "Why You Hate?" and in another track, "Becky," objectifies women, discusses sexual acts, and presents nihilistic attitudes. For my purposes, I have classified political rap as a subset of the larger rap genre. Identifying a subgenre is essential for this work and future studies of rap music. As discussed earlier, political rap is rap music that details political strategies, injustices, and grievances.

While many scholars discuss the importance and existence of political music, conscious or message rap, there is no categorization for identifying political rap as a specific subgenre that can be quantitatively analyzed. Ernest Allen, Jr. (1996) posits that political rap does exist and has a direct connection to two important nationalist sects, the Nation of Gods and Earths (NG&E) and the Nation of Islam (NOI). Allen asserts that there are three categories of political rap: "(1) the Islamic nationalist orientation of rappers such as Pete Rock and C. L. Smooth . . . (2) the cultural-political nationalism of Public Enemy . . . and (3) specific, message-oriented expressions embedded in the more earthy gangsta rap" (162). He also suggests, as does Errol Henderson (1996), that message or nationalist rap has contributed to greater political and racial consciousness. However, neither author attempts to define political rap nor empirically tests his claims, although both give examples of rappers they believe present political nationalist lyrics.

Still, Decker asserts that two categories—Afrocentric Nationalist rap and a 1960s-inspired Nationalist rap—exist within the subgenre of message rap. Afrocentric Nationalism, he argues, is more culturally based and views Africa, specifically Egypt, as the foundation for Black culture (Decker 1993). In contrast, the 1960s-inspired Nationalism focuses more on political and social power. Therefore, he believes that the differences in message rap rest on whether lyrics emphasize viewpoints of a specific time (1960s) or space (Egypt) (Decker 1993).

Likewise, The Centre for Political Song at Glasgow Caledonian University states that its focus is defining political music.[7] This Centre defines "'political song' as an umbrella term that incorporates a variety of different, and often quite disparate, strands." Essentially, the term refers to "any song containing a political thread." The Centre asserts that campaign and protest songs, as well as historical or blatantly political songs, all comprise the category of political songs. Inclusion depends not on whether the music is overtly political but on context. Similarly, Mark Anthony Neal describes political songs as those "that contained distinct political commentary" (Neal 2006: 624).

When describing political music, others have grouped political songs with socially relevant songs and labeled them message songs.[8] Others simply refer to artists who have made some message-oriented music and label those artists political (Decker 1993; Rose 1994; Allen 1996; Perry 2004). Nevertheless, identifying political rap is more complicated than simply observing political references because it is so difficult to agree on what is political. While the inclusion of political references is essential to identifying political songs, other aspects must be present for a song to be considered a political rap song.

In this book and in contrast to former works, I will not label artists. It is my belief that musicians change and grow and should not be confined to labels like pop, message, and gangster etc. Therefore, an artist such as Trick Daddy, who began his career rapping with Luther Campbell and 2 Live Crew[9] and classifies himself as a "thug,"[10] also creates political songs such as "America" and "Thug Holiday." For this reason the basis of examination later in this manuscript is the individual songs and not the artists. Using the songs will allow for inclusion of political rap songs from artists who are not known for producing political rap music. This categorization gives rappers flexibility while still observing the use of their art to participate politically, as well as giving examiners a larger sample of rap music to analyze. For instance, top selling rapper Lil Wayne is not known for proffering his political beliefs in his music. In other words, Wayne is no Yasiin Bey, but he still released political rap songs such as "Georgia Bush" and "Tie my Hands" in relation to the devastation of New Orleans during hurricane Katrina. Both songs discuss the lack of support and response from the government in the wake of Katrina, which impacted Lil Wayne's hometown, New Orleans. Allowing for the inclusion of artists who may not be known for producing political rap music, but who have released political music, demonstrates that, despite what critics and other artists say, Hip-Hop is not dead and still produces politically and socially relevant music.

Therefore, a criterion of political rap is necessary to analyze rap's effects on political attitudes, ideology, and behavior and to establish what songs are political. The criteria for political rap used here were developed

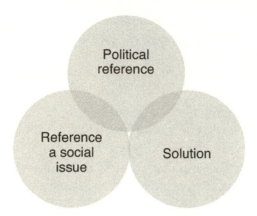

Figure 2. Categorizing political rap songs.

using the combination of previous attempts to classify rap music. These include the vague definitions proffered by Neal and the Centre for Political Song, which suggest that a political song must contain a political reference, and Robert Walker's (1974), Decker's (1993), and Allen's (1996) attempts to identify message music of the civil rights and post-civil rights eras. Walker gave the most detailed categorization by suggesting that there are three main criteria to identify message songs: (1) songs with implicit or explicit ethnic symbolism; (2) references to "social class problems"; and (3) references "to groups other than ethnic or social class" (Walker 1975: 39).

My categorization of political rap is similar to Walker's classification of message songs, but it differs in that it focuses on political references instead of references to sociological issues. While messages are asserted in many rap songs, for my purposes a song is only political if it displays an implicit or explicit political reference in the lyrics. This prioritization of political references also distinguishes my definition from other attempts to categorize rap as message rap. Therefore, political rap is rap music that must include the first criterion below, plus either the second or third criterion (This categorization can be observed visually in Figure 2):

1. Displays a political reference in the lyrics, such as directly referencing a political leader, political office/institution, political activity, political events or political position.

2. Makes reference to a social problem or issue and discusses it in the lyrics, thereby raising awareness about specific issues or disparities, nationally or globally.
3. Advocates a solution to injustices or problems in society.

Veteran New York rapper Nas' song, "I Want to Talk to You" satisfies at least two of the above criteria and features the following chorus:

I wanna talk to the mayor, the governor, the motherfuckin president
I wanna talk to the FBI, and the CIA, and the motherfuckin
    congressman

In this chorus Nas references the mayor, the governor, the president, and other political organizations and positions. This song satisfies the first condition by displaying explicit political references. However, all political references may not be explicit. Sometimes they will be implicit, using coded language, a popular element of Black vernacular, such as references to the system, the man, or other coded words (Scott 1990; Gates and McKay 1997). When coded words are present the listener is responsible for decoding and interpreting the meaning based on knowledge of the coded terms and the context.

Mr. Mayor imagine if this was your backyard
Mr. Governor imagine if it was your kids that starved
Imagine your kids gotta sling crack to survive

Here, Nas brings to the forefront the poverty rampant in many inner city neighborhoods. He invokes a common theme in rap music, the illicit drug trade, as the number one employment opportunity in the hood. This refrain implicitly decries the economic deprivation and blighted conditions found in many American inner cities. The lines satisfy the second condition because they make a reference and discuss the social condition of poverty. However, Nas' song is rare because it also satisfies the third condition with the following verse:

I wanna talk to the man understand
Understand this motherfuckin G-pack in my hand

In this verse, Nas expresses that his concern for the social conditions of his community is so great that he would use artillery to insure he is heard by his political leaders. His suggestion of discussion with political leaders and others who assist in making political decisions is an example of presenting a solution to the injustices the Black community faces. This call to arms expresses his frustration that political leaders will not listen to him except by force. His advocacy for this type of action, in his belief, guarantees that his community's voice is heard and considered.

The category of political rap is not all-inclusive. Some songs that may be classified as message songs are not political. For instance, "Beautiful Skin" by Goodie Mob would be classified as a message song because it exalts and praises Black women. Examining this song using my political rap criteria demonstrates how the song is not political.

> At one time, my mind, just, couldn't conceive
> A woman had to dress a certain way to believe
> But, in the same breath, allow me to say
> That, if you believed young lady, you wouldn't dress that way
> And I, was attracted to your class, I couldn't see all yo' ass

This verse from rapper Cee-lo, member of southern rap group Goodie Mob, represents one of the many songs written specifically for Black women (albeit, this song does take a sexist leaning by covertly attempting to dictate the type of clothes a woman wears). While this song clearly presents a positive message toward Black women, its lack of political reference excludes it from the subgenre of political rap. However, it can be argued by many that the song satisfies the other two criteria by discussing relationship issues within the Black community and advocating a solution to the relationship "problems" within the Black community. Nonetheless, this song does not satisfy my first criterion, which is necessary for political rap classification.

Political rap music, therefore, assists in this information transference by providing political information and social commentary. The information is in turn received and interpreted by listeners. Political rap represents an information source that many segments of the population do not have regular access to. Therefore, minority rap fans may possess first-hand experiences that give them the perspective to understand and interpret the information presented. These artists become influential because their audiences understand the sentiments in their music. This is not to say that all individuals who consume or are exposed to rap have experienced the issues discussed. But, to follow the logic provided by Dawson's Black Utility Heuristic (1994), a lack of direct experience does not equal a lack of familiarity or perspective. In some cases, while individuals will not share the experience the artist discusses, they may have a relative, friend, or peer who has had those experiences, enabling them to empathize with the artist's lyrics. This results in psychological changes for the listener and the adoption consciously or subconsciously of some of the same attitudes that the rap artist shares in his or her music.

For instance, violent and defiant rap has been recognized as a source of music that changes behaviors and affects attitudes. Exposure to violent rap videos increased support of violent acts, including greater acceptance of violence against women (Johnson, Jackson, and Gatto 1995) and the acceptance of stereotypical views about Blacks (Johnson, Trawalter, and Dovidio 2000). Similarly, deviant traits such as rebelliousness, hostility, and disinhibition were related to defiant rock and rap music (Carpentier, Knobloch, and Zillman 2003). Just as exposure to violent rap impacts attitudes and behaviors, so should exposure to political rap music. It is suggested that some attitudes, beliefs, and actions are socialized through rap music (Cohen 2010; Spence 2011). But it is still up for debate whether these attitudes are blatantly articulated in rap music or stem from other political information sources.

Conclusion

The study of rap music can broaden the analysis of the development of some political attitudes, thoughts, and ideologies. Originally rap was a phenomenon among youth. However, currently rap has a large audience that encompasses a majority of the Black population as well as large followings among segments of other racial groups worldwide. According to the Black Youth Project at the University of Chicago, 58 percent of Black, 45 percent of Latino, and 23 percent of White youth state that they listen to rap music every day (Cohen 2007). Because of rap's widespread influence, it is imperative to study the political attitudes that may be asserted through rap as predictors of a wide range of political attitudes and thoughts nationally.

There is a long history within political science of discussing ideological formations. This work adds to that discussion by asserting that culture is one way that political attitudes are transmitted and that culture assists in ideological formation. Understanding various means of political communication methods assists political scientists and others in examining and discussing how political ideas are transmitted. This book will assist the discipline in its discussion of the political attitudes, ideologies, and activity of future generations.

Chapter 2

Music and Political Resistance: The Cultural Foundation of Black Politics

If slaves were permitted to sing as they toiled in the fields and to incorporate music into their religious services, it was because the slaveocracy failed to grasp the social function of music in general and particularly the central role music played in all aspects of life in West African Society. As a result Black people were able to create with their music an aesthetic community of resistance which in turn encouraged and nurtured a political community of active struggle for freedom.
   —Angela Davis, *Women, Culture, and Politics*

Because my mouth
Is wide with laughter
And my throat
Is deep with song,
You do not think
I suffer after
I have held my pain
So long.
   —Langston Hughes, "Minstrel Man"

Fire burning inside my eyes, this the music that saved my life
Y'all be calling it Hip-Hop, I be calling it Hypnotize
   —Kendrick Lamar, *Section.80*, "Fuck Your Ethnicity"

In 2008, in the midst of the political campaign to elect the first African American president of the United States, Nas, a New York rapper who has produced many political rap songs led a protest outside Fox News Studios. He claimed that the network, specifically anchor Bill O'Reilly, was racist and presented racist ideas on his news show, especially in reference to President Barack Obama, which could be detrimental to Obama's campaign and life. O'Reilly featured guests on his show who stated that the fist bump between Obama and his wife Michelle Obama was a "terrorist fist-jab," claimed Obama was a Muslim by emphasizing his middle name, Hussein, and referred to Michelle Obama with the derogatory and racially associated term "baby mother."[1] To organize this protest, Nas worked with Colorof Change.org and Moveon.org. Petitioners presented signs that crossed out the Fox News slogan "Fair and Balanced" and replaced it with phrases such as "Fairly Racist" or "Your Choice for Racist Smears." Nas claimed to have the signatures of over 600,000 participants opposed to Fox News, collected on the two abovementioned sites (Chung 2008). Fox News would not accept the petitions or interview Nas, who wanted to talk with O'Reilly, but Nas was given the opportunity to have his voice heard on the pseudo-conservative news show, The Colbert Report, where Nas stated that the fearmongering that occurred on O'Reilly's show was worse than any rap lyrics he had ever heard. Nas concluded his interview with a performance of a song from his new untitled album "Sly Fox," in which he raps:

> Watch what you're watching
> Fox keeps feeding us toxins
> Stop sleeping
> Start thinking outside of the box
> And unplug from the Matrix doctrine

In this song, Nas detailed the way he believes the media control your mind and keep individuals ignorant to what is really occurring in society. Nas specifically focused on Fox News, although he also discussed big media corporations such as Viacom and media owners such as Rupert Murdoch. Nas was following in the tradition of Black culture that uses music as a form of resistance, in this case against media control and manipulation.

Political information is presented in popular culture, namely rap music. Music as a persuasive media source should therefore influence the acceptance of these attitudes among people exposed to rap music. With the significant impact Hip-Hop has not only on American culture, but on other cultures, the study of the relationship between Hip-Hop culture, political behavior, and political ideology is necessary when observing what factors may influence political attitudes. Therefore, examination of the relationship between Hip-Hop and Black Nationalist ideology in the United States can add another important variable to the theory of attitude formation and the support of certain ideologies in the Black Community. The inclusion of rap music exposure is a variable that should be considered when examining Black public opinion data and attitudes that may lead to specific political behavior of African Americans.

Music as Resistance

Minorities and other oppressed groups often use culture as a resistance mechanism, a platform on which to assert their attitudes and discuss issues relevant to them. The above example demonstrated the use of culture to resist dominant ideologies and oppressive situations—something that oppressed American Blacks have taken part in since slavery (Hechter 1975; Davis 1989; Mitchell and Feagin 1995; Zillman et al. 1995; Martinez 1997). Researchers have argued that as they toiled "through songs slaves could comment on their problems . . . they could voice their despair and hopes and assert their humanity in an environment that constantly denied their humanness" (Southern 1997: 156). Enslaved Africans instituted a system of hidden transcripts through culture, including music, to resist.

The most obvious way to resist slavery was to escape. Culture assisted in this blatant form of resistance by using hidden messages in songs to organize escape. These were usually manifested as coded language, symbols, or signs that expressed actual sentiments without the risk of retribution. This tactic was a staple of the Underground Railroad. For example, the song "Go Down Moses" alerted slaves seeking escape to the impending arrival of Harriet Tubman (who led over three hundred enslaved Africans to freedom), and "Follow the Drinking Gourd" served as a map instructing listeners to follow the constellation of the Big Dipper to freedom (Southern 1997). These songs are unique because, although they seemed like typical work songs and spirituals, they "often functioned as coded messages that called for blatant acts of resistance" (Neal 1999: 2).

With the dismantling of slavery and the addition of the Thirteenth, Fourteenth, and Fifteenth Amendments to the U.S. Constitution, some argued that the use of culture to fight for inclusion and consideration was no longer required. But slavery was not the only oppressive institution in which Blacks had to fight for their rights and inclusion as citizens in this country. With oppression and exclusion still occurring in many facets of life, culture continued to play a major role in fighting for political inclusion in the United States. Thus, the power of music did not stop being important after Blacks were emancipated.

Harlem Renaissance figure and legendary African American poet Langston Hughes was influenced by the antebellum period and in his short stories and poems often used characters that demonstrated the way music enables individuals to express their views about various political issues.[2] He used his infamous character Simple B. Simpleton to display the use of music and resistance in the Black community during his era. This character uses humor and wit to address positive and negative aspects of the African American experience. In one story, Simpleton details the creation and appreciation of Bebop as it relates to Blacks' interaction with the police:

> Then I have to go into my whole pedigree because I am a Black man in a white neighborhood. And if my answers do not satisfy them, BOP! MOP! . . . BE-BOP! . . . MOP! If they do not hit me, they have already hurted my soul. *A dark man shall see dark days.* Bop comes out of them dark days. That's why real Bop is mad, wild, and frantic, crazy—and not to be dug unless you've seen dark days too. Folks who ain't suffered much cannot play Bop, neither appreciate it. They think Bop is nonsense-like you. They think it's just *crazy* crazy. They do not know Bop is also MAD crazy, SAD crazy, FRANTIC WILD CRAZY— beat out of somebody' head! That's what Bop is. Them young colored kids who started it, they know what Bop is. (1961: 118)

Bebop, a form of jazz that includes scatting and a quick tempo, was a new form of music during this era. Many wondered where the name came from and what it actually meant. Hughes's attempt to answer this question was relayed in this short story. Though relayed in a humorous tone, the passage clearly relates a sometimes deadly and common event of the "Black experience." He jokingly describes these acts of violence, saying, "Every time a cop hits a Negro with his billy club, that old club says, 'BOP! BOP! . . . BE-BOP!. . . . MOP!. . . . BOP!'" 1961: 118). Simpleton's description of the origin of the musical genre, though fictitious, displays one form of resistance that has often been invoked in the African American community. Resistance is embedded in this story by detailing the importance of a counter-narrative and a counter-public. Here the counter-narrative— Simple's explanation of the creation of bebop music—was provided in Hughes's use of a counter-public, Black literature. One can deduce from Hughes's story that feelings such as pain and anger are asserted in this form of music. This is worth noting because it displays how attitudes have been presented in music. For some, culture—music, art, and film—was a platform to provide commentary of political, racial, or social injustice. This story is one fictional example of the possible relationship between music and political attitudes in the Black community. It also supports the contention that Bebop was a response to racism as it manifested in the north (Neal 2004b). It has been argued that the music represented rebellion for Bebop artists, deviating from the form of jazz that was becoming very popular and mainstream (Kofsky 1970). This revitalization of cultural forms occurred consistently in the Black community—from gospel to soul to R&B to funk—as some examples of these transformations. In essence, culture, specifically music, offered a safe space among a marginalized community to assert fears, concerns, attitudes, and dissatisfaction.

Billie Holiday's musical adaption of the poem of a similar title, "Strange Fruit" (1939), is also an example of an artist using music to express frustrations and injustices. This song conveyed anguish at the widespread lynching of African Americans during the early part of the twentieth century. However, Holiday did not write the lyrics. They were written by Jewish New York school teacher Abel Meeropol, who also used the alias Lewis Allen.[3] Meeropol was inspired to write the poem after seeing the photograph by Lawrence Beitler of the lynching of Thomas Shipp and Abram Smith in 1930 (NPR 2010; Blair 2012). Holiday was able to capsulate the sentiments of the original poem with the lyric

> Southern trees bear a strange fruit,
> Blood on the leaves and blood at the root,
> Black bodies swinging in the southern breeze,
> Strange fruit hanging from the poplar trees

Music continued to embody the strong relationship between African American suffering, oppression, and the fight for political inclusion during the Civil Rights era. Black music became more popular among mainstream

American audiences because of its political emphasis. Many artists used their songs to provide commentary on the racial issues of the day. For instance, in "Mississippi Goddamn!" singer Nina Simone vented her outrage about the deaths of four little girls in a Birmingham church and other violent acts committed against Blacks in the South during this time (Iton 2008; Neal 1999). Similarly, songs such as The Impressions' "This Is My Country,"[4] and "A Change Is Gonna Come" by Sam Cooke talked about citizen rights, racism, and discrimination (Neal 1999). Music not only provided information and attitudes, but also encouraged dedication, loyalty, and persistence during the difficult, contentious times of the Civil Rights Movement (CRM) (Morris 1984). Accounts of the CRM detail the use of music to motivate marchers and reinforce nonviolent responses, raise consciousness, provide comfort during times of incarceration, murder, and violence, and to express emotions during times of pain, suffering, sadness, joy, and celebration (Morris 1984; Garofalo 1992).

Cultural Art Forms and Oppositional Resistance

Music for African Americans has various uses. It not only has been a resistance mechanism but is also used to uplift individuals psychologically and emotionally. Though there are many examples, one song in particular has symbolized solidarity for all members of the Black community and was eventually adopted as the Black National Anthem. "Lift Every Voice and Sing," written by James Weldon Johnson, began as a poem written as a replacement to a speech that was to be given at a celebration in commemoration of Abraham Lincoln. It was later adopted by the NAACP as the Negro National Anthem (NPR 2002). Today this song is sung at various African American events, either to begin a program or at its closing. This anthem is a song of empowerment, hope, sorrow, and struggle.

African Americans were not the only group of people to use music and culture as resistance. The U.S. national anthem, "The Star-Spangled Banner," was written by Francis Scott Key after he learned of America's victory over the British at Fort McHenry in Baltimore during the War of 1812 (Sonneck 1972). The "Star-Spangled Banner" is played at graduations, sporting events, and national ceremonies and remains a symbol of American courage, loyalty, and patriotism. Other examples of songs that are used as assertions of political attitudes, particularly patriotism, in the United

States include George M. Cohan's "You're a Grand Old Flag" and "Yankee Doodle Dandy," Woody Guthrie's "This Land Is Your Land," Julia Ward Howe's "Battle Hymn of the Republic," Bruce Springsteen's "Born in the U.S.A.," and Toby Keith's "Courtesy of the Red, White, and Blue." These songs also illustrate the use of culture as resistance, solidarity, and upliftment.

Nevertheless, Americans have not been the only ones to embrace culture as a viable resistance mechanism. Other oppressed groups globally have also used culture to express discontent. This is evident in reggae music, as seen in songs by Bob Marley, who is known for his political commentary. Songs such as "Get Up, Stand Up," "Redemption Song," and "400 Years," all discuss the issues of slavery, assassination, racism, indoctrination, and fighting against injustice.

Still, one of the most prominent examples of the use of music for resistance and upliftment globally is seen in the anti-apartheid movement of South Africa. Apartheid (1948–1994), the legal segregation and oppression of Blacks in South Africa, was very similar to Jim Crow in the United States. Resisting or speaking out against policy or the oppressive regime often resulted in fines, harassment, prison, and even death. Again, there was a need for coded language to relay plans and important information, and to maintain the morale of those who were fighting against injustices. Examples of hidden transcripts were found in many songs during apartheid. One such song was "Asimbonang" by Johnny Clegg and Savuka, which translates into "We have not seen him," and discuses Nelson Mandela and other political prisoners who were incarcerated or went missing during the fight against apartheid (Shoup 1997). Another popular song of this movement was "Safa Seph'isizwe," which is often referred to as the funeral song and was featured in the South African play Sarafina!, which detailed aspects of the student-led Soweto Uprising of 1976 (Shoup 1997). Music in South Africa in later years was highly influenced by the U.S. Black Consciousness, Black Power, and Black Arts movements.

Back in America, music continued to be a viable resistance mechanism. Songs like "Hurricane," "If I Had a Hammer," "Respect," "Ball of Confusion," and "Heaven Help Us All" by artists Bob Dylan, Pete Seeger, Aretha Franklin, The Temptations, and Stevie Wonder respectively, voiced discontent with federal policies including the Vietnam War, police brutality, disenfranchisement, racism, sexism, and other injustices against people of color, women, and poor people (Neal 2004b; Iton 2008). Similarly, songs such as Marvin Gaye's "What's Going On" and "Inner City Blues," Sly and the Family Stone's "Everyday People," and Curtis Mayfield's "Keep on Pushing" and "We the People Who Are Darker Than Blue" took a stance against poverty in America and celebrated cultural pride, equality, and determination (Neal 1999). James Brown's "Say It Loud: I'm Black and I'm Proud" not only served as background music for the Black Power movement, but also increased racial solidarity and consciousness among African Americans (Walker 1975). Throughout history, music has been used as a voice and method of resistance, both political and social, for various groups at various times.

Changing Times

The Voting Rights Act of 1965 absolutely represented a victory and achievement for African Americans, but Blacks were still systematically marginalized in the American political system. With changing issues and a changing environment, the end of segregation and denial of voting rights, the issues of the Civil Rights Movement, which took aim at blatant racism and injustice, were not ubiquitous any more (Devine 1989; Kinder and Sanders 1996). The shift from overt racism, discrimination, and segregation was also observed in campaign language and messages. While explicit and blatant racism was deterred and abhorred, discrimination and racism occurred in other implicit institutional ways, often blanketed in politicians' coded language; they now discussed class instead of racial differences (Mendelberg 2001; Williams 2003; Hill-Collins 2006). Class differences were often much easier to mask in America because of its values of liberty and capitalism, which suggest that one can obtain a different status if she only tries harder.

After the Civil Rights movement, the 1970s and '80s ushered in persistent poverty for many African Americans (Wilson 1978, 1987; Walton and Smith 2000; Karenga 2002; Kitwana 2002).[5] Now, instead of being able to combat an observable face of racism that was explicitly notable through lynching, segregation, and racial epithets, activists had the task of identifying and combating an indescribable, almost invisible form of economic discrimination and institutionalized implicit discriminatory policies (Hill-Collins 2006). It proved difficult to persuade people of the connection between discrimination and poverty. A favorite argument by the opposition was that, with the passage of the Civil Rights and Voting Rights Acts, equality now existed, the playing field was level, and everyone had equal opportunity regardless of race.

Suddenly, laziness, inability, and incompetence were to blame for poverty as opposed to injustice and discrimination (Sniderman, Piazza, Tetlock, and Kendrick 1991; Gaertner and Dovidio 1986; Sniderman and Piazza 1993). Simply put, the discourse shifted from African Americans suffering from a legacy of discrimination and racism to "African Americans should try harder to succeed." This view was readily accepted by many white Americans who were weary of years of demonstration and conflict. However, Blacks living in poverty obviously had a different outlook on their economic situations, which was detailed in the culture of this time.

This was not the only attitudinal shift observed during this era. One of the common justifications for slavery was the supposedly inherently violent nature of African Americans, with slavery touted as a means of controlling enslaved Africans. This allowed whites to deny slaves' humanity and treat them as property. This ideology continued into the 1970s under a different paradigm. Instead of the label uncivilized brutes, in the '70s Blacks were labeled as violent, uncontrollable, and persistent drug users, again freeing white society to treat them unjustly (these characteristics were, of course, still in line with the uncivilized brute paradigm). The result was discriminatory drug policies and the recurrence of racial stereotyping of Black men as "Black Brutes" and Black women as lascivious manipulators in the pattern of the "Jezebel."[6] As a result of integration, many white Americans attempted to divert the government-enforced integration of the races by leaving urban areas where Blacks were more prominent and moving to the suburbs. This migration away from urban areas often affected the educational systems severely because richer White Americans took with them a large percent of the tax base and school funding. African Americans did own homes and contribute to the tax base, but there were often obvious racial disparities in income; Blacks did not earn at the same rate and amount as their white counterparts. This transformation of ideology, attitudes, and behavior among White Americans created an environment of continued discrimination that fostered the continual use of culture as a political outlet for the marginalized Black community.

Black Arts Movement and Politics

The oral tradition has been used regularly in the Black community as a means to articulate feelings and attitudes. In fact, it is suggested that the "search for Black ideology must begin with the oral tradition" (Henry 1990: 7). Out of this oral tradition arose one of the most influential music genres, rap music. It is widely accepted that rap music began with the Last Poets and the poetry of Gil Scott-Heron in the early 1970's (Allen 1996; Henderson 1996; Woldu 2003; Ards 2004). Cultural figures such as The Last Poets ("Niggers Are Scared of Revolution") and Gil Scott-Heron ("The Revolution Will Not Be Televised") were premier poets of the Black Arts Movement of the 1960s and 1970s.[7] These poets developed unique incorporated styles in which they recited poetry over musical beats. While this style can be described as one of the foundations of modern rap, rap can also be traced to the oral tradition of African griots and to Black ministers who used repetition, call and response, and music to tell stories, contribute lessons, and record history (Kitwana 2002). This style of call and response, repetition and rhyming can be found in the speeches of leaders such as Malcolm X, Martin Luther King, Jr., and Jesse Jackson.

This book began by exploring the impact Dave Chappelle's *Block Party* had on my political psyche; this performance was in fact reminiscent of Black Power rallies during the late 1960s and early 1970s. During most of these rallies, more serious discussions were precipitated by music and poetry performances that sought to influence the attitudes and emotions of rally participants. One of the most popular Black leaders to incorporate the method of rhyming, storytelling, and call and response was Jamil Abdullah Al-Amin, formerly known as H. "Rap" Brown. In fact, Al-Amin received his nickname "Rap" from his great prowess at "playing the dozens," an African American tradition of trash talking or using words to demean and belittle an opponent. One of the most famous Al-Amin toasts is duplicated in the popular rap song "Rapper's Delight" by the Sugarhill Gang, in which Grandmaster Flash states:

Well, I'm imp the Dimp, the ladies pimp
The women fight for my delight
But I'm the grandmaster with the three MCs
That shock the house for the young ladies

Similarly, Al-Amin rhymes a decade earlier:

Yes, I'm hemp the demp, the women's pimp
Women fight for my delight.
I'm a bad motherfucker. Rap the rip-saw the devil's brother 'n law.

Al-Amin carried this technique into his world as a Black Nationalist activist. In his speeches addressing Black power, he would use rhymes to drive home his point. However, Al-Amin was not the only Black Nationalist leader to use this oratory technique. Fred Hampton, Sr., and Stokely Carmichael, both Black Panther members, were known for using rhyme and "toasting" throughout their speeches. They were able to entice the crowd through their use of imagery and poetry.

The combination of politics and rhyming continued in Hip-Hop culture. Similar to the Black Arts Movement, Hip-Hop demonstrated that African Americans did not have to adopt the popular culture of mainstream America, but could instead create their own cultural platform that allowed "truth" from the perspective of many young African Americans. Some African Americans had come to believe they needed to prove themselves worthy of the same rights as whites. For many this required assimilating or adopting the norms, appearance, and other perceived attributes of the dominant culture. This manifested itself in aspects as diverse as straightening kinky hair to the adoption of American English in lieu of a Black dialect, Gullah, or "Ebonics."[8] Part of the seduction of movements of the 1970s and early '80s was the belief that African Americans were a proud and regal people who did not need to assimilate. This was personified in natural hair styles, African garb, taking ethnic names, and embracing Black dialect and slang as a rejection of the influence of white dominant culture. Popularized by Al-Amin, rapping quickly became a tool to discuss figures and issues germane to the Black community.

All elements of Hip-Hop demonstrate resistance to American cultural sensibilities, lifestyle, and ideals. In addition to music, these include graffiti, breakdancing, and disc-jockeying (Stapleton 1998). Born out of Bronx house parties when disc-jockeys (DJs) would give an emcee a few minutes on the microphone, Hip-Hop has always been equal parts entertainment and education (Rose 1994; Pough 2004). The most dominant element of Hip-Hop culture today is rap music, and this element can be used to voice discontent and discuss issues relevant to the artist's segment of the population. While there is a long history of message or protest music, there was a noticeable change in the prominence of this type of music in mainstream culture beginning in the late 1970s and early 1980s. This change resulted from the significant shift in social and political conditions during this period. One of the most notable shifts was the rising drug epidemic in the Black Community and the subsequent war on drugs implemented by the

United States government. In order to comprehend exactly how rap music can influence political attitudes and behavior we must begin by detailing some attitudes and issues that are presented in rap music.

Political Rap and Political Information

One of the most recurrent themes in rap music is the use and distribution of drugs. While drugs were not new in any community, they became more prominent in Black communities during the 1970s, predominantly because of disparities in wealth and job attainment, as well as the increased availability of illegal substances. Many begin the discussion of a "war on drugs" with President Richard Nixon's use of the term in 1971 (Whitford and Yates 2009). The war on drugs began as an agenda to decrease heroin use in America, in large part because of the high number of U.S. soldiers returning from Vietnam addicted to the drug. Under Nixon, this "war" advocated methadone treatment instead of law enforcement.[9] Heroin use was so prominent that we still see popular culture exploration of heroin distribution and use in the 2007 film, *American Gangster*, which focused on the life of notorious heroin dealer Frank Lucas.

While this "war" was declared by Nixon, it was revitalized by President Ronald Reagan in 1982 by creating the Vice President's Task Force on South Florida, led by George H. W. Bush. This task force's emphasis was to deter cocaine trafficking primarily from Colombia to Miami, Florida. The biggest federal act in the war on drugs was Reagan's 1986 signing of the Anti-Drug Abuse Act, which instituted mandatory minimums and sentencing disparities varying across types of drugs, including a mandatory minimum of five years for possession of 5 grams of crack cocaine or 500 grams of powder cocaine. Mandatory minimums disproportionately affected poor, urban Black citizens who were often victims of crack abuse and crack distribution because of the availability and inexpensiveness of crack in comparison to powder cocaine (Jordan-Zachery 2003). The biases found in drug laws were a staple of rap lyrics:

A street kid gets arrested, gonna do some time
He got out three years from now just to commit more crime
A businessman is caught with 24 kilos

He's out on bail and out of jail
And that's the way it goes, raah!

The above lyrics, from the song "White Lines" by Grandmaster Flash and Melle Mel, demonstrate the biases in drug laws by equating an urban youth to a white-collar businessman. Both engaged in drug distribution, with one serving time and the other given freedom. Many Blacks see the justice system in this country as biased against African Americans and the poor and this is often reflected in their music.

It ain't a secret, don't conceal the fact:
the penitentiary's packed, and it's filled with Blacks.
But some things will never change.
Try to show another way, but they staying in the dope game.

In the song "Changes," Tupac Shakur comments on the impact these biased drug laws have on communities of color. He argues that prisons are filled with Blacks because of some African Americans' participation with illegal drugs, either through distribution or use. He decries disparities in laws, distribution, criminalization, and creation. Some musicians, like Big Boi of Outkast, feel that crack cocaine, the drug that elicits the highest sentence, was created and placed in the Black community in order to imprison a specific population. In "Mighty O," Big Boi rhymes,

The worse thing since Crack Cocaine distributed to the poor
By the government, oh I meant, don't nobody know
Conspiracy theory, you be the judge, nobody's slow

Because of the disparities in sentencing based on the type of drug an individual possessed, many have argued that the policy was constructed primarily to criminalize a specific segment of the community. This law implicitly reflects the differences in race among drug users and distributers: crack cocaine was more popular in Black communities. On the other hand, there has been support for the disparities in drug policy because of the violence that was published in association with crack distribution.[10] The portrayal was increased violence associated with crack cocaine compared to powder cocaine. In the early 1980s crack cocaine hit urban areas across the United States with a monstrous punch that predominately affected Black and Brown communities. Crack became popular because of the low cost associated with it; a single dose did not require as much pure cocaine, which resulted in lower costs to produce the drug. With crack's increasing popularity, there was considerable profit to be made from return users. Associated with the profit of the drugs was violence to maintain control over drug sales and territory to distribute drugs. This violence is what prompted a need for harsher drug laws, which had dire effects on Black and Brown communities. This policy saw to it that those who were drug users were persecuted and imprisoned instead of rehabilitated. These changes in policy and living conditions were reflected in Black music (Neal 1999).

There are numerous examples in the Hip-Hop community of rap music being used to discuss other issues as well, including discrimination, poverty, racism, and police brutality. The best example is the oft-labeled first political rap song, "The Message," by rap group Grandmaster Flash and the Furious Five, which describes the reality for many living in urban communities (Neal 2004b):

You'll grow in the ghetto livin' second-rate
And your eyes will sing a song called deep hate
The places you play and where you stay
Looks like a great big alleyway

In this song the artists detail the realities of living in harsh impoverished neighborhoods and the impact these conditions have on a person's emotional and mental state (Southern 1997). Like the Bebop of the previous era, rap music emerged as a response to the inequalities in housing and education felt in urban communities, primarily in the north. Some of these disparities are detailed in Los Angles rapper Too $hort's song, "The Ghetto":

Even though the streets are bumpy, lights burned out
Dope fiends die with a pipe in their mouths
Old school buddies not doing it right
Every day it's the same
And it's the same every night

Again, Too $hort used rap music to discuss social issues he observed in his community. Like Grandmaster Flash and the Furious Five's "The

Message," this song emphasizes urban, predominately minority communities. Too $hort explains problems with the infrastructures in the "ghetto," including bumpy roads and nonfunctional street lights. He also laments the lack of concern those both inside and outside this community have for the lives of those in the community. Finally, he asserts that in these communities little changes; each day and night is similar to the last. Such descriptions of poverty, neighborhood activities, and living conditions were common fodder for rap songs.

In "Project Windows," Nas presents elements of poverty, relationships with the criminal justice system, and rampant drug abuse.

> Reading's what I should've done, cus my imagination would run
> I was impatient to get out and become part of the noise out there
> I used to stare, five stories down, basketball courts, shot up
> playgrounds
> and I witnessed the murders and police shake-downs
> Yo, the hustlas and hoes, drugs and fo-fos
> This was the life of every kid, lookin' out project windows

Ronald Isley sums up Nas' feelings with the chorus, "looking out my project window/ Oh, I feel uninspired." Nas expresses how easy it is for urban youth to feel isolated and damned to a life of crime and poverty. Similarly, he harps on why some individuals may lack determination and efficacy if they feel that their future is bleak and already determined. Nas expresses the exasperation many individuals in urban communities may feel because they don't believe they have many opportunities. This sentiment is echoed in Young Jeezy's song "Trapped," where he rhymes:

> Even though we had a will, we ain't have a way, (way)
> They just told us how to live, we ain't have a say, (say)
> All I know is the other side got some cuffs for ya, (for ya)
> Fresh khaki suit, nigga that enough for ya, (yeah)

In this verse Atlanta rapper Young Jeezy discusses what life is like in the "trap." For many southern artists the "trap" is a term to describe their communities. Individuals who fall into dealing or using drugs become trapped in that lifestyle or trapped behind bars. As expressed in these lyrics, Jeezy does not believe there are many options for young Blacks, even if they want to do something different from what they observe in their communities. The criminal justice system often serves these individuals badly, and they end up in prison. Both he and fellow Atlanta artist T.I. call their form of music "trap music" because they discuss their lives as former drug dealers. But before T.I. and Young Jeezy popularized the term "trap" in reference to their style of music, Atlanta's rap group Goodie Mob clearly articulated this lifestyle in their song, "Thought Process":

> These laws got me ready to brawl cause I fall a victim
> So I still be slangin' them fat pillows
> To make 'em meet
> Each and every day as I comb my city streets
> Sometimes I wish I never had been apart of this mess
> Cause the system got us fucked up
> It put us to the test, women and men, if you black you in
> Food for the soul listen to what I tell you
> It don't matter
> Young or old, it's time we loc' up
> And do like we suppose
> We killin' each other over this bullshit and some clothes
> We're trapped off in this world and society with no place else to go

Here Goodie Mob explains that selling drugs (pillows) is a way to supplement income, but is not enough to live off. He also details the frustration of being Black and poor in America and how the "trap" has indoctrinated a particular survival ideology, lifestyle, and consequence among Blacks. While these depictions are dreadful, they are the reality for many urban youth. Yet poverty and drugs are not the only issues discussed in political rap music; women and motherhood are also addressed.

Young Blacks seized on rap as an outlet to discuss the everyday reality of their lives. This use of alternative information sources was necessary as the images propagated in mainstream media only presented a "prototypical" Black character, eliminating a diversity of experiences, thoughts, and behaviors (Neal 2004b). One of the most popular examples of this form of stereotyping was the "welfare queen." Former President Ronald Reagan created the negative image generally referred to as the "welfare queen," a Black woman with multiple deceased husbands and addresses who used various aliases to deceive the government and used taxpayers' dollars to receive welfare and veterans benefits that she spends on living lavishly, including the purchasing of a Cadillac. This fictional perpetrator of fraud never existed. There was no woman who made "150,000" tax free dollars a year with a number of aliases, as Reagan detailed (Hancock 2004). The fictional image emerged from the story of a woman from Chicago who was facing charges of fraud of around $8,000 because of similar circumstances (Mink 1998; Hancock 2004; Alexander-Floyd 2007; Jordan-Zachery 2008).

Embracing the notion of a counter-narrative, many rap artists have used their lyrics to paint another image of single Black mothers. Rapper Queen Latifah's track "Evil That Men Do" discusses the interaction between race, class, and sexism in the reality of Black single motherhood in America while simultaneously dispelling Reagan's imagined "Welfare Queen." She rhymes,

A woman strives for a better life, but who the hell cares?
Because she's living on welfare
The government can't come up with a decent housing plan
So she's in no man's land.
It's a sucker who tells you you're equal

With its references to inadequate housing, the government, and the social issue of single motherhood, this verse typifies political rap at its finest. Queen Latifah is able to discuss society's marginalization of poor women who receive welfare benefits. She raps that no one cares about a woman's attempt to work for a better life if that woman is poor and receiving welfare benefits. This plays into the image of the welfare queen, which was used to rally numerous Americans against government-sponsored assistance programs. Thus, women receiving welfare benefits and Black women in particular are viewed as lazy and irresponsible. In these few lines, Queen Latifah presents discrimination, an intersection of race, gender, and class. She acknowledges the stereotype of the welfare recipient Reagan painted as an undeserving, manipulative, lazy, and conniving woman. And through her lyrics and the adoption of the moniker "Queen," Latifah provides an alternate image of Black women. Queen Latifah is one of many "Black women rappers [that] interpret and articulate the fears, pleasures, and promises of young Black women whose voices have been relegated to the margins of public discourse" (Rose 1994: 146).[11]

Like Queen Latifah, mainstream rappers and New York natives Nas and Tupac (later associated with West Coast rap) are known for examining political issues, racism, and social events in their lyrics. These two artists discuss events from the Vietnam War to the election of President Obama. For instance, in "Panther Power" Tupac details the core American values of freedom, equality, and liberty, but from the perspective of minorities who have not always experienced these values:

> As real as it seems the American Dream
> Ain't nothing but another calculated schemes
> To get us locked up shot up back in chains
> To deny us of the future rob our names
> Kept my history of mystery but now I see
> The American Dream wasn't meant for me
> Cause lady liberty is a hypocrite she lied to me
> Promised me freedom, education, equality
> Never gave me nothing but slavery

In this short verse Tupac criticizes American values of equality and liberty in relation to the treatment that African Americans faced in this country, including slavery and the dehumanization that resulted from that institution. Once again, political rap is used as a voice to assert views and opinions about political and social issues in the United States, here American values that all citizens are supposed to embrace and enjoy. Similarly, Nas continues in the tradition of music as an outlet to express political attitudes with his song "Doo Rags" from the *Lost Tapes*:

> Political thugs in shark suits persuade us to pull triggers
> in army boots, yellin "Join the armed forces!"
> We lost the Vietnam War, intoxicated poisons
> Needles in arms of veterans instead of bigger fortunes

In this verse Nas discusses a specific political event, the Vietnam War. He details the apparent differences between those who participated in the war through combat and politicians or "political thugs." Similarly, he discusses the sacrifice of troops fighting in the war and the consequences of those that "survived" the war. Growing up in the Post-Vietnam society, especially in urban areas, could make one very aware of the psychological and physical effects the war had on veterans. It was not atypical in some communities to see a veteran on a corner outside a liquor store or in an alley. Nas believes that it was the effects of the war, specifically "poisons" of heroin and other drugs, that turned these soldiers into victims when they returned to the states.

Conclusion

Rap continues the tradition of using art and culture to critique under-recognized problems in American society. Rap literally brought a voice to a segment of the community that was often alienated and dismissed. Rap allowed urban youth to detail their stories and lives at a time when they often saw distorted images of themselves in media, as portrayed by politicians and other leaders (Rose 1994; Allen 1996; Pough 2004; Norfleet 2006). These rappers represented a counter-public from which attitudes are developed. Yet, many still wonder: does rap really have the ability to affect political attitudes? And if it does, what types of attitudes are influenced, suggested and advocated by political rap, specifically?

In this chapter I examined the tradition of using culture to express the beliefs of marginalized individuals. Now, however, many assert that Hip-Hop is dead, meaning that the original position of rap music as a critique of political and social ills is no longer common. In fact, in a recent album titled *Hip Hop Is Dead*, Nas states in the title track,

> Everybody sound the same, commercialize the game
> Reminiscing when it wasn't all business
> It forgot where it started
> So we all gather here for the dearly departed
> Hip-hopper since a toddler
> One homeboy became a man, then a mobster
> If it dies, let me get my last swig of Vodka
> R.I.P., we'll donate your lungs to a rasta
> Went from turntables to MP3s
> From "Beat Street" to commercials on Mickey D's
> From gold cables to Jacobs
> From plain facials to Botox and face lifts
> I'm looking' over my shoulder

It's about eighty people from my hood that showed up
And they came to show love
Sold out concert and the doors are closed shut

These lyrics summarize much of the debate about the death of Hip-Hop. Many argue that because of the increased commercialization and commodification of the genre it is no longer considered a resistance mechanism, nor does it have the ability to influence political attitudes because the political content, if existent, is watered down compared to the rap music that was produced during Hip-Hop's "golden era." These sentiments are expressed not only in some rap songs but also in other popular cultural avenues such as Black films.

Brown Sugar, an urban film, has two congruent plots. One of the storylines deals with the relationship of two childhood friends who later fall in love, the other, with the growth and changes of Hip-Hop. For these friends, Hip-Hop was the foundation and thread that kept them connected from childhood into adulthood, and these characters grew and changed with Hip-Hop. In one scene, the main male character, Dre, an artist scout for a major label (A&R), is introduced to an aspiring rap duo Ren and Ten, who jokingly refer to themselves as the "Hip-Hop Dalmatians" because of the races of the artists, one white and one black. These artists are depicted as a mockery of the genre. In fact, they can be categorized as the "minstrelsy" type of rap Ogbar (2009) discusses in his text, *Hip Hop Revolution*. The rap duo are signed by Dre's label, Millennium Records, because of their potential commercial success despite lacking any lyrical sophistication or substance. Many argue that the type of rap presented by this duo in the film is a reality for the current state of rap music. In other words, rap has lost its political edge and thus should no longer be considered a voice for the people and instead as another source of racial stereotypes, inaccuracies, and hyperboles about the lives of young urban minorities.

The remainder of this book will debunk these assertions and demonstrate that, in 2014, there is still a segment of political rap music that is alive, thriving, and well. These sentiments are expressed by various artists. New York native and multimillionaire rap mogul Jay-Z and Eminem, the highest grossing White male solo rap artist, for example, wrote the song "Renegade," which discusses their rejection of conformity, and being ostracized and labeled. In "Renegade" Jay-Z[12] presents a critique of those who attempt to label rap music: "Do you fools listen to music or do you just skim through it?" He suggests that those who listen to rap will see that materialism and violence are not the only themes asserted within the genre. Many major African American movements were supported and fueled by music, and rap is not an end in this history of resistance and cultural importance. As Rose comments, "rap continues the long history of Black cultural subversion and social critique in music and performance" (Rose 1994: 99).

Political rap continues to exist, but its ability to influence political attitudes and behaviors is still up for debate. Does a listener actually adopt and believe the political information and critiques that are asserted in this subgenre of rap? Empirically, that question still remains, but what we can observe is that materialism, sexism, and misogyny are elements presented in rap music that have translated into observable behaviors. For instance, rap socializes capitalist ideas and values such as materialism. This sort of value is present in songs such as Drake's *I'm On One*, Kanye West's, *All Falls Down*, Gucci Mane and Young Jeezy's *Icy*, and Nelly's, *Grillz*.

An example that demonstrates how individuals adopt or accept certain attitudes presented within rap is evident in the "snowman" phenomenon. Children throughout the country, but predominantly in the South, began wearing t-shirts asking, "Got Snow?," which were subsequently banned in many public schools because of the reference to the illegal drug, cocaine (Scott 2005). The word "snowman" was coined by Young Jeezy, which connected ice to diamond jewelry. Jeezy raps, "Get it? Jeezy the Snowman, I'm iced out, plus I got that snow, man" (Scott 2005). The trend of wearing "Got Snow?" shirts became news when many schools attempted to ban the shirts due to the obvious drug reference. However, the need to ban them demonstrates the popularity of the message and how it was adopted by youth. These songs can influence large groups of individuals to value diamonds, jewelry, and even gold teeth, but can this genre politically educate, inspire, and push people to political action?

Hip-Hop apparently has some socializing powers, but does it have the ability to socialize political attitudes or inform individuals about political issues? We rarely evaluate the socializing effects of rap upon political attitudes. How can rap affect some behaviors and not others? I don't believe it can. Different types of rap affect different types of behaviors and attitudes. Advertisers know this, as evident when they use rap to sell items as varied as cars, beverages, and food, but social scientists often dismiss this cultural expression as something that can have real impact on social and political stances.

It's Bigger Than Hip-Hop: Rap Music and Black Nationalism

Black Nationalism ha[s] been more likely to engage politically active
Black youth than ideologies of racial integration and socialism."
  —Patricia Hill-Collins, *From Black Power to Hip-Hop*, 13

Never let the system use me, my duty is my passage
Watch the homies in your army, they don't always show their badges
Keep your family living healthy, teach your children 'bout their
    blackness
Teach your wifey how to use the ratchet, this shit is classic
Get your food, clothes and shelter, fuck the system pimp it backwards
I ain't hating, I'm just saying if you wanna be a rapper study Malcolm
    Garvey Huey
Dead Prez
  —Malcolm, Garvey, Huey, *Turn Off the Radio: The Mixtape Vol. 4:*
    Revolutionary but Gangsta Grills

In 2004, rapper Jadakiss's political song "Why," was discussed on *The O'Reilly Factor,* a right-leaning news show hosted by conservative commentator Bill O'Reilly on Fox News. O'Reilly, a vocal critic of rap music, featured the song because he believed it was an "atrocity" and offered a biased view of the Republican administration (Heim 2004). Jadakiss's song, a top 20 single on the Hip-Hop charts, posed many titillating political questions about former president George W. Bush, the Republican administration, the 2000 national election, and the events of September 11, 2001 (Heim

2004). Some of the most controversial questions implied Bush's involvement with the 9/11 events, including the line "Why did Bush knock down
the towers?"[1]

In his defense, Jadakiss stated "I think that before 9/11 the intelligence
agencies weren't communicating a lot of the important information. And
ultimately, at the end of the day, he's the boss. The buck stops with him"
(Heim 2004). Previously Jadakiss commented to Billboard.com that he "felt
[Bush] had something to do with it. That's why I put it in there like that.
A lot of my people felt he had something to do with it. Jadakiss continues
by asking other political questions about Arnold Schwarzenegger's election
as California's governor and Bill Clinton's signing of the Violent Crime and
Law Enforcement Act of 1994, which gave grants to states that implemented
a statute requiring prisoners to serve at least 85 percent of their sentence
before being eligible for parole.[2] Still, these are only some of the political
issues discussed in the song.

After controversy erupted over the original version, a remix featuring
rappers Styles P, Common, and Nas was released. While the initial song
had focused on the events of 9/11, the remix touched on themes as diverse
as partisanship and race, the 2000 presidential election, George W. Bush,
the war on terror, Barack Obama, Malcolm X, and the education system.
More importantly for my purpose here, the remix presented aspects of
Black Nationalist ideology. For instance, Styles P, member of the New York
based rap group the L.O.X. with Jadakiss, asks, "Why vote Republican if
you Black." In this lyric, Styles P questions the logic of voting for the
Republican Party if you are Black because of the belief that the Republican
Party does not advance issues relevant to African Americans. This is supported by Michael Dawson's linked fate theory, which argues that African
Americans tend not to support parties that do not align with issues relevant
to the Black community (full employment, welfare reform that includes a
guaranteed income, comprehensive health care, and minority business set
asides) regardless of individual class differences (Williams 2003; Dawson
2004; Walton and Smith 2010).[3] In fact, the Republican Party has been
known to advance implicit racial messages advocating against African
American participation (Mendelberg 2001). Examples can be found in the
Republican ads against Michael Dukakis in 1988 and Harold Ford in 2006,
as well as the location and "state's rights" rhetoric in Reagan's announcement of his presidential candidacy in Philadelphia, Mississippi, in 1980
(Mendelberg 2001). However, the Republican Party didn't always have a

contentious relationship with African Americans. In fact, African Americans gained freedom, citizenship, and protection from the Republican Party after the Civil War and during the Reconstruction era. Yet, after the election of 1948 and through the urging of South Carolina's senator and Dixiecrat candidate Strom Thurmond, southern whites defected to the Republican Party. By 1964, many southern Whites began voting Republican. Because of this history and lack of support for Blacks by either of the major parties, Black Nationalists believe Blacks should form their own independent party. Styles P continues in this vein; although he does not directly advocate for the formation of an all-Black party, he does invoke Black Nationalist beliefs of self-determination, Black consciousness, linked fate, and unity.

Another rapper who was featured on the remix of "Why" and was later reviewed by Bill O'Reilly was Chicago rapper Common. O'Reilly's critique of Common came after Common was invited to a poetry event at the White House. O'Reilly and other conservative pundits and politicians were upset with Common's invitation to this event because of content of a poem performed on HBO's Def Poetry, "A Letter to the Law." His metaphorical line "burnin' a Bush" was framed by O'Reilly and others as controversial and violent, and they categorized Common as a gangster rapper. However, Common is not a gangster rapper, even by the loosest of definitions; he can be categorized as a socially and politically conscious rapper, in part because this was not Common's first and only reference to former president George W. Bush. In the remix of "Why," Common voices his discontent with Bush and his assertion of Black Nationalist attitudes in the lines,

Why is Bush acting like he trying to get Osama
Why don't we impeach him and elect Obama

Common's solution to the possibility of entering wars, including the war on terror, was to impeach Bush and elect Senator Barack Obama president of the United States. He supported a Black candidate as a means of inclusion and empowerment within the political system, a common sentiment of Black Nationalists. Common could have proposed another solution to the problems with the Bush administration, but instead he chose to appeal to Black sentiments and beliefs that electing a Black official had the potential to eliminate problems and gain concessions for African Americans as well as other groups. Finally, Nas, who was also subjected to O'Reilly's critique, is more obvious with his Black Nationalist appeals. He makes a direct reference to Black Nationalist leader Malcolm X in his verse suggesting that Blacks should continue Malcolm X's mission. Black Nationalism is a very common theme within rap music and specifically political rap.

Black Nationalism has stimulated increased empirical research of the construction, adoption and impact on political behavior and public opinion (Dawson 2001; Brown and Shaw 2002; Davis and Brown 2002; Harris-Lacewell 2004; Price 2009; Spence 2011). Nevertheless, many empirical areas of this ideology remain untested, such as the examination of the relationship between Black Nationalism and political rap music. This chapter assesses the relationship between listening to rap and Black Nationalist ideology, positing that (1) some rap songs do present Black Nationalist attitudes; and that (2) there is an increase in Black Nationalist support among those who are exposed to rap compared to those who are not exposed to rap; and 3) subgenres of rap matter, and political rap specifically increases support of Black Nationalist attitudes more than nonpolitical rap or no exposure to rap music. Based on Zaller's (1992) RAS model, Black Nationalist attitudes are received, accepted, and sampled by those exposed to political rap music. While exposure to Black music increases racial solidarity, I assert that political rap provides more political information than other subgenres of rap music and positively influences one's adoption of Black Nationalism.

Black Nationalism

Black Nationalism as an ideology calls for the cultural, political, and economic independence of African Americans. Specifically, Black Nationalism is interested in self-determination, self-reliance, Black pride, unity, and consciousness (Dawson 1994; Henderson 1996; Brown and Shaw 2002; Davis and Brown 2002; Karenga 2002; Hill-Collins 2006; Price 2009). There are many different types of nationalist ideology. For instance, there is *racial solidarity*, which refers to organizations based solely on race; *economic nationalism*, which advocates a "Black capitalist economy and the support of Black-owned businesses"; and *revolutionary Black Nationalism*, which "views the overthrow of existing political and economic institutions as a prerequisite for the liberation of Black Americans" (J. Bracey et al. 1970: xxviii). Finally, *territorial separatism* is the Black Nationalist belief that Blacks should have their own part of the country and separate from other groups (xxix).⁴ Although there are different types of nationalist groups, they all support "distanc[ing] themselves politically, socially and culturally from what were seen as the hegemonic, racist narratives and practices of a corrupt system of White supremacy" (Dawson 2001: 90). Historically, the most popular Black Nationalist organizations were Marcus Garvey's Universal Negro Improvement Association, Elijah Muhammad's Nation of Islam, and Huey Newton and Bobby Seale's Black Panther Party for Self-Defense (BPP).

Born in Jamaica in 1887, Marcus Garvey created the Universal Negro Improvement Association (UNIA) in 1914. Two years later, Garvey moved to New York and opened the first American branch of the organization. Garvey declared the purpose of the UNIA was "to promote the spirit of race pride" (Hill-Collins 2006: 117). He helped raise the racial pride of Black Americans by insisting that, "Black stood for strength and beauty, not inferiority" (Franklin 1967: 490).

The Nation of Islam (NOI) is an Islamic group founded by W. D. Fard in 1930 and led primarily by Fard's protégé Elijah Muhammad. This group believed Blacks were Allah's chosen people and that Whites were a race of unruly and unenlightened people created by mad scientist Yacub (X 1964a). NOI believed Blacks in America should fight for self-determination and community control. Besides Elijah Muhammad, the NOI boasted two dynamic speakers and national leaders throughout its history, Malcolm X (El Hajj Malik Shabazz) and Louis Farrakhan, current leader of NOI.

Another prominent Black Nationalist organization was the BPP, founded in Oakland, California, in 1966 by Huey Newton and Bobby Seale. BPP emphasized self-defense and Black Nationalism. It instituted protection from police, self-defense, and numerous community programs including political education and free breakfast for children. The Panthers campaigned for issues of economic equality including employment equality, adequate housing, ending police brutality, and an equal justice system (Karenga 2002).

Why do I choose to focus on Black Nationalism? First, because Black Nationalism promotes racial solidarity and is "the dominant ideology in contemporary Black Politics," so it should also be an ideology represented in the smaller rap community (Alexander-Floyd 2007: 3). Second, since Black Nationalism is the most popular Black ideology, one can argue that being a Black Nationalist makes one more aware of issues that solely affect the Black community because of the Black, racial, or Afrocentric lens used to examine issues. A Black Nationalist typically is more aware of solely racial issues than a disillusioned liberalist or Black Feminist who uses other frames of reference that include dimensions other than solely race. Therefore, adopting this ideology should influence political behavior. Finally, Black Nationalist sentiments are the most identified political attitudes found in rap songs (Decker 1993; Henderson 1996; Dawson 2001; Lusane 2004; Miyakawa 2005).

Black Nationalism and Hip-Hop

Within Hip-Hop culture, Black Nationalism is a very popular ideology due to the prominence of nationalistic organizations in urban areas such as the Nation of Gods and Earths (NOG&E or Five Percenters), the NOI, the BPP and cultural movements like the Black Arts Movement. In fact, it has been asserted that Five Percenters deliberately used rap as a means of disseminating their culture, ideas, and beliefs, for example through rappers such as Brand Nubians, Rakim, Nas, Big Daddy Kane, and Wise Intelligent of Poor Righteous Teachers (Perry 2004; Miyakawa 2005; Norfleet 2006). In the sub-genre of political rap, there is evidence of direct connections between NOI, NOG&E and BPP philosophies establishing a relationship between nationalist sects and Hip-Hop that is identified in rap lyrics (Lusane 2004: 355).

To observe the introduction of Black leaders we can turn to the rap song "Thug Holiday" from Florida rapper Trick Daddy, in which he references Black Nationalist leaders Malcolm X and Louis Farrakhan:

And, I read your books know all the remixes to the bible
What about a verse for the thugs, a cure for drugs and survival
Let's add some chapters name them Martin, Malcolm and
        Farrakhan

In this verse Trick Daddy references religious inconsistencies and variations of Christians' holy text, the Bible, noting the lack of references in the Bible to thugs or those who are impoverished, targeted, labeled, and marginalized, as well as the issue of substance abuse, particularly drugs and a succinct plan for survival. Instead he suggests additional chapters of the Bible that detail the histories of esteemed Civil Rights and Black Nationalist leaders Martin Luther King, Jr., Malcolm X, and Louis Farrakhan. Two of these, Malcolm X and Louis Farrakhan, can be labeled Black Nationalists, especially after their interaction with Elijah Muhammad and the Nation of Islam. This verse rapped by Trick Daddy can be associated with Black Nationalism because of the direct referencing of Black Nationalist leaders.

Similarly, the song "Who Shot Rudy" by New York rap group Screwball references Black Nationalist leaders who may have had a role in detailing a fictional shooting of former New York City Mayor Rudy Giuliani. Screwball asks

Did Sharpton and Farrakhan make the shit real?
Was it Khalel? You know he keep mad steel
Did the Bloods or the Crips smoke Rudy on the hill.

Screwball lists people or organizations that may have played a role in this fictional shooting, including the notorious Bloods and Crips gangs and popular Black Nationalist leader Louis Farrakhan. This song not only detailed a fictional shooting of Rudy Giuliani but it expressed the disgust many urban New Yorkers felt about Giuliani's mayoralship and his policies. Further these authors also suggested Giuliani's possible replacement in the song with the lines

Knowing he was gone for good, dead stinking
It got me thinking
Ay-yo, where the fuck Dinkins?

These lines were referencing the replacement of Giuliani with previous New York city mayor, the only Black mayor of New York, David Dinkins to reign again.

This type of referencing of Black Nationalist leaders is popular among many artists. For instance, in "My Country," Nas invokes the memories of Malcolm X (El Hajj Malik Shabazz), one of the NOI leaders, Patrice Lumumba, a revolutionary leader from Republic of the Congo who fought for independence of his country. Bobby Seale and Huey Newton, Black Panthers co-founders and leaders, were referenced in "You're da Man." Not only does Nas make numerous political references to George W. Bush in "What Goes Around" and Colin Powell in "Rule," but he also explicitly makes nationalist references. For instance, in "You're da Man" Nas rhymes "Wish

I could flap wings and fly away / To where black kings in Ghana stay." In these two simple lines he is invoking a Black Nationalist attitude of repatriation and separatism, some of the more militant aspects of Black Nationalism.

While these songs make specific references to Black Nationalist leaders, not all the Black Nationalist references are as obvious. Sometimes the allusions are to Black Nationalist attitudes such as self-reliance, self-determination, racial consciousness, and racial solidarity, as expressed in Nas's song, "Black Zombie":

> What do we own? Not enough land, not enough homes
> Not enough banks, to give a brother a loan
> What do we own? The skin on our backs, we run and we ask
> For reparations, then they hit us with tax
> And insurance if we live to be old, what about now?
> So stop being controlled, we Black zombies

In this song, Nas invokes the Black Nationalist attitude of self-reliance. He advocates Black-owned businesses, banks, and land as a remedy for dependence on American political, social, and economic systems. In other words, owning, investing, and controlling businesses, the economy, and land, according to Nas, will help end the control and oppression and the "zombie"-like, walking dead state of African Americans. Throughout this song he discusses various ways he believes African Americans are "zombies," without the ability to reason and control their own desires, thoughts, and actions. While Nas primarily describes self-reliance and self-determination, he also summons racial consciousness and solidarity. Yet Nas is not the only political rapper who has achieved commercial success and produced political rap music.

Los Angeles rapper Too $hort, who does not typically discuss political or social issues, also appeals to racial consciousness, pride, and solidarity in his political rap song "The Ghetto":

> So much game in a Too $hort rap
> Blacks can't be White and Whites can't be Black
> Why you wanna act like someone else?
> All you gotta do is just be yourself
> We're all the same color underneath
> Short Dog's in the house you'd better listen to me

Never be ashamed of what you are
Proud to be Black stand tall at heart
Even though some people give you no respect
Be intelligent, when you put em in check
Cause when you're ignorant, you get treated that way

Here the rapper expresses his racial pride, a prominent trait of cultural Black Nationalist sentiment. While this song does not specifically address nationalist leaders, it still calls on nationalist ideas by referencing racial pride and the relationship between Blacks and Whites in America, including lack of respect of the former by the latter. Too $hort acknowledges that although he may not get the respect he deserves from others, he will maintain his pride and dignity and learn to rely on himself. These sentiments illustrate perfectly the internalized marginalization and hostility felt by many African Americans and the adoption of Black Nationalist attitudes in response.

Frustration, anger and discontent with the political and social system in the United States are widely-addressed issues within rap music. One of the most blatant expressions of frustration and anger concerning life as a Black youth in America is observed in New York rap group Wu-Tang Clan's song "I Can't go to Sleep." This song features 1970s icon Isaac Hayes singing the chorus:

Don't kill your brother, learn to love each other
Don't get mad, cause it ain't that bad
Look at who you are, you've come to far
It's in your hands, just be a man
Get the jelly out your spine
Cobwebs out of your mind.

In this chorus Hayes is portraying the voice of a wise elder telling these young men to refrain from anger, to embrace love instead of violence, and to continue striving because life has never been easy. He is offering comfort and encouragement to a segment of the population that has constantly endured struggle, frustration, violence, crime, and poverty. With the line "get the jelly out your spine," he encourages young Blacks to "be a man" and grow a backbone. In other words, don't falter. Finally, he encourages young men to think with the metaphor of removing cobwebs from the mind. What is interesting about this verse is the concept of masculinity which follows ideas presented in many Black Nationalist sentiments and organizations. Later in the song, by suggesting that the listener "stop all this crying and be a man," Hayes demonstrates a certain aspect of masculinity—that a man cannot cry or complain and must accept his lot in life and make the best of it. He is also indirectly asserting the Black cultural value that men take care of their families. Thus, the man cannot complain, cry, or be upset about his situation, but instead has to "be strong" and a "man" for the rest of his family, thus equating strength with masculinity.

This song also directly details Black Nationalist sentiments by referencing and recalling the consequences of famous Black leaders, some of whom held and presented Black Nationalist ideologies. In the third verse, New York rapper and one of the founders of the Wu-Tang Clan, RZA (riz-zah), recounts the murders, assassinations, and deportation of those leaders who were associated with the advancement of Black liberation in the United States.[5]

Numerous rap artists including but not limited to Dead Prez, Talib Kweli, Yasiin Beg, Kendrick Lamar, Drake, Kanye West, Lupe Fiasco, Jay-Z, Lil Wayne, Snoop Dogg (now known as Snoop Lion) and Common, have all referenced Black Nationalist leaders or used soundbites from Black Nationalist leaders. Some have incorporated Black Nationalist ideology and attributes into their stage names and album titles, such as Lord Jamar's *The Five percent Album* and Mos Def and Talib Kweli's duo BlackStar, taking from Marcus Garvey's successful shipping company called the Black Star Line. Others have aligned themselves with Black Nationalist traditions and customs of earlier generations by adopting African and Islamic names that invoke meaning (primarily those adhering to the teachings of the NOI and the Nation of Gods and Earths (Five Percenters)), including rappers U-God (member of the Wu-Tang Clan), whose name is influenced by Five Percent's custom of referring to Black men as God, and another rap artist Culture Freedom, which is the meaning of the number 4 in the Supreme Mathematics of the Five Percent nation.

For some, referencing Black Nationalist leaders and organizations may be simple, without any additional context, history, or significance. A telling example of dropping the name of a Black Nationalist leader in a song for lyrical purposes can be found in Canadian-born rap artist Drake's song "Forever," in which he states "labels want my name next to an X like Malcolm." In this lyric Drake references Malcolm X but does not give details of the person and his history. He simply uses Malcolm X's name as a lyrical strategy to show the avidity of record labels to sign him as an artist with their company and uses the symbolism of an X to signify where a person should sign. Similarly, in his verse in Lil Wayne's song, "Mr. Carter," Jay-Z states,

Now my name's been mentioned with the martyrs
The Biggie's and the Pac's, and the Marley's and the Marcus'
Garvey, got me a Molotov cocktail

Here a Black Nationalist leader, Marcus Garvey, is referenced, with only the information that he is considered a martyr. There are no details of who he was, his politics, or what organization he ran. However, the mere mention of these leaders could prompt others to research Marcus Garvey or Malcolm X, especially considering the popularity of these two rap artists.[6]

On the other hand, some artists provide context when they cite Black Nationalist leaders. This is portrayed in Chicago rap artist Common's "A Song for Assata," which details parts of the life of escaped political prisoner Assata Shakur. Assata Olugubula Shakur is a political activist who was a member of both the Black Liberation Army and the Black Panther Party.[7] In 1977 Shakur (previously known as JoAnne Deborah Bryan [Chesimard]) was convicted of first degree murder of a New Jersey State Trooper, Werner Foerster, on the New Jersey Turnpike. She details the case and the court proceedings as a mockery because she knew she would not receive a fair trial. Shakur escaped from prison in 1979 and ultimately moved to Cuba for political asylum (Shakur 1987). She became the only woman on the FBI's list of Most Wanted Terrorists in 2013 with a reward of 2 million dollars for her capture. Shakur's story was detailed in Common's song in her honor.

Common goes even farther on his song featuring rapper Ceelo, a previous member of the Atlanta based rap group Goodie Mob, by including a soundbite of Assata Shakur at the end of the song. The song concludes with Shakur's remarks to an assumed question of "what is freedom?"

While the names and speeches of many Black Nationalist leaders and advocates are featured in political rap songs, Malcolm X reigns supreme as one of the most often cited leaders in rap music. Among the most famous allusions is the cover of KRS-ONE's album *By All Means Necessary*, in which KRS-ONE draws on the popular image of Malcolm X protecting his home from those threatening his life by peering out of the window with a rifle in his hand. KRS-ONE uses this prominent image as well as one of the most famous quotes by Malcolm X, "by any means necessary," to invoke a memory of the man, his teachings, his life, and his prominence in New York. On this album cover, instead of holding a rifle, KRS-ONE, in Hip-Hop apparel (Malcolm X wore a suit and tie in his famous picture) holds an Uzi machine gun, a weapon that invokes a subliminal reference to the symbolism of drug related crime in many urban areas. Thus, while Malcolm X was protecting himself and his family from outside threats in the 1960s, it can be inferred that KRS-ONE uses this imagery to point to gang and drug violence in urban areas and the idea that a man must still protect his family from outside enemies.

Any discussion of the connection between Black Nationalist ideology and rap music is not complete without the mention of two important groups, Public Enemy and Dead Prez. Public Enemy openly advertised its connection to the Black Power movement of the 1960s, specifically the BPP and the Nation of Islam. The group was the "first overtly and consistently politically oriented group in Hip-Hop" (Norfleet 2006, 360). Often Public Enemy expressed nationalist ideology in its music by including snippets of speeches by leaders such as Malcolm X and Louis Farrakhan. Similarly, Public Enemy was able to demonstrate Nationalistic imagery through its security team, led and formed by band member Professor Griff and called S1Ws, the Soldiers of the First World. They dressed in all-black attire that mimicked that of the Black Panthers, including black berets, and they often performed military drills at shows. Angela Ards argues that "from PE and others like KRS-ONE, X-Clan and the Poor Righteous Teachers, urban youth were introduced to sixties' figures like Assata Shakur and the Black Panther Party, then began to contemplate issues like the death penalty, police brutality, nationalism and the meaning of American citizenship" (Ards 2004: 313).

Dead Prez used Black Nationalist images as well. They used red, black, and green on their album covers, signifying the Black liberation (red, black, and green) flag created by Black Nationalist leader Marcus Garvey. Like Common and other artists, Dead Prez has also dedicated entire songs to Black Nationalist leaders. In their song "Malcolm, Garvey, Huey," Dead Prez discusses Malcolm X, leader of the Nation of Islam and founder of the Organization of Afro-American Unity (OAAU or OAU); Marcus Garvey, leader and founder of the Universal Negro Improvement Association; and Huey Newton, founder and Chairman of the Black Panther Party. As is evident, numerous rap artists have infused their music with Black Nationalist ideas, images, philosophy, and soundbites while simultaneously maintaining some degree of commercial success. Dead Prez is among a group of artists who consistently produced complete political rap albums.

Although many may disagree on the time span, many fans and critics alike agree that there was a golden era of Hip-Hop, when rap songs had more meaning and were more politically and socially relevant. Specifically, Perry argues, "in the late eighties and early nineties politically conscious rap music flowered that vociferously critiqued White supremacy, classism and racial exploitation" (Perry 2004: 28). A common criticism of current rap is that it is shallow, misogynistic, clichéd, overly-materialistic, hypermasculine, and generally devoid of social commentary.

On the contrary, Lupe Fiasco's 2011 controversial album *L.A.S.E.R.S.*, which was listed as the most purchased album on Amazon.com and peaked on several Billboard charts as the number one album (Billboard's top 200, Rap Albums, R&B/Rap Albums), featured many political rap songs including "All Black Everything" and "Words I Never Said." This album was controversial because of Fiasco's battle with his record label,[8] the types of songs featured, and the political lyrics. In "All Black Everything," Fiasco describes an alternate timeline wherein Black people have never been enslaved or oppressed. He rhymes:

> We ain't work for free, see they had to employ it
> Built it up together, so we equally appointed
> First 400 years, see we actually enjoyed it
> Constitution written by the W. E. B. Du Bois
> Were no reconstructions, Civil War got avoided.

He envisions a role for Blacks in the creation of the United States, including W. E. B. Du Bois's involvement in the Constitution and an America where slavery, the Civil War, and Reconstruction did not exist. Additionally, in "Words I Never Said," Lupe Fiasco takes aim at the War on Terror, 9/11, budget cuts, and the education system:

> I really think the war on terror is a bunch of bullshit
> Just a poor excuse for you to use up all your bullets

How much money does it take to really make a full clip?
9/11, Building 7, did they really pull it?
Uh, and a bunch of other cover ups
Your child's future was the first to go with budget cuts
If you think that hurts, then wait, here comes the uppercut
The school was garbage in the first place, that's on the up and up
Keep you at the bottom but tease you with the upper crust

Lupe Fiasco's album, laced with politically and socially relevant content, was still a commercial success. This success can be attributed to rap fans who continue to purchase albums from artists who have a history of producing politically-relevant albums. In fact, Lupe Fiasco's fans were so supportive of his music and creative originality that they even staged protests outside Atlantic Records to support Fiasco's creative control.

Lupe Fiasco was not the only commercially successful artist to produce political music in 2011. That same year also saw the release of *Section.80*, an album by critically-acclaimed rapper Kendrick Lamar. On "Hiii Power" he raps:

Who said a Black man in the Illuminati?
Last time I check, that was the biggest racist party
Last time I check, we was racing with Marcus Garvey
on the freeway to Africa 'til I wreck my Audi
And I want everybody to view my autopsy
So you can see exactly where the government had shot me

This song deals with various political attitudes, including the increasingly popular discussion within the rap community about an Illuminati conspiracy theory and the group's relationship with political parties.[9] Lamar also references famed nationalist leader Marcus Garvey.

Although both "Words I Never Said" and "Hiii Power" aggressively take on political themes, the issues presented in these songs differ. Most importantly, both Kendrick Lamar and Lupe Fiasco represent a sample of rap artists who have found commercial success releasing political songs, despite criticism that political rap is no longer a viable component of rap music. Yet, the myth persists that popular rap artists will not be well received among mainstream media if they produce entire political rap albums. In 2010, Nas provided proof to the contrary by producing a successful political rap album in conjunction with reggae artist Damian Marley, son of notable political reggae artist Bob Marley. Nas's and Damian Marley's album reached number one on various U.S. Billboard charts.

There are also political rap songs that espouse Black Nationalist sentiments and even complete political rap albums by artists not as popular within mainstream rap but still attracting many followers, especially with the technological advances of Amazon MP3 sales and social networking sites such as Twitter, Facebook, and Youtube. As a result of many artists abiding by Black Nationalist ideology, in addition to the continuous references in political rap music to Black Nationalism, it is reasonable to expect that Black Nationalism will be a supported and accepted ideology of those who are exposed to political rap.

Cultural Influence

The early 1990s was a time of great expansion and innovation for Hip-Hop. It had been several years since LL Cool J's releases "I'm Bad" and "I Need Love" had gotten heavy rotation on MTV. Yet, the first inclusion of rap music as a variable in national studies occurred in the 1993–1994 National Black Politics Study (NBPS).[10] At the time NBPS was conducted, rap music was reaching new heights, greater mainstream exposure, and of course garnering more criticism.

In the years leading up to the study (1989–1993), rap had come to the attention of executive level politicians; C. Delores Tucker and former Vice President Dan Quayle both labeled the genre "misogynistic." Rap was also used to point to violence and racist sentiments when former President Bill Clinton called rap artist, author, and political activist Sistah Souljah a racist because of her comment, "If Black people kill Black people every day, why not have a week and kill white people? So if you're a gang member and you would normally be killing somebody, why not kill a white person" (as quoted in Chang, 2005). Many suggest that the focus on these comments, often referred to as the "Sistah Souljah moment," was a political strategy Bill Clinton used to distance himself from African American leader Jesse Jackson in order to gain support of Ross Perot voters (Chang 2005). Many other controversial issues surrounded rap during this time, including West Coast rappers Tupac and Snoop Dogg's prison sentencing and rapper Eazy-E's receipt of an invitation to attend a Republican luncheon. At the same time, evidence of rap's far reaching influence was evident in the debut of the sitcom *The Fresh Prince of Bel-Air*, featuring wholesome rap artist Will Smith, and the march of Hip-Hop-centered movies such as *House Party*, *CB4*, and *Who's the Man?* The same year of 2 Live Crew's legal woes, white rapper Vanilla Ice gave Hip-Hop its first Billboard chart topper in the form of the catchy song "Ice Ice Baby." In 1993, music icon Quincy Jones founded Vibe, which spotlighted Hip-Hop artists, actors, and other entertainers, and it became a leading source of information on Hip-Hop.

The popularity of Hip-Hop during this period provided rationale for the inclusion of rap variables in a national survey examining African American attitudes. However, the NBPS was lacking in that it categorized rap as a monolithic genre of music, rather than parsing out its many subgenres. Contrary to popular belief, rap music has never been a monolithic genre. Even at the time of its origin, there were multiple genres including battle rap, message rap, breaking rap, and party rap. Thus, the NBPS was not able to capture the separate impact of these different subgenres of rap on individual attitudes. It is instead necessary to go beyond general survey questions and conduct experimental analysis to observe the effects of exposure to rap music. I have conducted original experiments to differentiate between subgenres in rap music, allowing a more intensive examination of the relationship between specific subgenres of rap and Black political attitudes.

I argue that those who listen to rap are exposed to the beliefs and ideologies expressed by the artist and will demonstrate more support for Black Nationalism than those who do not listen to rap. 52 percent of those surveyed in the 1993 NBPS reported that they had not listened to rap, versus the 48 percent who had within the previous week. Among young people surveyed, those who were a part of the 'Hip-Hop generation' as identified by Bakari Kitwana (between eighteen and twenty-eight at the time of the survey), 78 percent said they had listened to rap within the last week.[11] While this survey was completed during the early 1990s when rap was just beginning to gain popularity nationally, the percentages among this age group remained relatively consistent. According to the Black Youth Project, in 2008 71 percent of young people (fifteen-twenty-five) listened to rap at least once a week, 4 percent once or twice a month and 10 percent rarely or never (Cohen 2007).

But what does all this mean for Black Nationalism? Considering the popularity of Black Nationalist sentiments in rap music, one must consider whether these attitudes are accepted and used as ideological foundations by those who are exposed to this type of music and these types of messages. Specifically, is Black Nationalism an ideology accepted by those exposed to political rap? With rap music being a part of the Black information networks of which Harris-Lacewell (2004) asserts affect Black political attitudes and ideology, then understanding the specific sole impact of political rap is essential to studying Black political attitudes. Thus, examining whether rap, alone, can influence political attitudes is a very important question especially considering the popularity of rap music.

Black Nationalism, Rap Music and Causal Relationships

One may wonder whether the previously demonstrated relationship between political rap and Black Nationalism is spurious. In other words, does listening to rap affect an individual's adoption of Black Nationalism, or does the acceptance of Black Nationalism make one more apt to listen to a specific type of rap music? It is easy to confuse correlation and causation. Experimentation is the best way to sort out the differences between the impact of political rap music and nonpolitical rap on Black political attitudes.

Black Nationalism can be measured a number of ways. Some researchers measure Black Nationalism by focusing on community control and self-reliance using a measure of Black autonomy (Dawson 2001). Others measure aspects that emphasize community or separation from the United States; these type of Nationalisms are called community nationalism and separatism (Brown and Shaw 2002). Still others analyze many strands of Black Nationalism together, including cultural, political, and social measures (Davis and Brown 2002) as part of a 10-variable scale. This nationalism focuses on self-reliance, self-determination, and cultural nationalism. The scale consists of the following variables:

- *Blacks should shop in Black-owned stores*
- *Blacks should rely on themselves and not others*
- *Blacks should participate in Black-only organizations whenever possible,*
- *Blacks should form their own political party*
- *Blacks should support all male schools*

- *Blacks should have control over the government in mostly Black communities,*
- *Blacks should have control over the economy in mostly Black communities.*
- *Black children should study an African language*
- *Blacks should vote for Black candidates whenever they run*
- *Blacks should form a separate nation*

The Black Nationalist variable used in this experimental analysis is an additive index that combines the ten aforementioned Likert scale variables ranging from strongly disagree to strongly agree (1 to 4).[12] For each item, higher values represent more agreement with Black Nationalist strategies on a 40-point scale. A respondent who strongly agrees with all 10 items would score ten 4s, a Black Nationalism score of 40. Conversely, a respondent who scored all 1s on the items, for a combined score of 10, would strongly disagree with all the Black Nationalist measures. I examine the overarching themes of Black Nationalism as they are presented in rap music: self-reliance, self-determination, cultural nationalism, racial pride, and racial unity.

An original experiment was conducted at Benedict College, a historically Black college in Columbia, South Carolina, to examine the effects of exposure to political rap music on the acceptance of Black Nationalist ideology. The overarching question in this experiment was whether political rap significantly influences one's adoption of Black Nationalism compared to exposure to nonpolitical rap or no music at all.

To recap, political rap is defined as rap music that has met the first element detailed below *and* satisfies either the second or third element:

1. Display political references in the lyrics, such as directly referencing a political leader, political office/institution, political activity, or political position.
2. Make reference to a social problem or issue and discuss it in the lyrics, therefore raising awareness about specific issues or disparities nationally or globally.
3. Advocate a solution to injustices or problems in society either through violent or nonviolent means.

The experiment examines a sample of students from Benedict College, a predominately Black (roughly 99 percent) private, liberal arts college; 90

percent of Benedict's students are first generation college students and a little over half of its students are women.[13]

In political science, experiments using college students may be contested due to a belief that students are not a representative sample. However, this is the beauty of experimentation. Good experiments stem from correct manipulation rather than from representative samples. In certain situations, it can be difficult to obtain a representative sample to participate in an experiment and field or lab work; therefore, the emphasis here is placed on having the best manipulations and model to measure exactly what the study needed and attempt to control for all other factors.

Benedict was chosen as the study site for a number of reasons. First, I am interested in the impact of rap on Black political attitudes, so it was necessary to choose an experimental site and population that would offer a large number of Black respondents. Using a college population was also beneficial because it is widely believed that the younger you are the less likely you have sustaining political ideologies. For someone interested in the impact political rap music has on Black political attitudes and ideologies, college students are the ideal subject. They are old enough to be able to accurately assess the political attitudes they may adopt and young enough to not hold any previous sustaining attitudes. Benedict is also the largest undergraduate private college in South Carolina and representative of students from every county in the state. The diversity of counties represented, the gender proportion, and the concentration of Blacks made Benedict an ideal place to study Black political attitudes.

The experiment conducted at this college observed the relationship between political rap music exposure and political attitudes, using four conditions and a control group. The four conditions were political rap, nonpolitical rap, rhythm and blues, and pop. The artists and songs chosen represented regional, lyrical, and temporal diversity. The artists represented the three dominant regions from which rappers originate, and the songs were produced between 1995 and 2005. The subgenre of interest in this study was political rap, which was represented by three songs that met the criterion of a political rap song.

The first political rap song used in the experiments was "Georgia . . . Bush" by New Orleans rap artist Lil Wayne. This song was written after the devastation of New Orleans by Hurricane Katrina. It is a commentary on government officials' slow response to the victims and survivors of this natural disaster. The song is classified as political rap because it satisfies the first and second criteria. This first verse and chorus reference a political leader, President George W. Bush. The song is filled with references to extensions of political institutions, such as the police department, as well as direct references to politicians like former president Lyndon B. Johnson, who was in office when Hurricane Betsy flooded New Orleans in 1965. The song satisfies the second criteria by raising awareness about the lack of government response to New Orleans residents from the perspective of a New Orleans native and rapper. This song represents a Southern perspective within rap and, with the album's 2006 release date, is relatively current.

The second song used in this subgenre is "Police State" by rap duo Dead Prez, consisting of rappers M-1 and Stic. Man, who formed their group in Tallahassee, Florida. Dead Prez, which is vehemently anti-government, is one of the most popular contemporary political rap groups.[14] While most of their records have not had much radio play, they have had some commercial success with their songs "Hip-Hop" and "Mind Sex," both of which had videos featured on Black Entertainment Television (BET). These artists are typically very militant and espouse Black Nationalist and anarchist sentiments. "Police State" represents a mixture of northern and southern perspectives based on the artists' hometowns and sits in the middle of the time range identified, with an album release date in 2000. This song presents a depiction of Black life and injustice in America. Law enforcement, specifically the prison system, is the focus. The song discusses the grave reality of prison life and the disproportionate number of Black men who are incarcerated,

The average Black male
Live a third of his life in a jail cell
Cause the world is controlled by the white male
And the people don't never get justice.

The song begins with a political reference in the introduction by Omali Yeshitela, African People's Socialist Party Chairman and an advocate of the Uhuru ("freedom" in Swahili) movement. In the introduction the chairman defines a state:

The State is this organized bureaucracy
It is the po-lice department. It is the Army, the Navy

It is the prison system, the courts, and what have you,
This is the State; it is a repressive organization

Dead Prez use their artistic platform to discuss the resistance and anarchist tactics they argue can be used against the government to change the injustices they describe. One verse includes vivid imagery of the fictional bombing of a police station, thereby positing anarchy as a plausible alternative to the perceived "Police State." Dead Prez also critiques the American governmental system by detailing the possibility of invasion of privacy and the prevalence of a capitalist hierarchy. They discuss the realities of prison, economic disparity, and sexism while exerting the acceptance of a socialist ideology. Thus, this song satisfies all three categories of the political rap criteria.

The last song in the political rap condition, "Us" by West Coast rapper Ice Cube, takes a different stance by critiquing the Black community instead of the government. This song can still be considered political rap for several reasons. First, "Us" makes reference to Uncle Sam, a common national personification of the American government. Second, this song raises awareness about disparities and problems in the Black community in the voice of a critic of that community.[15] This is significant because while many songs that identify problems in the Black community exist, this type of internal criticism is not very popular. Ice Cube's approach is important because it displays another type of voice within political rap from the blatant critique of government. Instead this style emphasizes ideas of self-determination and self-reliance that are key elements of Black Nationalism. This relation to Black Nationalism is no coincidence, as Ice Cube has been linked to the Nation of Islam and has stated that NOI is the "best place for any young male," and although he says he was not directly affiliated with the organization, he has acknowledged his religious background as a Muslim (*Guardian* 2000).

In addition to political rap, the experiment made use of three other conditions and a control group. The nonpolitical rap condition consisted of party songs or songs whose emphases are celebratory. In this condition subjects were exposed to the songs "Walk it Out" by DJ Unk, "In Da Club" by 50 Cent, and "Gin and Juice" by Snoop Dogg. Within the rhythm and blues condition, subjects heard "Love" by Musiq, "Let it Burn" by Usher, and "This is How We Do It" by Montell Jordan. Finally, within the pop condition participants listened to the songs "What I've Done" by Linkin

Park, "Saving Me" by Nickleback, and "This Love" by Maroon 5. Again note that the songs are all from male artists, represent the three popular regions of Hip-Hop (North, South, and West), and represent the time frame 1995–2006.

Procedures

Subjects for this sample were solicited via flyers, emails, and handbills distributed before and during the experiments. The students were promised compensation of $5 on completion of the survey. While there was no randomization of the potential subject pool since all subjects were students of Benedict College, there was randomization of the manipulation each participant encountered. Each subject was randomly assigned to one of five groups and sent to the respective classrooms, which were designated by numbers 1, 2, 3, 4, or 5. The subject was given 20–30 minutes to listen to all the songs and complete the short questionnaire to measure their political attitudes. The questionnaire consisted of 64 mixed response questions of which 10 questions represented the Black Nationalist attitudes previously presented. The survey was self-administered after respondents listened to the preselected songs. Those in the control group did not hear any music but instead read an article about technological advances before completing the survey.

The sample size of this experiment was 191 participants, with ages ranging from 18 to 48. The racial breakdown of the participants was African American 175; Latino 2; Arab, 1; Native American, 1; and Multi-Ethnic, 8. The study was conducted over the course of two days for a total of 6 hours. Once there were at least 20 participants in the designated manipulation the experiment began. In each classroom, an experimental proctor would start the series of songs, and after all the songs were played in their entirety the participants received a paper survey they completed. In the control group there was also a requirement of a minimum of 20 participants before the survey packet was handed out.

Results

The experimental analysis suggests that music does cause the acceptance of some political attitudes. Nationalist scores were averaged and the means of support were compared to assess the relationship between support of Black

Nationalism and exposure to music.[16] The results support my hypothesis that exposure to political rap causes increased support of Black Nationalism. Comparing the manipulation of the control condition, it is clear that political rap had the greatest significant impact on support of Black Nationalism, with a mean difference of -2.21 for those in the control group compared to those in the political rap group. (Those in the control group, who did not hear music, were on average 2.21 degrees lower in their acceptance of Black Nationalism compared to those in the political rap group.) This result is significant at the .05 level of a two-tailed means difference test. Compared to other manipulations to political rap music, participants in the nonpolitical rap, pop, and control group were significantly less supportive of Black Nationalism. Specifically, exposure to nonpolitical rap resulted in a 2.05 decrease in acceptance of Black Nationalism on the 10-point scale. These results demonstrate that exposure to political rap actually increases one's acceptance of Black Nationalism, particularly compared to no music exposure or exposure to nonpolitical, celebratory rap music.

This is important because it supports my hypothesis that political rap is more important to the acceptance of a Black Nationalist identity than nonpolitical rap. Thus, all rap music is not the same and all rap music does not influence Black Nationalist sentiments similarly. These results are significant in light of criticism that rap only leads to negative attitudes and viewpoints. Black culture, specifically political rap music, represents a counter-public that influences Black political attitudes.

Alternatively, these results demonstrate identifiable political consequences of exposure to political rap for African Americans. Exposure to political rap *causes* one to be more accepting of Black Nationalist attitudes. Surprisingly, results showed no statistical difference between the agreement with Black Nationalist attitudes in participants in the rhythm and blues and political rap conditions. This lack of statistical difference may be contributed to the long history of political music that is part of the rhythm and blues genre, or the R&B songs chosen may have activated other attitudes among the participants that were not examined. Chapter 2 detailed the use of music as a resistance mechanism throughout Black history, and R&B songs follow in this tradition. Perhaps the soulful tunes in the R&B songs used in this experiment primed an increased racial consciousness and solidarity simply because they can be categorized in this tradition of Black music that has had political and social meanings, especially through the Civil Rights and Black Power era.

Conclusion

Political science research rarely analyzes rap as a media outlet that provides political information and affects political attitudes. This chapter has made the case for consideration of rap as a relevant and powerful factor in the formation of political ideology. Rap music can frame an idea or viewpoint, set an agenda on a political issue, or prime certain ideas. Powell (1991: 245) asserts that "in addition to entertainment, rap music provides a significant form of informal education for adolescents . . . that extends far beyond the confines of the classroom and into their peer group circles." This chapter provides vital information about the relationships between rap music and Black Nationalism. Another interesting observation was that men who listen to rap showed stronger significant relationships with Black Nationalism than women do, which will be further explored in the next chapter. Similarly, this chapter has demonstrated that political rap increases support of Black Nationalism, especially in comparison to exposure to pop music, nonpolitical rap, or no music. Hence, political rap is different from nonpolitical rap. Therefore, people will have to clarify the type of rap referred to when criticizing the genre.

Harris-Lacewell (2004) correctly contends there are various avenues through which African Americans receive political information that assists in the formation of political attitudes; rap music is one of those avenues. Observing that exposure to political rap causes Black attitudes among Black participants establishes that not only is rap important but the type of rap one listens to may have more influence on political attitudes. However, a potential shortfall of this research and these results is that the reaction of exposure to rap is immediate. This book does not detail if continual exposure to political rap will have lasting attitudinal effects that shape long-term political ideologies, but this research demonstrates that there is evidence to think that this may be a possibility. Research on long term effects of rap should be considered in future studies.

Why haven't we observed this in political science research before? One possibility is that politically laced rap is believed to be less popular than nonpolitical rap, and therefore not as prominent in mainstream society. Another is that the actions and attitudes that stem from political rap have been attributed to other political sources. However, this is not a reason to discount the influence of the subgenre. The understanding of marginalized communities must include the examination of marginalized cultural forms within the community. Chapter 4 continues this discussion by observing the effects of rap music on Black Feminism.

Chapter 4

Beyond the Music: Black Feminism and Rap Music

> Black people come together to worship; organize around communal
> problems; sit together to cut and style one another's hair; pass news
> about each other through oral and written networks; and use music,
> style and humor to communicate with each other.
> —Melissa Harris-Lacewell, *Barbershops, Bibles, and BET*, 1

> U.N.I.T.Y., U.N.I.T.Y. that's a unity (You got to let him know)
>   U.N.I.T.Y. (come on here we go)
> U.N.I.T.Y., Love a Black woman from (You got to let him know)
> Infinity to infinity, (You ain't a bitch or a ho)
>   —Queen Latifah, U.N.I.T.Y.

In 2007, controversial radio host Don Imus described the Rutgers University women's basketball team as "nappy headed hos." In response to widespread criticism, he claimed that the term was derived from Hip-Hop music and thus should not be considered racist or offensive. Imus's attempt to justify his blatant use of divisive, abhorrent language by using rap music as a scapegoat sparked many discussions about the effects of explicit lyrics in rap music. Many organizations and leaders were outraged at the disrespect the Rutgers women endured.

Many people embraced Hip-Hop as the scapegoat and turned the discussion to the influence and language of rap music.[1] Television stations such as BET (*Hip Hop vs. America*) held forums about misogyny, sexism, nihilism, and violence in rap music. Oprah Winfrey dedicated two shows to a discussion about censoring rap music, the damage of the lyrics, and sexism and misogyny in Hip-Hop; guests included record label executives, rap critics, rap supporters, a panel of women from Spelman College, and one rap artist, Chicago native Common. The record executives denounced the use of the word "nigga" in rap songs played on the radio. However, the fact that only one rapper was present in the panel limited the discussion on freedom of speech and an artist's agency and control over his artwork, as well as generalizable views about how rap artists view women and the language used to reference women within the genre.

We can certainly characterize some rap music as misogynistic, abhorrent, and sexist, but this classification does not apply to all subgenres of rap music. For instance, some rap music is misogynistic while some espouses pro-feminist sentiments. As a result, one might expect listeners of different types of rap music to embrace vastly different attitudes about women. Do rap music listeners believe the characterization of Black women presented by rapper Snoop Dogg, whose persona is one of a pimp and whose lyric "Bitches aint shit but hoes and tricks" is considered classic among Hip-Hop listeners? Considering the relationship between political attitudes and political ideology, one may wonder if Black Feminism is an ideology embraced by rap music listeners, especially considering the misogyny and patriarchy presented by many rap artists, both men and women. Is there a distinction between the subgenres of rap and the listeners' acceptance of Black Feminist attitudes? Specifically, how does exposure to nonpolitical rap compare to political rap when observing Black Feminist attitudes and attitudes about women?

The first three chapters have detailed the relationship between music and resistance, attitude formation, and Black Nationalist ideology. Still, we must observe how this contentious cultural outlet relates to women and gender attitudes. In this chapter, I explore these relationships quantitatively and demonstrate that rap music influences the development of some political attitudes, thoughts, and ideologies among those who listen to it. There is a relationship between exposure to rap and acceptance of Black Feminist attitudes.

While feminist attitudes may be present in some rap music, listening to rap music in general should not correlate with the acceptance of Black Feminist ideology. This is because there are not enough alternative, positive images of Black women presented across the many rap subgenres. The few positive references and assertions of some aspects of feminist ideology or female perspectives are often marginalized by the dominance of hypermasculinity, misogyny, and sexism in the genre. However, treating rap music as a nonhomogeneous cultural form and observing different subgenres of rap music reveals differences in the treatment of women and topics related to women in the lyrics. As a result, we should observe a difference between the effects of nonpolitical rap music and political rap, a more progressive form of rap music. Those exposed to political rap have a more positive relationship with Black Feminism than those exposed to nonpolitical rap.

Rap Controversy in Reference to Women

As I have noted, rap is no stranger to controversy. Over the years, church groups, moguls, politicians, and even everyday people have taken aim at the genre for its perceived celebration of sexism and misogyny. Well before Oprah Winfrey discussed the issues of rap, misogyny, and sexism on her popular talk show, activists C. Delores Tucker, Calvin Butts, Al Sharpton, and others denounced the demeaning aspects of rap music. Specifically, in 1994 C. Delores Tucker led a hearing in Congress with William Bennett, Joe Lieberman, and Sam Nunn to denounce rap as pornographic, disrespectful, and misogynistic (Hess 2007).

Similarly, rapper Uncle Luke (Luther Campbell) and his group 2 Live Crew are known for their chauvinistic lyrics in songs such as "Face Down, Ass up," and "We Want Some Pussy," which include misogyny, sexual abuse toward women, and disrespect of women. For instance in "Face Down, Ass Up" 2 Live Crew raps,

> I bust a nut, and then I'm breakin' out
> So when you're naked, down on all fours
> You better make sure that you get yours
> 'Cause a nigga like me will love ya and leave ya
> I got mine, hoe! SEE YA!

It is clear that these rappers have very little respect for the females with whom they engage in sexual relationships. In fact, the artists detail using women for their own sexual pleasure without concern for the sexual pleasures of these women. Women are seen only as sexual objects. Similarly, in the song "We Want Some Pussy," the artists describe "running a train" on a girl, in which a group of men take turns having sex with one girl and not stopping even when the girl asks them to quit, demonstrating not only a lack of respect but also invoking rape as an allowable act. "The girls would say "Stop!" I'd say "I'm not!""

Several of Luther Campbell and 2 Live Crew's songs were banned for their extremely misogynistic and sexually explicit lyrics as well as their stated acts of violence. As a result, the band engaged in a battle with the courts to argue for freedom of speech. In 1990, a Florida state court ruled that 2 Live Crew's album *As Nasty as They Wanna Be* violated decency laws, but the 11th Circuit Court of Appeals overturned the ruling two years later by determining that the original judge in the case, Judge Jose Gonzalez, did not have sufficient evidence that the work did not present any artistic value (Powell 1991; Deflem 1993). In response to this case, the group created the album *Banned in the U.S.A.* One of the songs featured on the album was directed to Bob Martinez, governor of Florida, who had originally requested that the state look into 2 Live Crew's music for violating the state's obscenity laws. In the song "Fuck Martinez," 2 Live Crew employs a call and response style to disparage Martinez and Sheriff Nick Navarro, while also disrespecting Martinez's wife by telling her to suck dick and eat pussy.[2]

To offer another example, in 2004 a group of Spelman College women (the same group that later appeared on Oprah Winfrey's town hall Hip-Hop special) led a protest against St. Louis rapper Nelly for his offensive "Tip Drill" video in which he displayed the image of sliding a credit card through a woman's buttocks. Nelly, who was scheduled to hold a bone marrow drive at the college, was met with student activists who requested that in addition to the bone marrow drive, the artist also serve as a panelist in a forum to discuss sexism, misogyny, and disrespect of women in rap music and videos (Reid-Brinkley 2008). Because of the student body's outrage and insistence that he take responsibility for the images he portrayed of Black women, Nelly declined participation in the panel and canceled the bone marrow drive. Later, the BET show that played this video on the show "Uncut" was cut from the station's lineup.

Meanwhile, rappers such as Mississippi native David Banner and Louisiana native Master P appeared before Congress in attempts to defend the cultural form. This congressional hearing was initiated by Chicago, Illinois, representative and former Black Panther Bobby Rush. Before Congress, these artists described the positive effect that rap music had on their lives as well as their resignation with the way the music spoke about women. David Banner commented that rap saved his life and kept him out of trouble because it was an outlet for his childhood aggression and anger, and Master P apologized to women for the rap he and the rest of his No Limit family produced.

Rap music has clearly suffered from much protest and controversy. Yet, the type of music that is typically protested is not political rap but the various genres of nonpolitical rap, including "gangsta" rap. By studying these oppositional rap subgenres (political versus nonpolitical rap), one can begin to measure whether a specific subgenre has an impact on an individual's support of Black Feminist attitudes.

Black Feminism and Hip-Hop

As observed through the lives and works of historical figures such as Sojourner Truth, Ida B. Wells-Barnet, and Anna Julia Cooper, Black Feminism has a long history in Black political thought. Black Feminism considers the intersection of identities, specifically of race, class, and gender (Hill-Collins 1990; Crenshaw 1991a; Dawson 2001; Harris-Lacewell 2004; Simien 2006). The three main components of Black Feminism are intersectionality, activism, and community orientation (Dawson 2001). One key element of Black Feminist practice is dispelling the misogyny and sexism that erode policy and the everyday lives of people. Rap is one place where misogyny and sexism are prevalent. However, the relationship between Black Feminism and rap music is rarely quantitatively studied (Harris-Lacewell 2004; Spence 2011).[3] This book goes farther than previous studies by examining differences between subgenres of rap and its impact on Black Feminism.

Adams and Fuller (2006) demonstrated that while different words may be used in society today in reference to Black women, ideology has remained constant. The terms and images of the *Jezebel* and the *Sapphire* correlate to the modern terms "ho" and "bitch" respectively. While Black women are no longer referred to as Jezebels or Sapphires, popular culture, specifically rap music, still uses misogynistic terms and images in reference to them (Adams and Fuller 2006). Pough asserts that "by the time we reach the Hip-Hop era, Black women have generations of conditioning to stay in the background. . . . [there also exists] a history of seldom speaking out against Black manhood even when it poses a direct threat to Black woman-hood" (Pough 2004a: 75). This statement is especially true when observing the misogyny in some Black Nationalist sects and the support of Black Nationalist attitudes within rap music as demonstrated in Chapter 3. Nevertheless, some rap is positive in the construction of Black women's images and attitudes.

Numerous women rappers disrupt the dominant attitudes promoted in this genre, including Monie Love, Lauryn Hill, Salt-N-Pepa, Bahamedia, Trina, Tiye Phoenix, and Eve. These female emcees have taken a stance as subjects instead of objects within Hip-Hop culture, as exemplified through the songs they create. For instance, Grammy award winning rapper and singer and New Jersey native Lauryn Hill discusses her objections to aborting her unborn child in her song "Zion," revealing that abortion was the recommended course of action because of her career.[4] Baltimore emcee Tiye Phoenix, in her song "Half Woman, Half Amazin,'" exclaims her lyrical prowess as a female emcee, an attribute not freely given to many rappers, but one she claims for herself. Many women emcees spread Black Feminist attitudes through their songs. For instance, rap artist Queen Latifah's single "U.N.I.T.Y." discusses misogynistic language and "challenges those males who use bitch/ho appellations in their lyrics" (Keyes 2004: 273).

Yet the acceptance and advocacy of Black Feminist ideas by some rap artists does not result in acceptance of the label Black Feminist. Via her Twitter account, popular emcee Jean Grae states that she is not and will never be a feminist. In fact, many female rap artists have asserted that Feminism was a "movement that related specifically to White women" (Rose 2004: 303). These Black women believed that by adopting Feminism they would be abandoning their Black brothers or putting their struggle for legitimacy before that of Black men, thus betraying "the cause." However, this feeling of solidarity with Black men is in fact a Black Feminist sentiment, according to the Combahee River Collective. Thus, to examine Black Feminist attitudes in rap songs, we must understand the pillars of Black Feminism as described in this Collective.

The Combahee River Collective was a group of Black Feminists who drafted A Black Feminist Statement in 1977. The statement details the beginnings of Black Feminism, the beliefs and problems with organizing Black Feminists, and Black Feminist issues. According to the statement this collective attributes the origin of Black Feminism to historical activists and scholars such as Harriet Tubman, Sojourner Truth, and Anna Julia Cooper, whose previous attitudes were embraced more fervently during the 1960s and culminated in a "politics that was anti-racist, unlike those of white women, and anti-sexist, unlike those of Black and white men" (A Black Feminist Statement). They believe in the value of Black women and the necessity of liberation from sexual, gender, class, and racial oppression, which they believe are inseparable for Black women. They "reject pedestals, queenhood, and walking ten paces behind." They are against sexual oppression, including criteria that define how a "lady" should act, look, and dress. Instead these women are interested in humanity, socialism, understanding how the personal is the political and solidarity with Black men. They simultaneously oppose separatist lesbian attitudes and oppression from white women, white men, and Black men. Some of the issues identified in the Statement that Black women have been focusing on are sterilization, the right to choose or reproductive rights, domestic violence, health care, rape, privacy rights, and issues that affect those of Third World nations.

However, because of the intersectionality of various oppressions, it has been hard for Black Feminism to set a specific political agenda, although some have tried. Following the work of the Combahee River Collective and the demands of the Black Panther Party Platform, members of the Black Feminist Working Group (BFWG) created their own set of plans in their twelve-point platform. BFWG states that Black Feminists want freedom and an end to violence against Black children, control over reproductive health, diversity in media, reformation of the criminal justice system, equal housing, an end to poverty, educational liberation, safety and security, an end to homophobia and violence against homosexuals, an end to sexism and sexist practices, and more respect for nature and the environment (Black Feminist Working Group 2011).

Similarly, in Hip-Hop and Hip-Hop scholarship there has been a designation of Hip-Hop Feminism by Joan Morgan (1999), Aisha Durham (2007), Kamala Price (2007) and others. Joan Morgan (1999) suggests that women who listen to rap understand that the lyrics may be sexist but continue to listen to and support the artists. While Durham and Price argue that Hip-Hop Feminism is the feminism that women who were born after 1964 and were supporters of Hip-Hop culture and feminism embraced. Specifically, Durham (2007: 305–6) states that Hip-Hop Feminism is "a socio-cultural, intellectual and political movement grounded in the situated knowledge of women of color from the post-civil rights generation who recognize culture as a pivotal site for political intervention to challenge, resist, and mobilize collectives to dismantle systems of exploitation." While Black Feminism is in depth and covers many issues within the intersection of race, gender, and class, I am not debating any specific form of Black Feminism or Womanism in this text. Instead, I am arguing that when considering the intersection of race, gender, and sex within Hip-Hop music and culture, differences in attitudes are presented that relate to Black women, Black Feminism, and Womanism. In the following sections I examine how Black Feminism (or Womanism), generally, and Hip-Hop Feminism in particular have been demonstrated within rap music by observing three elements that intersectionally affect abuse, both domestic and sexual, reproductive rights, and objectification.

Women, Hip-Hop, and Violence Against Women

Keeping in mind the multifaceted demands of Black and Hip-Hop Feminists, I now turn to songs that identify some of the issues discussed on these two statements. Female rappers often sing about issues that disproportionately affect women, such as domestic violence, as exemplified in Philadelphia rap artist Eve's song, "Love Is Blind." In a narrative format, Eve describes the mental, physical, and verbal abuse her friend endures in a relationship:[5]

She was in love and I'd ask her how? I mean why?
What kind of love from a nigga would black your eye?
What kind of love from a nigga every night make you cry?
What kind of love from a nigga make you wish he would die?
I mean shit he bought you things and gave you diamond rings
But them things wasn't worth none of the pain that he brings
And you stayed, what made you fall for him?
That nigga had the power to make you crawl for him
I thought you was a doctor be on call for him
Smacked you down cause he said you was too tall for him, huh?

This song struck a chord with many women who had been abused or had witnessed abuse, as well as those organized against domestic violence. While Eve may not identify herself as a Black Feminist rap artist, it can be argued that she wrote about an issue that is addressed within some elements of Black Feminist ideology. This song discusses the intersection of gender,

race, relationships, motherhood, and class by detailing a domestically violent relationship between a man and the mother of his child that results in
the death of the mother. Eve does an excellent job bringing in the dynamics
of motherhood and what impact this tumultuous relationship has on the
couple's child. She also incorporates the level of control the man had over
this woman, her friend, because of economic constraints, and describes the
way this man was able to "make up" with his partner through the purchase
of lavish jewelry. Eve is taking a stance not only by using her music to
discuss this issue but also in her music by attacking the abuser after he beat
her friend to death. "Love Is Blind," as a heavily played single, may have
empowered some women to leave abusive relationships while simultaneously bringing awareness to the issue of domestic violence. However, abuse
is experienced not only through domestic violence, but also through sexual
assault and child abuse.

Sexual assault is a fact that many women know too well and another
issue that has grave implications when observing the intersection of race,
gender, and class. Sexual abuse and rape are topics covered by Black women
throughout America's history. During slavery, Harriet Jacobs wrote in her
autobiography that she was unable to escape the sexual advances of her
owner because of her oppression and enslavement. Jacobs believed it was
necessary to give her account to dispel the myths and stereotypes of Black
women as licentious Jezebels enticing white slave owners to engage in sexual relationships with them. She saw her autobiography as an option to
detail the horror she experienced. She was not able to call upon authorities
to stop her rape or bring her abuser to jail because enslaved Black women,
men, and children did not have any rights that were to be respected,
acknowledged, or protected by Whites during this time. Even when Black
women resisted, they still did not have the support of the law, as evident in
a book entitled *Celia, a Slave*. Celia, an enslaved Black woman who killed her
owner because she was tired of fighting off his sexual assaults. However,
unlike Jacobs, Celia did not live to tell her story. Instead she was executed and
we know of her story through her trial documents. While enslaved Blacks, in
most cases, did not have rights that were protected, in some cases they were
brought to trial for acts against Whites. Black women have historically and
currently been painted as seductive temptresses who use their bodies and
sexual appetites for favors and advances. This attitude, especially prevalent in
rap music, is asserted not only by male rap artists through imagery of women
gold-diggers in their videos and suggested treatment of women in some rap

songs, but also by some female rap artists who relate their sexual appetites and conquests in the same manner as some men. This is not to say that female artists should not talk about sex or embrace these stereotypes in ways that can be empowering, but only to demonstrate that these stereotypes of Black women are pervasive in the American psyche.

Thus, there is no wonder that songs about sexual abuse are found in rap music. One example of a rap song that details sexual abuse is by Angel Haze, who describes her molestation at age seven and the impact it had on her life in the song "Cleaning Out My Closet," using the beat from the song with the same name featured on *The Eminem Show*, in which Eminem describes abuse against his longtime girlfriend. In her song, Angel Haze raps,

> I was afraid of myself, I had no love for myself
> I tried to kill, I tried to hide, I tried to run from myself
> There was a point in my life where I didn't like who I was
> So I'd create the other people I would try to become
> Sexuality came into play and with as scarred as I was
> I was extremely scared of men so I started liking girls
> I started starving myself, fucked up my bodily health
> I didn't wanna be attractive to nobody else
> I didn't want the appeal, wanted to stunt my own growth
> But there's a fucking reason behind every scar that I show
> I never got to be a kid so that's as far as I grow
> My mental state is out of date, and that's as far as I know

> My biggest problem was fear, and what being fearful could do
> It made me run, it made me hide it made me scared of the truth
> I'm not deranged anymore, I'm not the same anymore
> I mean I'm sane but I'm insane but not the same as before
> I had to deal with my shit, I had to look at my truth
> To understand that to grow you've got to look at your root.

In this song Angel Haze discusses being sodomized and made to perform fellatio at age seven. She speaks to her feelings surrounding the trauma she experienced and her self-hate and hate for men. She also discusses the anger she had, specifically toward her abuser, and how she wanted to harm him and herself. While not explicitly labeling herself feminist, Haze tackles an issue that also deals with her identity as a young Black woman in America.

Sexual abuse is a reprehensible act that affects 1 in 5 women in the United States, according to the National Intimate Partner and Sexual Violence survey of 2010 (Black et al. 2011). Still, above this 20 percent who are accounted for, it is believed that more Black women have experienced sexual violence and abuse that is undocumented because of the cultural norms of silence in the Black community and shame and marginalization. This song is unique because Angel Haze goes beyond the cultural norm by detailing her victimization and assault as well as sharing the psychological impact this trauma had on her (another disparity not widely discussed in the Black community). What is also unique about this song is that Haze uses the same beat from a song by Eminem where he describes abuse against his longtime girlfriend, one that lauds violence and abuse, a theme readily available within rap music. Instead, Haze uses this medium to empower herself and describe her own abuse. She discusses issues often silenced in the Black community, giving a voice to both women and men who are victims of sexual abuse. These abuses are not discussed from the perspective of male rap artists. Because of the hypermasculinity, sexism, and patriarchy in rap music, rarely will you hear songs about men being victims of sexual or domestic abuse. Thus, Angel Haze is able to discuss an issue that impacts Black women from the voice of a Black woman. However, sexual abuse and violence is not the only topic dealing with the intersection of race, gender, and class that is presented in rap songs. Issues of reproductive rights are also presented by both male and female rappers.

Women, Hip-Hop, and Reproductive Rights

Again, because of the history of subjugation and oppression Black women have endured in America, the rights of reproductive control are often advocated on behalf of Black Feminist activists and discussed in rap music. As detailed by Dorothy Roberts in her book *Killing the Black Body* (1997) and Harriet Washington in *Medical Apartheid* (2008), Black women have endured centuries of not having control over their bodies, which resulted in cases of forced sterilization and birth control use, especially among Black women deemed in some way incompetent either mentally or criminally because of drug use during pregnancy. This type of direct criminalization of mothers was not commonly applied to women of other races or who used other types of intoxicants (e.g., alcohol) that could have endangered an unborn child. Numerous incidences of rape and forced childbirth have occurred because other alternatives may not have been present, as a means of control, oppression, intimidation, and humiliation, not only during slavery but also as recently as the Civil Rights era, as documented by Danielle McGuire in *At the Dark End of the Street* (2011). Thus, reproductive and privacy rights issues encompass the intersection of race, gender, and class and are observed here as Black Feminist issues.

For instance, in the Combahee River Collective and the BFWG 12-Point Plan, many Black Feminists advocate for reproductive and privacy rights. Some songs that deal with reproduction, pregnancy, and privacy in rap music are "Abortion" by Doug E Fresh and the Get Fresh Crew, "La Femme Fetal" by Digable Planets, "Can I Live" by Nick Cannon, "Runaway Love" by Ludacris, "Autobiography" by Nicki Minaj, "Invetro" by Organized Konfusion, "My Story" by Jean Grae, "Real Killer" by Tech N9ne, "Retrospect for Life" by Common, "The Unseen" by Geto Boys "Happy Birthday" by Flypside "Lost Ones" by J. Cole and "What's Going On" by Remy Ma. In line with public opinion in larger society, some rap songs favor the rights of the unborn child and some support privacy and reproductive rights of the woman and her body. A majority of the songs listed above are in favor of the unborn child and these attract a great deal of attention from certain groups. One song that fits this description is "Happy Birthday" by Flypside, which has received over 600,000 views on youtube .com and news articles praising the position of the artists, primarily from conservative groups. The assertion of feminist attitudes, however, comes in the form of rap songs that advocate reproductive and privacy rights, notably "La Femme Fetal," by the trio Digable Planets, a group consisting of two men and a woman.

In this song, the artists describe the role that social and political ideologies play in the decision-making process of pregnant women. They tell a first-person story in which we learn about a pregnancy in the voice of the woman who is then given advice by the artists:

> You remember my boyfriend Sid, that fly kid who I love
> Well our love was often a verb and spontaneity has brought a third
> But due to our youth an[d] economic state, we wish to terminate
> About this we don't feel great, but baby, that's how it is
> But the feds have dissed me
> They ignore and dismiss me
> The pro-lifers harass me outside the clinic

And call me a murderer, now that's hate
So needless to say we're in a mental state of debate

Digable Planets respond:

The fascists are some heavy dudes
They don't really give a damn about life
They just don't want a woman to control her body
Or have the right to choose
But baby that ain't nothin'
They just want a male finger on the button

In this song, fascists are those who oppose abortion or a woman's right to choose, and the use of the term "dudes" indicates an anger specifically toward male anti-choice advocates. The group explains how these men want to control women's bodies by not allowing them to choose for themselves. Many Black Feminists promote freedom of choice so a woman can have autonomy and ultimately control over her own body. This, of course, has been a demand by Black women throughout the history of the United States, especially considering the aforementioned medical "practices" against Black women and the oppression of Black women. For instance, the profitability of Black children during slavery also left many Black women unable to choose their sexual partners, whether they had children, and whether they were able to raise their children. Thus, in the history of women's fight for control over their bodies, race complicates this right for Black women.

Still, many of the songs that deal with reproduction are complicated and do not take a specifically pro-choice or pro-life stance, but instead discuss emotions and outcomes based on decisions as well as the relationships among religion, health care, and anti-abortion advocates. Many artists indeed complicate the dichotomous pro-choice, pro-life stances in society by adding details to these positions, which are typically painted as either/or issues. An artist such as Jean Grae complicates this duality in her autobiographical song "My Story" by adding context, details, and imagery to the complexities of reproductive decisions. She details the rappers' ability to have and make a choice in having an abortion, the pros and the cons of her decision, and the thoughts preceding and following the abortion. Similar to Digable Planets, she explores reproductive rights, which are not about advocating for or against abortion, but for a woman's right to control her own body. Jean Grae also dispels the stereotype of the Jezebel by detailing how she was not lewd or promiscuous, further complicating previously held perceptions about Black women (Harris-Perry 2011).

Another female emcee, Remy Ma, also discusses her personal reproductive decision in the song "What's Going On?" In this song she raps,

> Politics and shit quit when the doctor says positive it's a life living
> In my body but it don't gotta live it's up to me but if I keep what
> The fuck I got to give I mean I'm still young and I don't really have
> Shit and if this nigga up and leave then my child a be a bastard
> This is drastic nobody really understands me and my mom don't
> Give a fuck and neither does the rest of the family they like
> Remy you can't afford it you expect us to support it
> I feel my seeds a part of me and I don't want to abort it

Here Remy Ma details the thoughts she had after finding out she was pregnant. Not only does she discuss her right to choose and the decisions she has to make, but also details some of the positives and negatives of her choice in either direction. According to her, if she decides not to have an abortion she may not have the money to take care of the child who may grow up without his father present, but she also questions what would have happened if her mother had aborted her. She experiences guilt, but feels she has no option other than abortion because of her current economic and mental situation. Remy Ma's song is a perfect example of how the intersecting identities of gender, race, and class affect reproductive and privacy rights. In some ways, Remy Ma has the choice to have a baby or not have a baby, but her choice is still limited by her economic situation and class.

Women, Hip-Hop, and Objectification

It's no secret that rap is a boys' club. Numerous female rappers have spoken publicly about the obstacles they face, including lack of respect in the industry. Hip-Hop culture avows hyper-masculine attitudes and male dominance that often diminishes the role of women, leaving women emcees with a fight to prove their talent and right for inclusion within the genre (Alexander-Floyd 2007; Pough 2004). In efforts to assert themselves within this arena, female emcees have tried varied lyrical styles from overt sexuality and sexual prowess (à la Lil Kim and Miami rapper Trina) to a more masculine lyrical style as exemplified through Philadelphia rapper and former Ruff Ryder affiliate Eve "aka the pit-bull in a skirt" and Lil Wayne's protégé Nicki Minaj, who refers to herself as the "Female Lil Weezy." While there are differences among these artists in lyrical content and style, they all emphasize their appearance and sexuality through dress.

Eroticism and images of the female body in rap are frequent topics of discussion in Black Feminist circles (Lourde 1984). Black women rappers deconstruct the objectification of Black female bodies by embracing their bodies lyrically and through their clothing. But these forms of agency can backfire, as observed through the cases of Lil Kim and Nicki Minaj. Both artists were known for their good looks and lyrical styles. Over the years Lil Kim's looks seemed to take priority over her lyrical content with the consistent plastic surgery she had to reinvent herself. Similarly, Nicki Minaj's physical appearance has evoked discussions of authenticity, amazement, and blatant disrespect concerning her physique, particularly her bottom— in some ways similar to the exploitation of Saartjie (also spelled Sara or Sarah) Baartman (Hottentot Venus).[6] In fact, late night talk show host George Lopez was so concerned about others' interest in Nicki Minaj's bottom that he presented her with a gift of a barbed wire "booty protector" when she appeared on his show. This was after daytime television host Regis Philbin grabbed Minaj's buttocks to examine its authenticity.

Likewise, many women rappers incorporate their own forms of eroticism through descriptions of their sexual relationships (Perry 2004). For instance, most of Lil Kim's repertoire details her sexual prowess. In her song, "Big Momma Thang," she raps,

> Can't tell by the diamonds in my rings
> That's how many times I wanna cum, twenty-one
> And another one, and another one, and another one
> 24 carots nigga
> That's when I'm fuckin wit' the average nigga
> Work the shaft, brothers be battin' me, and oh
> Don'tcha like the way I roll
> And play wit' my bushy
> Tell me what's on your mind when your tongues in the pussy
> Is it marriage

Baby carriage
Shit no, on a dime shit is mine
Got to keep 'em comin' all the time

The typical male rapper asserts his sexual conquests and the preceived sub-servience of women to him because of strength, power, money and swag (confidence and style). Lil' Kim details, instead, the power she believes women possess, as well as her own sexual freedom, by not being afraid to talk about her sexual desires. In this verse, Lil Kim details how many orgasms she would like to experience in one night with one man, twenty-four, which she states is significant because that is the number of diamonds in her ring. However, this number of orgasms is only satisfactory because the guy is just "average." In other words, the guy is not superior and thus doesn't deserve her best. She continues with a possessive and aggressive tone toward the man who is now performing oral sex on her and she believes he is in a position where she has power, enough power that his mind is conjuring a way he can keep her either through marriage or getting her pregnant. This synopsis of the eroticism and aggression that is displayed in Lil Kim lyrics applies to many other female rappers including Foxxy Brown, Trina, Nicki Minaj, Salt-N-Pepa and others. Not only are the lyrics of rappers beneficial to the discussion of sexuality and objectivity, but "Black women rappers' public displays of physical and sexual freedom often challenge male notions of female sexuality and pleasure" (Rose 1994, 166). A lot of these male beliefs of females' sexuality and desire were adopted and promoted by rap's relationship with some prominent Black Nationalist organizations. This relationship is examined in detail further in this chapter.

Male Rappers, Hip-Hop, and Black Feminism

Women in the rap community sometimes use rap as a space to assert feminist ideas (Hill-Collins 2006). Women use lyrical skills to disrupt male hegemony, tell their stories, create space, and disturb masculine discourse. For example, women emcees Queen Latifah, Salt-N-Pepa, and Yo-Yo, among others, have asserted Black Feminist attitudes through their lyrics and created organizations to increase gender solidarity, self-love, and self-esteem for urban women (Pough 2004). While some women rappers have asserted feminist attitudes in some of their songs, they are not the only

gender that is advocating feminist sentiments. Some male rappers participate in this tradition of disrupting dominant sexist attitudes by asserting
Black Feminist attitudes. For instance, rap artists Mos Def and Talib Kweli,
collectively known as Black Star, released "Brown Skin Lady," which exalts
and discusses the beauty of Black women.

> You fruitful, beautiful, smart, loveable, huggable
> Doable like art, suitable to be part
> Of my life, Coppertone owe you copyright infringement, pay
> You been this tan since way back in the day
> It's like I'm standing there you know appreciatin God's design
> And then you showed up, it's like you read my mind
> DAMN SHE'S FINE, I think I add the R-E, in front of that

Here the artists are expressing their love for and of Black women and the
attributes of Black women they believe are beautiful, often features that
oppose "traditional" features of White women. Still, some may wonder if
this song is a political song since the book primarily focuses on political
rap music. Indeed, this is a political rap song. It references political institutions, states, which are called out at the end of the song, and because of its
discussion of the social issue of beauty and self-love I classify it as a political
rap song.[7] This song is in complete contrast with critics' assertions that
presentations of women in the genre are negative (Rose 2008). The artists
close by detailing Black female beauty, both dismantling the image of
beauty promoted by popular media and suggesting that those women held
up as examples of perfection are actually dying to look like Black women.

> You know what some people put themselves through
> to look just like you?
> Dark stockings, high heels, lipstick alla that
> You know what?
> Without makeup you're beautiful
> Watcha need to paint the next face for
> We're not dealing with the European standard of beauty tonight
> Turn off the TV and put the magazine away
> In the mirror, tell me what you see
> See the evidence of divine presence

Black Star takes aim at the media's projection of white beauty standards, exuding respect and love of Black women.

Another rap artist, the late West Coast rapper Tupac Shakur, also created songs that were about uplifting Black women and detailed some of the traumas, violence, and marginalization Black women face as young girls and mothers. In one song, "Keep Ya Head Up," Tupac takes a stance in defense of Black women, stating that they should be respected and protected. This is a political song as well because of the use of the term "welfare," which has been highly politicized from Ronald Reagan, Bill Clinton, and other political leaders and policy makers (Hancock 2004). Specifically, he rhymes,

> And since we all came from a woman
> Got our name from a woman and our game from a woman
> I wonder why we take from our women
> Why we rape our women, do we hate our women?
> I think it's time to kill for our women
> Time to heal our women, be real to our women
> And if we don't we'll have a race of babies
> That will hate the ladies that make the babies
> And since a man can't make one
> He has no right to tell a woman when and where to create one
> So will the real men get up
> I know you're fed up ladies, but keep your head up

In this verse Tupac is speaking out against verbal and physical abuse of women. He supports protecting women from violence and respecting women as child bearers, mothers, and people. He suggests that a consequence of not respecting and protecting women is the creation of generational hate of women from their children, lovers, and friends. Finally, he offers some condolence and support by asking women to "keep your head up," keep persevering. In this verse Tupac is chastising all those who disrespect and are violent toward women, though he is specifically addressing men. But Tupac is not the only west coast artist who defends women and discusses the violence perpetrated toward women. Another West Coast rapper, Kendrick Lamar, also discusses violence against women, in "Keisha's Song," in which he takes a different perspective from that of Tupac.

Kendrick Lamar uses this song to explain how and why a particular woman became involved in prostitution that ultimately resulted in her death. Kendrick Lamar gives us a fictional psychological analysis by detailing the possible thought process that resulted from earlier traumatic experiences in her life. Specifically, he rhymes,

Sometimes she wonder if she can do it like nuns do it
But she never heard of Catholic religion or sinners' redemption
That sounds foolish, and you can blame it on her mother
For letting her boyfriend slide candy under her cover
Ten months before she was ten, he moved in and that's when he
    touched her
This motherfucker is the fucking reason why Keisha rushing
through that block away from Lueders park, I seen an El Camino
    parked
and in her heart she hate it there, but in her mind she made it where
nothing really matters, still she hit the back seat
And caught a knife inside the bladder, left her dead, raped in the
    street

In this verse, the subject, Keisha, is questioning if it is possible to quit the business of prostitution and live a life of abstinence, but she quickly dismisses that as an option because she doesn't know much about Catholicism. Next, Lamar explains how Keisha was ultimately introduced to prostitution, through the molestation she experienced from her mother's boyfriend at ten years old. Keisha's way of dealing with this early childhood trauma was to repress her thoughts and feelings and instead make herself believe that nothing mattered. Her lifestyle, similar to Brenda in Tupac's song "Brenda's Got a Baby," ultimately resulted in her death.

Lupe Fiasco also takes the psychological approach to addressing disrespect of women in his song "Bitch Bad." He elaborates on the impact media images and depictions of the term "bitch" have on a male and a female child who are exposed to these depictions via rap songs. Lupe Fiasco is critiquing the psychological impact that degrading rap has on young children's psyches. He gives the example of a young man who is watching his mother who raps along to a song where she refers to herself as a "bad bitch," someone that is "far above average." However, the young man does not understand the positive connotations that are given to bad and bitch in this song and instead understands the phrase as one of disrespect. In essence, in this verse his mother is teaching him to disrespect women because she does not understand the underdevelopment of his mind at this young age and his inability to understand the context and intention. Next, Lupe Fiasco compares this young male perception of bitch with a perspective of a young female watching a rap video. The young girl sees one of her favorite rappers rapping about "bad bitches" and in the video is a woman who is "acquiescent to his whims." Lupe Fiasco describes the girl in the video as

High heels, long hair, fat booty, slim
Reality check, I'm not trippin'
They don't see a paid actress, just what makes a bad bitch

Thus, this young girl has her own interpretation of what it means to be a "bad bitch": for her, someone scantily dressed who succumbs to the whims of a man, especially sexually, and should gain the respect of said man because of her sexual empowerment. She believes that this person, this depiction of a woman, should be respected, accepted, and loved by all because she is a "bad bitch," this time with positive connotations of the phrase. However, the problem arises when this young man and woman meet later in life as adults who have internalized these phrases based on their perceptions of the terms at a young age. Here, the male thinks disrespectfully of the female, while she thinks highly of herself, at least until he disrespects her. Lupe Fiasco ends this song with the lines,

Bad mean good to her, she really nice and smart
But bad mean bad to him, bitch don't play your part
But bitch still bad to her if you say it the wrong way
But she think she a bitch, what a double entendre (tell 'em)

Lupe Fiasco is taking on misogyny and sexism in society and specifically in the rap world by giving us a psychological illustration of how misogynistic rap can shape the perceptions of both males and females exposed to the music. Later in this chapter, I demonstrate empirically what Lupe Fiasco is able to show lyrically, that the type of rap music one is exposed to can have a psychological impact on one's attitude. Still, these are not the only examples of ways male rappers have championed women's issues, including disrespect of women, misogyny, and violence toward women.

Some songs are multifaceted and challenge many Black Feminist issues, such as Atlanta rapper Ludacris' "Runaway Love." Like most rappers, Ludacris is not typically viewed as supporting women's rights or issues. In fact, much of his music can be classified as misogynistic and sexist. But like most artists and people, Ludacris is multilayered, as demonstrated in "Runaway Love." Here, he details the stories of three little girls between ages nine and eleven who experience rape, molestation, pregnancy, child abuse, murder, drug abuse, and poverty, along with the feelings of loneliness, desperation, and fear. In turn, Ludacris discusses these experiences of neglect and abuse as detrimental for young, poor, girls of color.

However, the aforementioned instances of feminist sentiments promoted by male and female rappers are still insufficient to counterbalance the pervasiveness of misogyny and sexism in the genre. This genre emphasizes a hypermasculinity that typically results in abusive language and behavior. In fact, numerous instances of lyrics and behavior exemplify negative relationships between Black men and women, including dysfunctional and emotionally abusive relationships. One of the most popular and discussed examples of the violence associated with rap was the public beating of New York City talk show host Dee Barnes. She was accosted by rap artist Dr. Dre in retaliation for things she said on the radio about him. Dr. Dre used violence to command respect through a demonstration of hypermasculinity. Unfortunately, this is only one example of the violence, misogyny, sexism, and hypermasculinity asserted in rap music. Sexism can also be observed in the relationship between rap music and Black Nationalist ideology. We cannot understand and discuss feminist attitudes within rap music without discussing the relationship between Black Feminism, Black Nationalism, and rap.

Black Nationalism, Black Feminism, and Rap

As noted by Alexander-Floyd (2007), there is complicated history between Black Feminism and Black Nationalism, and rap continues in this direction. Rap's history with Black Nationalist organizations like the Nation of Gods and Earths (also referred to as the Five Percenters Nation) and the Nation of Islam allowed beliefs about subservient roles of women to survive in a new era (Miyakawa 2005). For instance, Lord Jamar, member of the rap group Brand Nubian whose members are openly affiliated with Five Percenters, describes women in this sect as subservient to men in his song "Supreme Mathematics," featured on the Billboard charting, *The 5% Album*.

> Wisdom is the wise words spoken by the wise Black man
> Who is God, Wisdom is symbolic to the Black woman
> Secondary, but, most necessary, to bring forth the seed of life

Lord Jamar breaks down the "mathematics" or the formula to a righteous lifestyle according to him as a Five Percenter. Specifically, Lord Jamar details the correlation between the number two in Five Percent numerology (referred to as the Supreme Mathematics) and Black women. Lord Jamar also explains the relationship between women and men based on this ideology by identifying women as "secondary but most necessary" and men as god Like many Black Nationalist sects, Five Percenters believe men should be the heads of households, with women as secondary yet necessary because they can bear children. This philosophy of women as caregivers and mothers, whose duty is to raise and bear children, can be found in many Black Nationalist philosophies, particularly those prevalent during the 1960s and 1970s (Hill-Collins 2006; Alexander-Floyd 2007). This type of thinking often juxtaposes Black Nationalism and Black Feminism as ideologies that cannot be held simultaneously. Feminists argue that this line of thinking limits the role of Black women and girls as child bearers and child nurturers, dissolving most of the responsibility of the men in the parenting process. But such seemingly conflicting attitudes have coexisted and continue to coexist.

Sexism and patriarchy were present in some chapters of the Black Panther Party, U.S. organization, the Nation of Gods and Earths, and the Nation of Islam (Hill-Collins 2006). Black women who espoused feminist attitudes in some of these organizations were labeled race-traitors who were bated, indoctrinated, and used like puppets by White women to divide the Black community. In fact, some Black Nationalist men subscribed to the beliefs asserted by Daniel Moynihan in his infamous Moynihan Report that Black women were often socially and politically constructed as Black Matriarchs who were too aggressive and only pushed Black men away from them and their households (Moynihan 1965; Alexander-Floyd 2007). In fact, many Black Nationalist organizations and leaders adopted the construction

of the Black Matriarch and later the "welfare queen" as the dominant reason for increased Black female-headed single families (Alexander-Floyd
2007).

Many of these assertions present in Black Nationalist doctrine are also
evident in rap music. Women who did not support nationalistic efforts in
rap music were labeled "ungrateful wives or gold-digging lovers" (Decker
1993: 68). Rapper Ice Cube commented in an interview that "Black women
have to wait for Black men to be uplifted first" (Lusane 2004: 359). Ice
Cube supported the position of "race first, women later" adopted by many
Black Nationalist leaders and members.

Examples of promoting sexism and Nationalism simultaneously can
also be found in many songs. For instance, Public Enemy, a rap group
known for its acceptance and support of the Black Panther Party and
Nation of Islam ideologies, also suggests sexist ideas about women under
the guise of "uplifting the race." In the song "She Watch Channel Zero?",
sung by Flavor Flav, Public Enemy details the impact they believe television,
specifically soap operas, have on Black women.

> Trouble vision for a sister
> 'Cause I know she don't know, I quote
> Her brains retrained
> By a 24 inch remote
> Revolution a solution
> For all of our children
> But her children
> Don't mean as much as the show, I mean
> Watch her worship the screen, and fiend
> For a TV ad
> And it just makes me mad

In this verse Public Enemy suggests that watching television is counter-
productive and will not assist in the "revolution" of the Black nation, again
illustrating belief in the role of Black women solely as nurturers of children.
The artists insinuate that a woman's television consumption is detrimental
to her family, specifically her children, who, they argue, are neglected. The
attitudes presented in this song are not only sexist but also nationalist. The
song proves to be sexist because TV-watching is equated specifically with
women while disregarding the oppositional myth that most men control

the remote controls in their homes. The song also implies that women are incapable of separating fantasy from reality, subtly hinting that men are smarter because they are able to watch television and decipher fact from fiction or smart enough to not watch television at all. These lyrics also contribute to the faulty characterizations of Black women as "welfare queens" and "crack mothers" because they insinuate that these women do not have jobs (Roberts 1997; Neal 2004a). Similarly, comparing the television-watching woman to a fiend alludes to the irresponsibility of crack mothers, an image that was popular in the late 1980s and early 1990s (Roberts 1997). This one verse is problematic on many fronts, specifically concerning sexism and patriarchy. The sexism continues in Flavor Flav's closing lines:

> Yo baby, can't you see that's nonsense you watchin'?
> Look, don't nobody look like that, nobody even live that, you know
>   what I'm sayin'?
> You watchin' garbage, noth'n' but garbage. Straight up garbage.
> Yo, why don't you just back up from the TV, read a book or some'in'
> Read about yourself, learn your culture, you know what I'm sayin'?

Not only is Flavor Flav saying that men must point out issues he deems harmful to the Black community, but he also offers women a solution by suggesting they "read a book or something. . . . learn about your culture." He embraces the patriarchal role of dictating to a woman what she should and should not do. This example demonstrates that even in groups like Public Enemy that are credited with highly political and positive lyrics, attitudes of sexism and patriarchy still exist. "Political" does not necessarily equate to positive or beneficial for all aspects of the Black community. Some political rap music can have negative effects on women as well as gays and lesbians (Ransby and Matthews 1995). Further, as I have shown, some "songs produced by the political, usually Black Nationalist rappers run counter to women's liberation" (Lusane 2004: 360).

While there are expressions of both Black Feminist and Black Nationalist ideals, rappers both male and female are less accepting of a feminist label because it is often believed to be in direct competition with the race-first doctrine alluded to by Ice Cube. For example, in reference to being labeled a Black Feminist, Queen Latifah commented she was not a feminist, "I know that at the end of the day I am a Black woman in this world and I gotta get mine. I want to see the rise of the Black male in personal strength and power. I wanna see the creation of a new Black community for ourselves and respect from others" (quoted in Pough 2004a: 89). Latifah appears to ascribe to the more popular Black Nationalist sentiment many women have asserted before her. Some have argued that equality in this country will result from the rise of the Black man first and the elimination of racism before sexism. Her comment suggests that Queen Latifah holds this opinion and does not believe racism and sexism can be eliminated simultaneously. However, based on Queen Latifah's music (U.N.I.T.Y. and Ladies First), her earlier attire and her activist work, one can contend she was rebelling against the label of feminist in general and not referring specifically to the ideology of Black Feminism.[8] With examples of both feminist and counter-feminist attitudes present in the genre, quantitative analysis will provide further examination of the support of Feminism in rap music.

Black Feminism and Rap Music: A Closer Look

Dawson (2001), Harris-Lacewell (2004), and Spence (2011) observed some aspects of the relationships between rap and Black Feminism. They concluded that there was no direct relationship between Black Feminism and exposure to rap music. However, these scholars failed to distinguish between the subgenres of rap music and thereby missed other possible relevant relationships between rap music and Black Feminist attitudes. The current study differs from others before it in two important ways. First, it identifies a specific subgenre of rap music and examines its impact on particular political attitudes by exposing subjects to music within a particular subgenre. Second, participants only listened to songs (rather than listening while watching a music video), simplifying the relationship between exposure to music and political attitudes.[9]

While Harris-Lacewell (2004) limits her assertions about the influence of rap music to the activation of discussions and how those discussions can lead to the formation of attitudes, this book goes farther and posits that rap simultaneously influences the formation and acceptance of certain Black political ideologies. Thus, the main thrust of this experiment examines whether political rap differs from nonpolitical rap in its impact on Black political attitudes. I argue that there is a relationship between rap and Black

Feminist ideology. Specifically, nonpolitical rap decreases listeners' support of Black Feminism, as compared to political rap.

Measuring Black Feminism has not always resulted in a succinct, agreed upon operationalization of the ideology. Some scholars have constructed Black Feminist attitudes using interaction analysis of responses to race and gender identification (Gay and Tate 1998). Others have examined Black Feminism utilizing traditional measures of White Feminism (Conover 1988; Cook 1989). Still others have observed a wide range of variables which, supporters argue, capture Black Feminist ideology (Dawson 2001; Harris-Lacewell 2004; Simien 2006). Similar to Chapter 3, experiments were conducted to examine the impact of nonpolitical versus political rap on Black Feminist attitudes.

Results

The sample for this study is the one described in Chapter 3: students from Benedict College, an HBCU in South Carolina. The experiment has four conditions and a control group. The four conditions were political rap, nonpolitical rap, rhythm and blues music, and popular mainstream music (pop music). The different genres of music were presented through three carefully selected songs that represented different styles, regions, and issues, and all songs are from male artists to eliminate variation.[10]

An examination of the data supports the hypothesis that exposure to political rap leads to more support of Black Feminist attitudes in comparison to other conditions. As previously discussed, although political rap can certainly be progressive in some ways, it can also be regressive in relationship to Black Feminist attitudes and beliefs. Exposure to nonpolitical rap significantly decreases an individual's acceptance of Black Feminism across all conditions. In fact, compared to the other types of Black music (R&B and political rap), nonpolitical rap is the most detrimental to the acceptance of Black Feminist attitudes. This confirms the hypothesis that there are differences in music genres and their effects on Black political attitudes, specifically among African Americans. The most profound conclusion that can be drawn from these results is that nonpolitical rap is significantly different from any other music group in the experiment, as demonstrated by the decreased support of Black Feminism by those exposed to nonpolitical rap compared to the other genres. This finding demonstrates what many have previously argued: the sexism and misogyny in rap can be detrimental to support of Black Feminism. But the findings also reveal the important distinction that only certain subgenres of rap music have such effects (Alexander-Floyd 2007; Pough 2004a; Perry 2004; White 1995; Rose 1994).

Conclusion

In 1999, the first rap artist to win a Grammy award for an album was Lauryn Hill, a female emcee (Spence 2011). She not only is a very fine lyricist but also stands up for social issues and issues relevant to women's empowerment and liberation.[11] Understanding female inclusion in this male-dominated genre, as well as how women are depicted, is essential to understanding how women are viewed, portrayed, and revered in the genre. Often, because female characterizations are largely negative in rap music, female artists have had to go against the grain to fight for inclusion and respect as emcees. These artists have asserted themselves and fought for their rights lyrically as well as through the creation of organizations, foundations, and campaigns. Consequently, in order to properly assess Black political attitudes about women, one must understand the portrayal of women in this clearly influential cultural form.

Rap music is not typically considered a communication source that provides political information or impacts a person's political attitudes, although some have commented on the possibility of such an influence (Spence 2011; Harris-Lacewell 2004; Dawson 2001). This chapter has demonstrated that this effect does exist. Among African Americans, music does affect one's support of Black political attitudes. Listening to political rap significantly increases support of Black Feminism when compared to nonpolitical rap. This shows that political rap is different from other rap and that, despite espousing sexist attitudes at times, it is significantly more positive in terms of feminist attitudes than is nonpolitical rap. Rap music has been characterized as a misogynistic musical genre, yet this chapter has demonstrated that not all subgenres are harmful to Black Feminist ideology and attitudes toward women. Of the various genres of music included here, nonpolitical rap has the greatest negative impact on acceptance of Black Feminist ideology. Therefore, distinctions are necessary when discussing this heterogeneous genre of music and its relationship to political attitudes and behavior. Not only is rap important to political attitudes, but the type of rap one listens to influences Black political attitudes differently. Observing that rap does impact political attitudes, the next question is how do these attitudinal changes influence behavior? Chapter 5 examines the relationship between Hip-Hop and behavior.

Chapter 5

The Future of Politics: The Implications of Rap Music and Political Attitudes

> Once you change your philosophy, you change your thought pattern.
> Once you change your thought pattern, you change your attitude.
> Once you change your attitude, it changes your behavior pattern and
> then you go on into some action.
>   —Malcolm X, "The Ballot or the Bullet"

> Y'all telling me that I need to get out and vote, huh. Why?
> Ain't nobody Black running but crackers, so, why I got to register?
> I thinking of better shit to do with my time
>   —Andre 3000 of Outkast, "Git up, Git Out,"
>   *Southernplayalisticadillacmuzik*

> My country shitted on me (My country)
> She wants to get rid of me (Naw, never)
> Cause the things I seen (We know too much)
> Cause the things I seen (We seen too much)
>   —Nas, 2001, "My Country" *Stillmatic*

The crowd gathering outside the 2006 Video Music Awards (VMAs) was no doubt surprised when Yasiin Bey, the rapper and actor formerly known as Mos Def, began an impromptu concert from the flatbed truck outside Radio City Music Hall. The VMAs are a big deal in the music industry; they are one of several music awards at which artists and label executives gather to celebrate those who have created chart-topping albums in the previous year. While these events often attract myriad celebrities, from actors to singers and songwriters, one group of artists is always visibly missing or underrepresented. Artists who primarily create and perform political rap songs are often excluded from consideration for awards because their songs typically do not appear high on Billboard charts, and rarely do these artists have music videos featured on music television networks. With a half dozen Grammys to his credit and a longer list of critically acclaimed appearances in movies, plays, and television, Bey is a notable exception to this rule. He performed his song "Katrina Clap" ("Dollar Day"), which discusses the devastation in New Orleans during and after hurricane Katrina, on a portable stage outside the highly publicized Video Music Awards to protest against the treatment of New Orleans and its citizens by the government. He had harsh words for the Bush administration's slow response to the mostly Black victims, asserting that the intersection of race and poverty resulted in lack of concern from America's governmental system. Specifically, Bey states,

> Listen, homie, it's Dollar Day in New Orleans
> It's water water everywhere and people dead in the streets
> And Mr. President he bout that cash
> He got a policy for handling the niggaz and trash
> And if you poor you Black
> I laugh a laugh they won't give when you ask
> You better off on crack
> Dead or in jail, or with a gun in Iraq
> And it's as simple as that
> No opinion my man it's mathematical fact
> Listen, a million poor since 2004
> And they got -illions and killions to waste on the war
> And make you question what the taxes is for
> Or the cost to reinforce, the broke levee wall
> Tell the boss, he shouldn't be the boss anymore
> Y'all pray amin

Bey was calling for the political incorporation and consideration of a marginalized segment of the American population, expressly, the Black urban poor. He lent his voice and fame to reflect the pain of those rendered voiceless and invisible in the aftermath of this natural disaster. In his lyrics, Bey raises a question that many political scientists have pondered since the beginnings of their discipline: Are some groups excluded from political consideration or does everyone have the opportunity to have their voices and concerns heard and acted upon? Specifically, does everyone experience a pluralist political society? If so, how are urban minority voices incorporated into American political society?

Although Bey was able to use his right to freedom of speech to assert his disgust with the U.S. government, he was subsequently arrested for not having permits for a public demonstration. This performance demonstrates a relationship between rap music and political behavior: specifically, the use of rap as a form of political protest. What resulted from this public performance also demonstrates the limits of relationships between rap and political behavior. Rap is a cultural form that uses alternative means to assert its voice and viewpoints because rap artists recognize that their voices have been silenced—simultaneously, they must abide by the rules of the dominant culture.

Bey wasn't the only rapper upset about the lack of governmental response to the victims of hurricane Katrina. As discussed in Chapter 1, popular rap artist Kanye West publicly declared his belief that president George W. Bush did "not care about Black people," in reference to the slow response of the government after Katrina. Additionally, a multitude of Hip-Hop artists, both mainstream and underground, released records that expressed discontent, anger, sadness, and pain in relation to hurricane Katrina or the victims of the disaster, including Jay-Z's "Minority Report," Lil Wayne's "Tie My Hands," Public Enemy's "Hell No (We Ain't Alright)," Papoose's "Tribute to Hurricane Katrina Victims," Jay Electronica's "When the Levees Broke," and 5th Ward Weebie's "Katrina Song." Not only have rappers led by example through political action, but they have also provided support to many programs aimed at helping the Black community. In the aftermath of Katrina, Hip-Hop artists on the southern coast provided much-needed support. Rapper Ludacris collected books to rebuild New Orleans libraries. Other rap artists, including superstars Nelly, T.I., and Young Jeezy, performed at a free benefit concert for relief efforts to the victims of Katrina in Atlanta. Many Hip-Hop artists realize that their fame is also a platform from which they can raise awareness and demand the help their communities so desperately need. In this chapter, I detail examples of both electoral and nonelectoral forms of participation that artists who have produced political rap have embraced.

Political Incorporation

Three dominant theories have been used to explain urban political incorporation and empowerment: pluralism, regime theory, and coalition theory. Pluralism is the belief that every group has equal opportunity to compete and receive full incorporation in the political systems of democratic governments. Dahl (1961) focused his discussion of pluralism on the urban community of New Haven. He was unique in that he argued that it was not the business leaders who ruled the political systems of the city, but instead that ordinary citizens could be incorporated in the political system and ultimately have a voice.

It is believed that most democratic nations offer a pluralist platform for those seeking to enter the political structures. The major contention for this viewpoint is that "The rules and procedures of democracy guarantee that the needs and concerns of minority groups will be accommodated by the agencies of government and the instrumentalities of the wider political system" (Nelson 2000: 13). However, Dahl's theory was refuted because he only examined the upper-class members of New Haven and left out the voices of the poor. Thus, all individuals did not have full access to the political system, nor were their issues recognized or part of the city's agenda.

As an anti-pluralist, E. E. Schnattsneider (1960) has suggested that some groups are systematically screened out of the political system through the use of police force to suppress democratic participation. This police force Schnattsneider refers to was embodied in a radical form for Blacks in the "Jim Crow" south, who were often lynched and terrorized if they attempted to participate in the political system by voting or registering to vote during the early twentieth century. COINTELPRO, a system created during the anti-communist era, was also a program utilized by by J. Edgar Hoover during his tenure with the FBI to stifle Black political movements and empowerment through infiltration, fraudulent arrests and charges, and surveillance. The protocol of COINTELPRO, as it related to Black organizations and movements, continued to be utilized in our modern society. Task forces staffed with "Hip-Hop cops" are created to follow and report Hip-Hop artists who may be involved in or associated with "criminal" activity or violence. This issue first came to light after *Miami Herald* reporters uncovered correspondence from New York Police and Miami-Dade Police Departments revealing that they were keeping tabs on certain artists when they entered and left these cities. The problem with this force is that it often keeps records of any Hip-Hop artist that has a large following, even when they may not be associated with any criminal activity, a problem detailed in the political Hip-Hop documentary, "Letter to the President."[1] Thus, pluralism has failed to be a sufficient political theory of incorporation for those whose issues never penetrate the political system and for minorities who were fully eliminated from the electoral process in many northern and southern cities.

Clarence Stone (1989) attempted to address the lack of an accurate theory of political inclusion through a case study of Atlanta, Georgia, where he asserted regime theory as a viable option for political incorporation for those who were excluded. Regime theory is "the informal arrangements that surround and complement the formal workings of governmental authority" (Stone 1989: 3). Stone builds on pluralist theory and suggests a form of government participation, the regime, that is more inclusive than the pluralist society described by Dahl (1961). He posits that a regime is the most viable source of political success for minority citizens. Elected officials must engage in relationships with members of the business community as well as members of political interest groups. Thus, coalitions between leaders who are involved with public and private sectors of the community must exist for minority citizens to be fully incorporated. Stone observes the political incorporation of some Black business interests in Atlanta during and at the end of the Jim Crow Era. He notes that some Black groups, particularly those with more resources, are able to assert their concerns and issues to some extent. Though Stone discusses these specific elements of political incorporation, he fails, according to Nelson, "to give adequate attention to the hierarchical racial structures and relations that systematically screen Blacks out of the arena of informal bargaining" (Nelson 2000: 17). Nelson suggests that a regime theory leaves out community-based organizations, which are the major backbone of Black agenda setting. Stone does not consider the power and influence of Black grassroots organizations that often suggest to the elite which issues are prevalent to the Black community and therefore should be on the city's agenda. Stone also fails to examine the relationship between local and federal government entities. Thus, the Black urban poor are still marginalized under this system. Neither regimes nor pluralism are fully inclusive theoretical structures, particularly regarding organizations that lack resources or have nonelectoral political power, such as disenfranchised grassroots organizations.

Finally, coalition theory—suggested by Rufus Browning, Dale Marshall, and David Tabb—is yet another that attempts to describe political incorporation. Coalition theory posits that Blacks can gain political incorporation if they align with liberal whites and form coalitions (Browning, Marshall, and Tabb 2003). After the passage of the Voting Rights Act, African Americans gained electoral political power, but many still wondered whether Black issues and interests would be fully incorporated into the larger political agenda. Browning, Marshall, and Tabb attempted to answer this query by observing ten California cities. They found that when Blacks entered into biracial coalitions, the city was more responsive to the Black community. Their theory suggests that Blacks can receive political incorporation if they align with liberal Whites and form coalitions. Browning, Marshall, and Tabb argue that two essential processes must occur before political incorporation is an option. The authors contend that demand-protest has to occur to increase political consciousness, which would in turn affect the political mobilization of minority groups and liberal whites.

However, this theory presents many problems, including the issues of forming and sustaining coalitions. Similarly the authors do not consider achievement of partial versus full incorporation, demonstrated through the ability to influence agenda setting. Mollenkopf (2003) demonstrated in his examination of New York City that with all the necessary requirements suggested by Browning, Marshall, and Tabb, coalitions were difficult to form. Mollenkopf found that in New York, where two-thirds of the residents are minorities and there is a history of coalition formation, it is still difficult to maintain and form sustaining coalitions and receive electoral representation. This is because many White liberals or Blacks may not be willing to join political coalitions because one group may feel no need for the other to attain office, or there may be internal conflict, as in New York. If coalitions are formed, they may be terminal coalitions that dissipate after a political office is won or an issue is resolved. Finally, if the coalition is formed and sustained, there is no guarantee that all members will have equal standing. One group may be systematically ignored once in the coalition, or given only small patronage to stay. Coalition building, while a good theory, has many particulars that Browning, Marshall, and Tabb overlook.

Still, none of these theories are successful in explaining full incorporation of members of submarginalized communities into the political scene. Particularly, individuals who do not have access to or the ear of political elites still do not have their voices and concerns addressed as part of the political agenda. The Hip-Hop community (young, urban poor who listen to rap music) is an example of a group of individuals who don't always have access to political elites. In fact, as detailed in earlier chapters, the urban poor are often criminalized, dehumanized, and dismissed by elites in their own community. Such has been the case with political leaders C. Delores Tucker, Calvin Butts, Bill Cosby, and even President Obama.[2]

With no succinct way of receiving full political incorporation, members of the Hip-Hop community have used various tactics in an effort to aggressively assert their voices, issues, and concerns to whoever will listen. The lack of a precise method to ensure political incorporation has contributed to the insufficient political incorporation of all African Americans even after the Civil Rights Movement.

The previous chapters have established the alternative methods that systematically ostracized community members use to be heard and included in our political system. Rap music continues the cultural tradition of using the power of the spoken word to discuss political and social issues, advance attitudes, raise consciousness, and assert a political voice. Observing that political rap music influences political attitudes is only one step in uncovering the precarious relationship between Hip-Hop culture, the Black community, and the political future. We must observe not only the ways rap music and culture have been examined and evaluated by political leaders, but also rap's response to the political world, including the political behavior of rap artists and audience members. Thus it is essential we examine the political participation, both electoral and nonelectoral, of the Hip-Hop community to fully understand the impact of political rap on political behavior.

Politics and Popular Culture

Since its beginning, rap has caught the attention of some of America's leading politicians because of the issues discussed in the songs and the often blunt, militant, or incendiary ways these issues are presented. For instance, Ice-T's "Cop Killer" invoked negative reactions from many leading political figures including Tipper Gore (wife of former vice president Al Gore), former vice-president Dan Quayle, and former president George H. W. Bush, who decried the song's characterization of law enforcement. Many believed these types of songs would provoke actual violence against police officers, especially after explicit acts of police brutality, as seen with the Rodney King beating and subsequent verdict (Rose 1994). While many have argued that listening to rap, specifically gangsta rap, leads to an increase in violence, this line of thinking has not been applied to the impact of political rap on political behavior.

Historically, marginalized groups have been alienated from the political, social, and economic arenas, but they are allowed to entertain those in power. Simultaneously, entertainers often use their platforms as a conduit of inclusion into dominant society and discourse (Iton 2008). For example, Atlanta rapper Big Boi (of the rap group Outkast) used a political rap song to encourage political participation in the form of voting in his song "Sumthin's Gotta Give" featuring R&B singer Mary J. Blige. In this song, Big Boi used lyrics and a music video to discuss political participation, as well as current economic problems and the effect the economy was having on many citizens. He described the despair that he argues many feel because they are not making enough to survive due to the steady rise of gas prices and unemployment. Because of the lyrics and the blatant advocacy for presidential candidate Barack Obama, this song was featured on CNN, and Big Boi was interviewed. With the help of CNN, Big Boi used his artistic platform not only to entertain but to include a perspective from the voiceless and to advocate for political participation among those who were disillusioned with politics because they believed their vote didn't count. Big Boi is a prime example of celebrities using their status or platform to fight against injustices and encourage political participation.

However, many celebrities have moved past using their voices and are actively participating on the ground in various social movements and causes. As an example, Kanye West and Russell Simmons's presence at the Occupy Wall Street (OWS) movement brought media attention to the movement that they perhaps did not intend, partly because of their celebrity and economic statuses. OWS is often described as a movement that resulted from protests occurring globally, such as the Arab Spring in Egypt and the occupation of Central Square in Spain (Hardt and Negri 2011). Specifically, OWS began in 2011 as a movement of the 99 percent, a diverse set of individuals who have suffered economic hardships such as, but not limited to, loss of jobs, homes, and retirement funds. This movement was to fight against the 1 percent said to control the political and social system because of their wealth. OWS was against concentration of wealth and power in the hands of the elite 1 percent while the other 99 percent of the population suffered. These rap celebrities' attendance at this event is unique because their wealth places them in the one percent. Considering that these demonstrations were about those who were economically distressed, some argued that West and Simmons were out of place and unwanted because of their economic status. In fact, many media outlets and bloggers questioned the sincerity of the multi-millionaires' attendance at this political demonstration. Ultimately, while their presence may not have been wanted, they were able to bring media attention the OWS was unable to receive previously. Other rappers in the area, including Immortal Technique and M1 of Dead Prez, also attended the demonstrations, with local rapper Talib Kweli giving an impromptu performance.

Hip-Hop and Politics: A Precarious Relationship

In recent years, there have been numerous events with political overtones and outcomes that have gripped and mobilized the Black community, including the Jena 6 trial of Black Louisiana teenagers who were facing adult second degree murder charges; the Stop the Violence campaign against gang and urban violence; and more recently the call by Common to rappers to assist in ending urban violence and specifically violence in Chicago. Other politically and racially charged events include hurricane Katrina, a natural disaster that rendered an entire city helpless; the Troy Davis trial of a young Georgia man facing death as the result of a contentious court case after he was accused of murdering a police officer; the election of Barack Obama, the first Black president of the United States; the killing of Oscar Grant by an Oakland police officer; and the murder of Florida teenager Trayvon Martin by a neighborhood watchman. Hip-Hop artists and their community have participated in various aspects of these important social and political issues.

Hip-Hop artists have volunteered during national disasters, campaigned for and with political candidates, organized around social and political issues, encouraged bone marrow donations, and created programs for underprivileged youth. We have also seen efforts to encourage rap artists and other urban youth to run for political office and participate with local government. Many artists have asserted the need for increased African American participation in the political arena. Many of the social and political problems that directly affect the Black community rarely enter mainstream media outlets. Further, many of the organizations involved and fighting on behalf of these issues were further marginalized and were rarely covered by the few remaining African American news enclaves because of their politics.

Hip-Hop's Formation of Political Organizations

With Hip-Hop originating at the end of the Black Power Movement and Black Arts Movement, the genre adopted many tactics used by those of the previous era. The organizational abilities of the Black Power and Civil Rights era had a profound impact on the organizations formed by Hip-Hop leaders, listeners, and artists. Conrad Muhammad, founder of Conscious Hip-Hop Activism Necessary for Global Empowerment (CHHANGE) stated, "we don't have colored-only water fountains or a Vietnam War, so we have to more carefully show young people how political issues are affecting them" (quoted in Kitwana 2002: 190). Politically driven Hip-Hop organizations used community building, assertion of political agendas, and both grassroots and electoral politics to raise awareness of concerns in their community which were conspicuously missing from the dominant political agendas. Russell Simmons's Hip-Hop Summit Action Network, the National Hip-Hop Political Convention, the Hip-Hop Caucus, and the Ella Baker Center are all examples of the adoption of tactics and ideologies from various Black Power and Civil Rights organizations to assert the voices of the Hip-Hop community in this current era.

Hip-Hop Summit Action Network

The Hip-Hop Summit Action Network is a nonprofit coalition of Hip-Hop artists, youth activists, industry leaders and civil rights and education activists who are "dedicated to harnessing the cultural relevance of Hip-Hop music to serve as a catalyst for education advocacy and other societal concerns fundamental to the well-being of at-risk youth throughout the United States" (HSAN 2001). HSAN was created predominately by music executives and community leaders. Currently only one actual Hip-Hop artist, P. Diddy, is a member of its board of directors (Spence 2011). HSAN believes that Hip-Hop can be influential in assisting social change to the benefit of the urban poor. This organization drafted a fifteen-point demand platform, entitled "What We Want," that is similar to the ten principles asserted in the Black Panther Party Platform and Program.[3] The similarities between these two platforms demonstrate the connection between the BPP and the philosophy/tactics of members of the Hip-Hop generation.

In fact, HSAN revives three of BPP's ten demands. The number one demand in both the BPP and the HSAN platforms is freedom and self-determination for the Black community. Similarly, point three from the BPP platform and point nine from HSAN both demand some type of reparations from the U.S. government as a result of slavery. Specifically, in item three of its platform, the BPP states, "We believe that this racist government has robbed us and now we are demanding the overdue debt of forty acres and two mules. Forty acres and two mules was promised a hundred years ago as restitution for slave labor and mass murder of Black people" (Black Panther Party Platform and Program 1966). Similarly, point nine of the HSAN platform states, "We want reparations to help repair the lingering vestiges; damages and suffering of African Americans as a result of the brutal enslavement of generations of Africans in America" (What We Want 2001). Finally, point seven in both platforms demands a stop to police brutality and mistreatment of Blacks in the criminal justice system. BPP states, "We want an immediate end to police brutality and murder of Black people" and in HSAN the point is, "We want the total elimination of police brutality and the unjust incarceration of people of color and all others." Not only do these points connect members of the Hip-Hop generation to a direct paradigm and agenda presented before the creation of Hip-Hop, they also demonstrate the issues continually being fought after the Civil Rights Movement and the political concessions Blacks received as a result of the Movement. Apart from the three mentioned points that correspond directly, other elements of both platforms are also similar. For instance, both platforms call for quality public education: the BPP asked for curricula that correctly detail an accurate non-hegemonic portrayal of American history and Blacks in society, while HSAN asks for "quality" education with no specification on exactly what factors will be used to determine quality. Similarly, both platforms call for revision of the penal system and policies. The BPP asked for all Black men (not women) to be released from prison and jail, while HSAN asked for a repeal of unjust policy and legislation that have had disproportionate effects on communities of color such as mandatory minimums, the three strike policy, and trying juveniles as adults. In contrast to its demands for education, here HSAN is explicit and detailed in what it demands in relation to the criminal justice and penal systems.

While similarities do exist between the two platforms, there are also numerous differences from and expansions on older attitudes and beliefs. For instance, unlike BPP, HSAN discusses issues of discriminatory policy and legislation, the need for HIV/AIDS education, universal health care, environmental disparities, and legislation that directly affects the Hip-Hop community. In contrast, the BPP was not concerned with legislation that affected Black arts, and some of the other issues for which HSAN advocates did not exist during the time of the BPP, including HIV/AIDS.

As a Hip-Hop-based organization, HSAN has been involved in numerous political activities. HSAN collaborated with Life on the Outside, NAACP, National Urban League, Southern Christian Leadership Conference, and Rap the Vote to increase voter registration in recent years. It has established numerous grassroots Hip-Hop summit youth councils that promote leadership development in many urban cities as well as having sponsored over 40 Hip-Hop summits. Its members have demonstrated against the Rockefeller Drug Laws in New York, which demand a mandatory minimum sentence of 15 years to life for the possession and distribution of small amounts of illegal substances. Their efforts eventually culminated in a federal lawsuit from HSAN against a New York lobbying commission to have their speech protected as they inform others of the problems with the 1973 Rockefeller Drug Laws (Fontaine 2009). Additionally, HSAN and numerous rappers including Jay-Z, Busta Rhymes, Fabolous and M-1 from Dead Prez participated in a protest that included over 60,000 people. This protest and HSAN efforts led to changes in the Rockefeller Drug Laws including giving judges discretion over sentencing and allowing drug treatment to occur in prison (Fontaine 2009; Gray 2009). In 2003 HSAN wrote an open antiwar letter to President George W. Bush requesting that he not engage in war with Iraq, instead demanding that he continue to advocate for the disarmament of weapons of mass destruction. Similarly, HSAN used its organizational voice to work to defend Hip-Hop culture against the United States Congress. Finally, in 2010 HSAN spread its network actions internationally, acknowledging the global impact of Hip-Hop and the global oppression of some communities. This internationalization was done in conjunction with the Music for Peace Initiative and Tour, which promotes a message of peace through the arts.

Alhough Hip-Hop organizations are active on multiple fronts, many argue that there is a lack of support for issues that disproportionately affect Black women. In fact, some have criticized Russell Simmons, CEO and founder of HSAN, for his recent allowance of the short sketch of the "Harriet Tubman Sex Tape" through his YouTube channel *All Def Digital*. The film is very insensitive to the legacy of Harriet Tubman and to women in general. The short sketch features a fictional depiction of freedom fighter Harriet Tubman's use of her body, particularly her vagina, as a means to negotiate the freedom of some enslaved people she helped escape to freedom from White slave owners. This video sent the message that the only way Black women could negotiate or in this instance fight for freedom is through the use of their sexuality, a popular theme suggested in rap music. Similarly, this sketch was not only offensive to women because of the assumption that a woman only means of power lie within her sexuality, it was also offensive to Black women because it suggested that the stereotype of the lascivious Jezebel was true. This skit suggested that Black women seduced White men in return for favors or power, eliminating the facts that Black women were raped and victimized as enslaved women with no options for recourse against their assailant.

Despite such controversies, Simmons has made important contributions to Black politics through HSAN. HSAN not only uses the methods and rhetoric of the BPP, but also follows the political process model described by McAdams (1982). McAdams states there are four key requirements to establishing a social movement: expanding political opportunities, broad socioeconomic processes, indigenous organizational strength, and cognitive liberation.

We can observe that HSAN has a sense of group goals by examining those goals that are identified in its platform. HSAN has also aligned itself politically with other groups. It has numerous members and relationships with various communication networks, including local radio stations and national television networks such as BET and MTV. The organization has effective leaders in Ben Chavis, past leader of the NAACP, and Simmons, CEO and co-founder of Def Jam records. Finally, the various programs and initiatives that HSAN carries out give its members and the Hip-Hop community it represents a greater sense of cognitive liberation, a confidence that the goals detailed in their platform are practical and can be achieved.

National Hip-Hop Political Convention

Another group invested in the cognitive liberation of the Hip-Hop community was the (now defunct) National Hip-Hop Political Convention

(NHHPC). NHHPC started in 2003 as an organization to promote voter registration and address issues that were affecting urban youth. Increasing membership and outreach culminated in a biannual conference with the purpose of discussing and creating a political agenda for the Hip-Hop community. The founders of this convention believed that the Hip-Hop generation's concerns and issues were not present on any other agendas and needed to be addressed. In essence, this organization recognized the sub-marginalization of members of the Hip-Hop generation. The first of the series of three conventions, which targeted individuals ages eighteen to thirty-five, was held in Newark, New Jersey, in 2004. More than 6,000 people attended that first convention and were involved in drafting the first five-point agenda, which focused on health and wellness, economic and criminal justice, education, and human rights (Spence 2011). The subsequent conventions were held in Chicago in summer 2006 and in Las Vegas in 2008.

I attended the 2006 convention in Chicago, where artists, activists, and fans gathered, not only to discuss relevant political and social issues, but also enjoy all the elements of Hip-Hop. This three-day event featured sessions covering topics that included women, sexism, and feminism in Hip-Hop; the individual's legal rights in relation to interactions with police; the media role in the Black community; and the four elements of Hip-Hop: break dancing, disc-jockeying, rapping, and graffiti art.

NHHPC is now dismantled, likely because of clashing visions and dwindling attendance. All the conventions included Hip-Hop activist Rosa Clemente, but at the last convention in Las Vegas, 2008, Clemente was vice-presidential candidate for the Green Party. At this convention Cynthia McKinney was the closing speaker, urging participants to support her and Green Party vice-presidential candidate Rosa Clemente's bid for the executive branch. Clemente suggested that the Hip-Hop community support McKinney's presidential bid to demonstrate their electoral power and because the Green Party was most aligned with the issues being discussed at the convention. Two factors worked against this plan. First, many voters in 2008 were more swayed by the opportunity to elect the first Black president, Barack Obama. Second, many felt their vote would be wasted by voting for McKinney and Clemente. Though it didn't necessarily result in a voting coalition, the NHHPC was successful in registering many young men and women to vote during its five-year existence. It provided an outlet for issues plaguing the Hip-Hop community and allowed those who love

Hip-Hop to convene, network, enjoy the cultural form, and share ideas about the political and social future and neglect of urban communities.

The Hip Hop Caucus

Community activist and minister Reverend Lennox Yearwood, Jr., founded the Hip Hop Caucus (HHC) in 2004. HHC's vision is to change the world by ensuring that young people (according to its website, between fourteen and forty) and people of color are involved in the political system and aware of the policy making process.[4] This organization uses culture and celebrities to engage individuals in community action such as voter mobilization efforts and voter registration campaigns, including partnering with T.I. in his "Respect My Vote!" Campaign. The mobilization campaigns from "Respect My Vote!" varied and included efforts from artists such as 2 Chains, who hosted workshops for ex-felony offenders to inform them of their voting rights. This is a particularly beneficial program considering the large percentage of Black and Latinos that are incarcerated on felony charges. HHC is now involved in wide-ranging projects. For example, HHC increased its presence in New Orleans after the devastation of hurricane Katrina by hosting town hall meetings and forming the Gulf Coast Renewal Campaign. HHC also has a presence in antiwar efforts and green movements; one of the most notable is the production of "Clean Energy Now!" Bus Tour in conjunction with Al Gore's Alliance for Climate Protection.

More recently, HHC has been involved in organizing and mobilizing young people around the 2013 Supreme Court decision on the Voting Rights Act, which stated that the previous formula to determine which states must submit to section 5 of the VRA is unconstitutional. Like HSAN and NHHPC, the Hip-Hop Caucus has also developed a list of issues it supports. In HHC's Justice: Civil and Human Rights section, goals include ending police brutality and the death penalty, fighting against Stand Your Ground laws, and supporting marriage equality, global peace, immigration reform, and Black male fatherhood. In efforts to support and fight on behalf of some of these issues, HHC has been vigilant in its fight for justice for the families of Trayvon Martin and Oscar Grant, organizing virtual town hall meetings with members of both Martin's and Grant's families and various cultural leaders and celebrities. HHC has had a real impact. It has provided educational programs on many recent issues that affect the

Hip-Hop community, on Troy Davis's execution, the government shutdown of 2013, and the anniversary celebration of the 1963 March on Washington.

Ella Baker Center

The Ella Baker Center in Oakland, California, is another organization that fights on behalf of members of the Hip-Hop community and addresses some of the same issues as HSAN and NHHPC. The center is named after Civil Rights leader Ella Baker and was founded by Van Jones, who served as the green jobs advisor for the Obama administration in 2009, and Diana Frappier, a San Francisco native and lawyer.

Ella Baker is one of the heroines of the Civil Rights Movement. She worked with many community organizations, including the NAACP and the Young Negroes Cooperative League in New York City, whose purpose was to foster Black economic stability (Ransby 2005). With the NAACP, Baker served as field secretary and director of branches for three years. However, she did some of her most notable work as one of the founders and organizers of the Southern Christian Leadership Conference under the leadership of Dr. Martin Luther King, Jr., SCLC and Baker hosted a student event at Shaw University that turned into the foundation of the Student Non-Violent Coordinating Committee (Ransby 2005). Baker was an avid grassroots organizer.

Continuing her legacy, the Ella Baker Center's mission is to support and work on behalf of low-income people and people of color. The center uses a grassroots approach of volunteers and community activists to carry out its mission. While the center does not focus specifically on Hip-Hop as do HSAN and NHHPC, it uses Hip-Hop and Hip-Hop artists to carry out its mission in the tradition of its namesake. For instance, one of the center's programs is the Third Eye Movement. This group of youth activists used Hip-Hop culture and lyrics to fight against California's Proposition 21, which among other things lowered the age at which a child could be tried as an adult for some offenses from eighteen to fourteen.[5] This new legislation was similar to the New York Rockefeller Drug Laws HSAN protested against in that both limited the discretion of judges for sentencing purposes and imposed mandatory minimums for specific crimes (Lucas 2000). However, unlike HSAN, the Ella Baker Center Third Eye Movement was unsuccessful in its efforts to defeat this legislation, which became law in 2000.

Similar to HSAN and the NHHPC, the Center also focuses on the penal system and works through numerous programs on behalf of youth who are incarcerated. One such program, Books Not Bars, has decreased the number of incarcerated youths in California by 75 percent, according to its website, by allowing the stories and experiences of those incarcerated in California's Department of Juvenile Justice to be featured in articles and books. The Center has also been instrumental in helping to eliminate five prisons that were abusive to children; leading campaigns that helped defeat California's Proposition 6, or the Safe Neighborhoods Act, which would have increased the number of youth in prison; providing support to family members of incarcerated youth; and working to ensure that justice is carried out for youth of color in California who are faced with criminal charges or police harassment.[6] While this organization does not specifically state that it fights on behalf of members of the Hip-Hop community, it focuses on many issues that disproportionately affect that community and its base of volunteers and participants are a part of the Hip-Hop generation.

Through HSAN, NHHPC, the Hip Hop Caucus, the Ella Baker Center, and other Hip-Hop organizations, the political involvement of the Hip-Hop community has been remarkable. Leading members have been able to speak before the U.S. Congress, Federal Trade Commission, and Federal Communications Commission to defend Hip-Hop culture. They have worked with the Recording Industry Association Alliance to support Parental Advisory labels on all compact discs, organized various public awareness forums about the unfairness of the Rockefeller Drug Laws in New York and Proposition 21 in California, and promoted public demonstrations against these laws. These organizations have continued to fight for their communities by organizing and working with Alliance for Quality Education to mobilize over 100,000 New York City public school students to protest at City Hall against proposed tax cuts from the city budget, which resulted in Mayor Bloomberg restoring over $300 million dollars back to the school budget. They have educated their members as well as other urban youth about their legal rights concerning law enforcement, financial stability, economic power, and voting power. These groups have encouraged rap artists and other urban youth to run for political office and to participate with local government. As a result, there has been an observable increase in political awareness and voter participation among members of the Hip-Hop community.

Hip-Hop's Political and Social Activism

The organizations detailed above are not the Hip-Hop community's only political outlet. Many Hip-Hop activists and artists have used grassroots activism to respond to some of the dominant issues facing their communities. For instance, Hip-Hop artists such as Ice Cube and Dr. Dre spoke out against the verdict in the case of the Rodney King beating, expressing the sentiments of many in the Black community regarding police brutality and racial profiling. Some of the most outspoken critics during this case and subsequent L.A. uprisings were west coast rappers Ice Cube, specifically in his song "We Had to Tear This Mothafucka Up," and Dr. Dre, with his "The Day the Niggaz Took Over." Years later, during an interview in which he discussed his thoughts on the Trayvon Martin case, Willie D, a member of the rap group Geto Boyz, stated, "we're politicians and the fans are our constituents." As he explained, he believes rap artists owe it to their fans to discuss social and political issues that affect urban communities and people of color (Paine 2012).

This was a very powerful pronouncement, akin to Chuck D's statement relating rap music to CNN. Even prior to prominent Hip-Hop organizations, members of the Hip-Hop community have used their voice and cultural form to address issues that affect the larger Black and Brown communities. One of the prevailing issues Hip-Hop has tackled is overt criminalization and injustice within the criminal system. The next section will describe artists' and activists' responses to some of the major contemporary political and social issues facing urban communities.

Hip-Hop Stopping the Violence

Unfortunately, violence is not new to the Hip-Hop community. In 1988, the stabbing of Julio Fuentes at a Nassau Coliseum concert became a rallying point (Rose 1994). Critics of rap attributed this incident and others that followed to the violent acts described in some lyrics of rap music. In response to this event and a broader pattern of rising violence, in 1989 leading artists in the Hip-Hop community launched the Stop the Violence Movement (STV). The STV movement was the brainchild of premier rapper KRS-ONE, who organized it in an effort to curb excessive violence in urban communities and to demonstrate that rap was not the overly aggressive violent genre depicted by the media and those outside the Hip-Hop community. Many believed this movement was necessary because of the negative stereotypes of rap fans, which were aligned with stereotypes of Blacks in this country as violent, aggressive, and lewd.

In order to counter the belief that all rap music promotes, advocates, and incites violence, STV released a song called "Self-Destruction" that stated emphatically the group's position. This song featured many prominent rap artists from the east coast such as KRS-ONE, Kool Moe Dee, Heavy D, MC Lyte, and Public Enemy. They came together to advocate an end to violence in a way that defied the stereotype. One of the major critiques of rap music is that it incites and promulgates violence (Rose 2008), but this movement was offering a different read of the genre, its fans, and its artists. The lyrics discuss a single rap fan who resorts to violence, which results in the entire genre and community being perceived as violent. The movement also organized various marches and produced a book, *Stop the Violence: Overcoming Self-Destruction*, which included statistics, photos, and accounts of violence (Rose 1994). The movement dissipated shortly thereafter, but in 2007, KRS-ONE re-launched the STV movement. West Coast rap artists made similar moves with the creation of the 1990 single "All in the Same Gang," an effort to address and curb gang violence.

Recently, Hip-Hop artists and members of the community have been involved in efforts to eliminate other kinds of violence, including bullying among young adults, racial violence, and injustice. Specifically, Hip-Hop artist and actor Nick Cannon is the spokesperson for the STOMP Out Bullying Campaign and created a rap song called "Die Young," in which he discusses stories of teenagers who were victims of bullying and cyberbullying. Similarly, Atlanta Hip-Hop artist Waka Flocka Flame has created his own anti-bullying campaign. Waka Flocka Flame used social networks to allow his fans to choose which cause he would advocate for in 2012. They chose anti-bullying and he agreed to donate 25 percent of the proceeds from the sale of his custom hats to the cause (Raze and Magic 2012). Even notorious "gangsta rap" artists such as 50 Cent are speaking out against bullying and violence among youth. 50 Cent wrote a book, *Playground: The Mostly True Story of a Former Bully*, which takes a different approach of speaking directly to the bully. Additionally, Atlanta rapper T.I. created a public service announcement to support a Facebook anti-bullying oath in conjunction with the organization Saving Our Daughters. More recently, Chicago native Common has called for more rappers and rap songs to denounce and fight against the mass violence that is plaguing many

American cities. Rap artists have supported anti-violence campaigns and efforts throughout rap's history by utilizing music, movements, demonstrations, and literature to speak out against violence.

Hip-Hop and Jena 6

One of the more controversial issues to recently affect the African American community was the case of the "Jena 6." The Jena 6 was a group of teenagers from fifteen to seventeen who were charged as adults with attempted second-degree murder. The charges stemmed from a fight involving the students and a fellow white student who allegedly hurled racial epithets during what was framed as a highly contentious racial atmosphere at the high school in Jena, Louisiana. It was later announced in the plea bargain that the racial epithets were never stated. What is interesting about the case is that these students were being tried as adults over a schoolyard fight. The facts and consequences brought national attention to Jena, garnering much support from the Black community.

One of the most vocal Hip-Hop artists who spoke about the Jena 6 case and encouraged demonstrations was Yasiin Bey, who not only wrote an open letter calling for more members of the African American community to get involved, but also called for highly visible rap artists like Jay-Z, 50 Cent, and Kanye West to become involved by donating time or money. Yasiin Bey took his message to television, repeating it on Bill Maher's late night political commentary show alongside professor Cornel West. Yasiin Bey was not the only Hip-Hop artist involved in the Jena 6 fight. Talib Kweli, Common, and M1 of Dead Prez, the Malcolm X Grassroots Movement (MXGM), NHHPC, and other organizations were also instrumental in orchestrating a student walkout throughout the country that occurred on October 1, 2007, to support the young Black men of Jena, Louisiana, who were facing criminal charges.

In Louisiana the Jena 6 demonstration was supported and attended by artists Bun B and Salt-N-Pepa, who documented their journey and participation on their VH-1 reality show, the *Salt-N-Pepa Show*. Similarly, Ice Cube and T.I. gave moral and financial support and David Banner discussed the case and his views on national radio shows while promoting his new album (Lang 2007; Sims 2007). Still, Yasiin Bey was disappointed that many of his fellow Hip-Hop artists did not travel to Jena to participate in the demonstration.

As an acknowledgment of the experiences of these young men, BET recognized some of the teenagers involved by asking them to present an award. Bryan Purvis and Carwin Jones received a standing ovation from the crowd of stars when they presented the award for the Hip-Hop Video of the Year award at the 2007 BET Hip-Hop Awards. The young men used part of their time on stage to discuss the facts of their case. Many argued that the Hip-Hop Awards was not the appropriate platform for the teens to make their case, considering the violence often described in the songs nominated. But at the same time, many believed this was the perfect platform to reach other urban youth who might still have been unaware of the case and to show solidarity between the Hip-Hop community and these six young men. Subsequently, the charges were reduced to lesser charges and five of the Jena 6 were sentenced to a fine and probation. Only one, Mychal Bell, was sentenced to prison time and served. Still, these charges, convictions and publicity led many of these young men and their families to leave their home town. Today, most are pursuing college degrees.

The Jena 6 case, of course, has not been the only criminal justice case to resonate with the Hip-Hop community and the larger Black community. Similarly poignant have been the cases of Troy Davis and Trayvon Martin.

Hip-Hop and Troy Davis

Troy Davis, a Savannah, Georgia, native, was charged with the 1989 murder of an off duty police officer, Mark McPhail, who was shot trying to defend another man against assault. Troy Davis was charged with the murder and maintained his innocence until his eventual execution. In 2011, Davis was executed in the state of Georgia, although many of the witnesses to the case had since recanted their stories, with many suggesting their testimonies were coerced by the police. While the details of what really happened that night are unknown, many supported an appeal of the death penalty on the grounds that Davis did not receive a fair trial. Davis's supporters included former president Jimmy Carter, Archbishop Desmond Tutu, the Rev. Al Sharpton, Pope Benedict XVI, and even conservative former Georgia U.S. representative and presidential candidate Bob Barr. Many popular rap artists also supported him. Georgia native Killer Mike spoke out against the injustice on Twitter, attended the protest alongside friend and fellow rapper Big Boi, and gave an interview in *XXL* magazine where he stated he could empathize with the officer's family because he is the son of an officer, but he also said, "If there's any doubt this could possibly be a mistake, if there's any doubt that he may not be the guy, we shouldn't do it. We should further investigate" (Lelinwalla 2011).

Many artists took to social media, predominately Twitter, to voice their support of Davis and concern for his impending execution. On Twitter Big Boi asked others to join him to protest against Troy Davis's execution in Jackson, Georgia, tweeting "Breaking News!!!!!!! We're not waiting until 4:00pm we leaving Atlanta RIGHT NOW #Troydavis meet me in Jackson Ga!!! 40 miles away" (@BigBoi). Questlove, Killer Mike, Q-Tip, Bun B, Diddy, Russell Simmons, Jermaine Dupri, DJ Drama, Busta Rhymes, and Talib Kweli, among others, expressed their support for Davis, and asked their followers to call Attorney General Eric Holder, District Attorney Larry Chisolm, Judge Penny Freesemann, or even President Barack Obama to voice their discontent and outrage over the pending execution.

Still other artists used their medium to express their views and support of Davis. One such artist, Jasiri X, wrote the song "I am Troy Davis (T.R.O.Y.)." This track samples the instrumentals from Pete Rock's and C. L. Smooth's song "They Reminisce over You (T.R.O.Y.)," which laments the death of a childhood friend. Jasiri X's song provides details of the case and the controversy that surrounded it, such as the police coercion and recanted testimonies. In addition, the video for the song includes interviews with Davis and his family. Jasiri X's song for Davis was not simply a song, but served as a public service announcement and brief introduction to the history of the case for many who might be unfamiliar with it. Even with all the notoriety around the case and the millions of people speaking out, Troy Davis was executed on 21 September 2011 shortly after 11 p.m. after a brief delay from the Supreme Court.

Hip-Hop artists did not give up voicing their opinions, regrets, and feelings about this execution. Again, many took to social media, usually Twitter, to express their sentiments and dismay at the criminal justice system and the execution of Davis. Wale lamented "This Troy Davis stuff is breaking my heart," and Busta Rhymes stated, "My heart hurts bad!!" Davis's case is not the only case of injustice that the Hip-Hop community has rallied behind. The Hip-Hop community has supported many prisoners, including Mumia Abu Jamal, Assata Shakur, Mutulu Shakur, and countless others. Not long after Davis's execution, the Hip-Hop community found itself rallying behind another cause in the tragic death of seventeen-year-old Trayvon Martin.

Hip-Hop and Trayvon Martin

Trayvon Martin was walking to his father's home from a local convenience store in Sanford, Florida, on 26 February 2012 when he was shot and killed by neighborhood watch member George Zimmerman. The case was highly political because of the Stand Your Ground policy in Florida, which states that an individual who feels threatened has the right to react in self-defense to someone perceived as threatening his or her life. This law was the legal explanation for why Zimmerman was not initially charged in the killing of an unarmed teenager.

As detailed in the many news reports and court proceedings, Martin was walking through the neighborhood where Zimmerman lived on his way back to his father's home after purchasing Skittles for his little brother and a can of iced tea for himself when Zimmerman spotted him. Zimmerman attests that because of the recent home burglaries in the neighborhood and reports of possible Black male suspects, he was suspicious of Martin, so he called the police. Zimmerman, however, did not follow police orders not to approach Martin. Instead, he followed and approached Martin and an altercation occurred that resulted in Martin's death. Particularly disturbing is the fact that Zimmerman did not go to jail, even though he killed a young man and was there when the police arrived. Zimmerman used Florida's Stand Your Ground policy for his explanation for killing Martin. The problem with this case, however, is that Zimmerman racially profiled Martin and took it on himself to police Martin even when told by actual law enforcement not to engage him. Zimmerman did not act because of a threat, but instead created and provoked a situation where Martin had to stand his ground, which unfortunately resulted in his death. Many in the Hip-Hop community found this to be particularly disturbing, and blamed Zimmerman for racially profiling Martin and provoking an unnecessary altercation.

Martin's case is interesting and resonates with many in the Hip-Hop community because of his race, age, and style of dress. Many Black men and women can relate to the experience of being racially profiled. As usual, there was the rush by some members of the public to brand the teen a "thug," while still others criticized rappers and other artists for not doing enough to raise awareness of the incident. The first characterization falls in line with common stereotypes about Hip-Hop, which is deemed a violent genre whose aggressive and hypermasculine songs incite more violence. It's not surprising then that the music favored by most young black men, often seen as a threat in American society, promotes views of danger for association with or being fans of the genre. Much has been made of the hoodie Martin was wearing at the time of his death. People of all ages wore hoodies at rallies and marches in protest of the Sanford Police Department's handling of the case. The teen's Twitter handle "No Limit Nigga," has also been dissected and used as support for the defense that Martin was an aggressor in the incident. New Orleans-based rapper turned entrepreneur and producer, P. Miller, better known as Master P, popularized the phrase "no limit" in the late 1990s with his record label and crew of artists of the same name. The phrase meant there were no boundaries to the actions of the artists and the label.

Like the Rodney King beating in 1991, the incident sparked conversations about racial profiling and police misconduct. Across subgenres, rappers seemed to agree that Zimmerman should have been charged immediately. In an MTV interview, Nas, Bun B, 50 Cent, Killer Mike, and others spoke on the case, many lamenting that Martin could have been their son, brother, nephew, or cousin. This incident especially hit home for Atlanta-based rapper Young Jeezy, who spoke about the fact that he had a son the same age as Martin and urged artists to be advocates for the youth in their home communities. Artists Wyclef Jean, Ghostface Killa, Killer Mike, Janelle Monae, Big Boi, and countless others took to social networking sites to rouse fans into action, circulating petitions as well as informing them of rallies and marches. As a direct response many celebrities, television personalities, and rap artists donned hooded sweatshirts (hoodies) in solidarity with the young man who was profiled based on his apparel.

Others also delved into their craft to express their pain and frustration. For instance, in his song "Skittles and Arizona Ice T," GdotO chronicles the events of Martin's last night alive, starting as the teenager leaves his father's house to make the short walk to the convenience store. This perspective is interesting because it allows rap listeners the opportunity to imagine what Martin may have been thinking or feeling as he was followed and then confronted by Zimmerman. Surely many listeners heard some of their own stories in the song and were reminded of times when they were profiled or victimized. This particular case resonated with the Black community because it brought up the feelings of helplessness and victimization often detailed in rap songs and other resistance songs.

Similarly Yasiin Bey, Dead Prez, and MikeFlo created a track "Made You Die" using the beat from Nas's "Made You Look." In this song, the artists discuss a lack of community protection in the urban community, racial profiling, and ineffectiveness of protests and demonstrations, while mentioning other victims of police brutality. Similarly, they advocate retaliation in instances of violence against members of their community and biases in the criminal justice system. Other songs inspired by Martin's death include: Florida's own Plies song "We are Trayvon," Reef The Lost Cauze's "The Prey (For Trayvon and my Son)," Jasiri X's "Trayvon," Mistah F.A.B.'s "God Don't Love Me (RIP Trayvon Martin)" and Wyclef Jean's "Justice (If you're 17)."

Hip-Hop and Electoral Politics

The aforementioned social movements, political organizations, protests, and demonstrations were and are important because they have provided many minorities the opportunity to participate in nonelectoral politics, as well as demonstrating that many issues were being ignored and needed to be addressed in urban communities. However, nonelectoral politics was not the only means of recourse used by the Black community. The CRM and other social movements also led to increased political and racial consciousness among many minority citizens, as well as increasing minority mobilization and cohesive voting as minority politics shifted from protest to politics. With this form of political strategy, minority constituents were able to receive incorporation in urban areas by electing representatives who were both symbolically (descriptively) and substantively representative (Tate 1994). This tradition of using electoral politics continues today and is one of the dominant forms of political participation among citizens. Over the past twelve years, social scientists have observed an increased emphasis on mobilizing and informing youth voters, due in great deal to mobilization efforts by Hip-Hop organizations and artists.

Hip-Hop moguls, Bad Boy Records CEO Sean Combs (Diddy, Puff Daddy, P.Diddy), along with Def Jam Records and Rush Communications founder Russell Simmons were intensely involved in mobilizing young Hip-Hop voters during the 2004 presidential election campaign. The two created and championed mass voter mobilization drives called "Vote or Die" and "Rap the Vote" respectively, which targeted urban voters between ages eighteen and twenty-four. Four years later, in 2008, Atlanta-based rapper T.I. and the Hip Hop Caucus launched the "Respect My Vote" campaign. That same year, T.I, who has been convicted of several felonies in past years, voted for the first time. However, the electoral politics does not stop here.

Hip-Hop and Barack Obama

In 2008, a historic election placed a Black man in the Oval Office. Many of the voters of this election were brought into the fold as a result of the Barack Obama campaign's savvy use of social networking media, grassroots mobilization, and celebrities including Hip-Hop celebrities. Hip-Hop music was prominently featured in Obama's campaign. He declared he was a fan of Hip-Hop and even had a private meeting with controversial southern rap artist Ludacris. Obama has shared that he has various Hip-Hop artists on his iPod playlist, including Jay-Z, Lil Wayne, and Ludacris. He has also mentioned many rap artists in passing, including southern rapper Young Jeezy. But 2008 was not the POTUS's first encounter with Hip-Hop.

Before his famous introduction to the American public at the 2004 Democratic National Convention, Obama was backstage giving political participation and efficacy advice to Southern rapper Andre 3000, part of the duo Outkast, a conversation featured in the political documentary film *The After Party*. During this interview, Obama explained why people should be interested in political participation regardless of their economic or celebrity status because "Uncle Sam is taking part of your check." Obama elaborated on the importance of sophisticated political participation, primarily voting. Andre 3000 had previously rhymed in Outkast's song "Get up, Get Out," "Y'all tellin me that I need to get out and vote, huh. Why? Ain't nobody black runnin but crackers, so, why I got to register? I'm thinking of better shit to do with my time." Andre 3000's disillusionment with the electoral process and system is noticeable from this verse. Obama contended that it was important to understand how politics and voting relate to the individual's personal situation, receiving nods in agreement from the rapper. But Andre 3000 was not the only person in the Hip-Hop community to speak with Barack Obama that night. Sean Combs, who also created the Vote or Die campaign, was able to interview Obama while working as a reporter for MTV News at the DNC, and spoke with him about informed political participation on 16 January 2009. At the end of the interview Diddy stated he understood Obama's points. Diddy offered to provide his support and a platform for Obama and assured him MTV would do the same.[7] Early on, Obama was already making headway with some of the top members of the Hip-Hop community.

Similarly, in September 2007 Obama was featured in the Hip-Hop magazine *Vibe*. The magazine sported a double covered profile that represented the intrigue and enthusiasm young people felt about Obama's campaign and potential as the first Black president of the United States.[8] This feature also covered Obama's own beliefs about Hip-Hop and the duality of the genre as one that described life in many urban communities while also presenting a pseudo-reality and glorifying aspects of drug culture, violence, materialism, and sexual encounters. The article gave *Vibe* readers a solid introduction to Obama's past and beliefs. Continuing and using his link to the genre during his 2008 presidential campaign, Obama used the notorious Hip-Hop symbol of brushing dirt off his shoulders in reference to his opponents. The symbol comes from Jay-Z's song, "Dirt off Your Shoulders," in which he describes how to deal with those who oppose or offend you: simply brush it off and move on. Obama took his cue from this song and used the symbol without uttering a word to show how he felt about his opposition and their strategy, specifically that of rousing hateful, moblike crowds.

Many rappers campaigned for presidential candidate Obama and wrote songs that used his name as synonymous with success, pride, and manhood. In 2008, Will. I. Am. created the song "Yes We Can," which featured direct Obama quotes, and he later donated the song, along with three other songs, to the album *Change Is Now, Renewing America's Promise*, officially adopted by the Presidential Inaugural Committee. Similarly, Nas released his song "Black President," which opens with a part of an Obama speech from election night 2008, and gave his full support of Obama through his lyrics. Additionally, several news outlets covered a group of elementary students who created and performed a rap about the candidates to the tune of a popular rap song by Hip-Hop artist T.I. And on election night, CNN spoke with a hologram of rap artist Will. I. Am. for his analysis of the election returns.

Grammy Award winning Atlanta rappers Ludacris and Big Boi of Out-kast were very vocal about political and social issues during the 2008 elec-tion season. These artists both created political rap songs, which are not typical of the type of rap they usually produce. Ludacris is widely known as a comedic rapper whose songs often include misogynistic lyrics like "I got hoes, in different area codes," part of the chorus in "Area Codes," a 2001 single from his second album *Word of Mouf.* While Big Boi's work with Outkast (comprising himself and childhood friend Andre 3000) frequently includes commentary on social and political issues, his contributions just as often exalt big butts and casual sex. Both artists received a lot of attention during the 2008 presidential campaign for their songs, but the songs were received differently. The media praised the positive message propagated by Big Boi's lyrics in "Sumthin's Gotta Give." Through these lyrics Big Boi summarizes the pain and economic strain many felt during this economic recession. He raps about his hope that the problems plaguing many minor-ity communities will be solved with the election of senator Obama. At the same time, Big Boi voices his doubt, shared by many African Americans leading up to the election, that a Black man would ever be elected president. Displaying the cynicism endemic in minority communities in regards to the political system and the equality of American society. The song ends with R&B singer Mary J. Blige referring to the many political promises that have been made throughout Black history but have not been upheld.

> And I heard him say that every man, woman, child was gonna be ok
> I heard him say that they would bring our soldiers home in one
>   piece today, hey!
> But its not that way
> They been tellin us a dream
> Tellin us we[']re on the same team
> Now we all gotta deal with the lies.

"Sumthin's Gotta Give" invokes imagery from the Civil Rights Move-ment era and Martin Luther King, Jr.'s "I Have a Dream" speech. This song pays homage to the gains made by the Civil Rights movement while acknowledging that the political struggle continues. Big Boi voices a com-mon sentiment among the Hip-Hop generation when he contends that the promised equality is simply a lie.

In contrast, Ludacris found his song "Politics as Usual" the subject of derision on numerous television news broadcasts, primarily as a result of the harsh words he had for Obama's opponents, including senators Hillary Clinton and John McCain. Less controversially, the song encouraged people to register to vote. Ludacris starts off by detailing his relationship with Obama, how the future president acknowledged Ludacris as a great rapper and had the artist's music on his iPod playlist.[9] Specifically,

> With a slot in the President's iPod, Obama shouted him /
> Said I handled my biz and I'm one of his favorite rappers.

But by the end of the song Ludacris puts Obama's support of him in a compromising situation through his misogynistic lyrics toward Hillary Clinton and derogatory statements about John McCain and George W. Bush. Ludacris states,

> McCain don't belong in ANY chair unless he's paralyzed
> Yeah I said it cause Bush is mentally handicapped

The song prompted criticism from many organizations and leaders including presidential candidate Obama himself.

Rappers have been seen campaigning with and for political candidates in increasing numbers recently. Politically involved artists include Young Jeezy, Ludacris, Big Boi, Jay-Z, Will. I. Am., T.I, Nas, Common, Scarface, Ice Cube, Chamillionaire, Souljah Boy, and Bow Wow. Many of these artists have publicly supported candidates other than Obama on the campaign trail. For instance, T.I., Ludacris, and Young Jeezy supported Georgia's Democratic senatorial candidate Jim Martin in his run-off election. Unfortunately, this endorsement did not help Martin secure the 2008 senatorial seat. In 2008, many Hip-Hop artists gathered to assess Obama's viability as a candidate and their support for him. But they were also mindful of how their endorsement or association could hurt his campaign. Specifically, rappers Scarface, Young Jeezy, Jay-Z and Ice Cube spoke candidly about avoiding the mistakes of Ludacris' "Politics as Usual" in their associations with the candidate. Because of the characterization of rap music as misogynistic, sexist, materialistic, lewd, obscene, violent, and destructive, many believed that a public association with Hip-Hop and its artists would adversely affect Obama. Former NWA rapper turned actor Ice Cube stated,

I think the first thing [the hip-hop community has to] do is let the man become president," Ice Cube opined. "They gotta work in other ways to get him in the White House. It's not really about doing a song right now. He has to separate himself from that stuff; he's in a political race. Everybody should kick back for a minute, see what happens in November. If he becomes president, he wouldn't have to separate himself as much from some of these statements. Because Obama can't come as hard-core as Ludacris as far as his message right now—he can't do that. Us rappers might have to hold our tongues for a few months. (quoted in Reid 2008)

Likewise, Texan rapper Scarface suggested that rappers withhold endorsements and not release songs in support of Obama until he was elected (Reid 2008). "[Rappers] need to be quiet, super quiet on Barack," he continued, "All it takes is for a mutha----er getting out there being real [ghetto] and people will be like, 'We don't wanna f--- with Obama'; they'll wanna smash on him because of what somebody else said. [Someone] speaks for himself and its Barack's fault? What did Luda say—that's Barack's fault? Is it Barack's fault what *I'm* saying? I don't wanna be the reason he don't get [the presidency] . . ." (quoted in Reid 2008). As a compromise, some artists endorsed Obama at their events or concerts but did not actively participate in his campaign for fear that their presence would hurt it. Jay-Z even went as far as to state at his concerts that his messages and support of Obama are not "Obama sponsored" (quoted in Reid 2008). As it turns out, support and endorsements from rap stars positively affected support for Obama by making voting popular among a typically alienated, disenchanted and nonvoting segment of the population. Hip-Hop fans were taking cues from some leading rap stars about not only whom they should vote for but concerning the very fact of political participation. In less than two years, Obama became Hip-Hop's newest trend.

But not all rap artists supported Obama. Some artists who are left of center produced songs that criticized Obama. British rapper Low Key produced the songs "Obama Nation" (Parts 1 and 2), which discussed the continued oppression of the American government, capitalism, racism, imperialism, colonization and wars on Islamic nations as well as his disillusionment with Obama's presidency. Part Two, which featured artist M-1 from the rap group Dead Prez, discusses the lack of impact Obama's race or heritage had on his politics and instead argues that Obama is still a part of an American system that is oppressing and killing minorities. The two versions of the song were very harsh criticisms of America's government and President Obama. Still others, such as Lupe Fiasco and Immortal Technique, have also offered lyrical critiques of President Obama. In fact, Lupe Fiasco is one of the more outspoken critics of Obama, so much so that he shared his decision not to vote for Obama in his song "Words I Never Said." It has been reported that Lupe Fiasco was kicked off-stage after rapping at an inaugural ball in 2013, "Gaza Strip was getting bombed, Obama didn't say shit. That's why I ain't vote for him, next one either. I'm a part of the problem; my problem is I'm peaceful" (Peralta 2013; Weiner 2013). Lupe Fiasco continues his critique of Obama in interviews and through his Twitter account as well. In an ABC interview Lupe Fiasco stated, "To me, the biggest terrorist is Obama in the United States of America" (quoted in Nielson 2012).

Some of the positive and supportive relationships between Obama's campaign and the Hip-Hop community did change between the 2008 election and his second election in 2012. For instance, when Obama released his campaign playlist for 2012 and no rap artists were included, many were shocked. Additionally, in 2012, many of those who had been enthusiastically supportive of Obama in 2008 no longer carried the same hopeful flame. Rap artist Speech of the rap group Arrested Development and Snoop Lion (Dogg), who were both previously supportive of Obama in 2008, threw their support behind Ron Paul in 2012 (Nielson 2012). Similarly, Nas commented, "The historic part of him being elected president was got, and everyone was happy about that, and I'm glad I lived to see it. The flipside is, after we get over that, it's back to the politics, and it's something, which doesn't have time for people. It's its own animal" (quoted in Nielson 2012). The most prominent rap supporters of Obama's 2008 campaign also expressed their disappointment in Obama's first term (Nielson 2012).

Nonetheless, Obama has maintained a very visible relationship with some rap artists, especially Jay-Z, who performed a concert in Ohio for Obama's last campaign stop for 2012. Jay-Z performed his song "99 Problems," and changed the chorus to reference Mitt Romney the Republican candidate running against Obama. Instead of the original lyrics, "I got 99 problems but a bitch ain't one." Jay-Z rhymed, "I got 99 problems but a Mitt ain't one." This slight interjection of a different word, while simple, was profound, based on the attention this change received in the media. In fact, on various news broadcasts that night, many were upset that the derogatory term bitch was replaced with Mitt. Many believed it was disrespectful and in bad taste to have Jay-Z, a rapper, perform this song at the last campaign rally.

After both elections, President Obama continued to acknowledge the influence and importance of Hip-Hop culture in American society. A star-studded inaugural concert on January 18, 2009, featured Queen Latifah, and Will.I.Am. During his first term Obama continued to include, acknowledge, and use Hip-Hop by inviting Pharrell and Diddy to celebrate Cinco de Mayo at the White House in 2010. He also employed Hip-Hop imagery and references at the annual Correspondents Dinner in 2011 and 2012 and was associated with First Lady Obama's invite of Chicago rapper Common for the Night of Poetry event.

The Correspondents Dinner is an annual event that hosts reporters, writers, and other press members and is also attended by various celebrities and politicians. The main feature of the dinner is a comedic speech by the president. It was through these jokes that President Obama was able to reference Hip-Hop music and culture. At the Correspondents Dinner in 2011 Obama began by facing the birthers movement, led by Donald Trump, that questioned Obama's nationality. At the dinner Obama referenced Trump by saying, "Donald Trump is here tonight! Now, I know that he's taken some flak lately, but no one is happier, no one is prouder to put this birth certificate matter to rest than the Donald. And, that's because he can finally get back to focusing on the issues that matter like, 'Did we fake the moon landing?' 'What really happened in Roswell?' 'And where are Biggie and Tupac?'" Obama was referencing popular conspiracies and included a Hip-Hop reference by mentioning the conspiracy beliefs about the murder of Tupac and Biggie Smalls. He ended his segment with a mock-umentary detailing his life without a teleprompter. In this mockumentary Obama goes to Vice President Joe Biden for help on how to live without prepared remarks. The background music displaying Biden's gaffes was a tribute to Hip-Hop with the song "Shimy Shimy Ya," by Ol' Dirty Bastard (ODB), famed member of rap group Wu Tang Clan. The short vignette highlighted the segment of the song, "yeah, baby I like it raw," in reference to Biden's gaffes.

Similarly, at the 2012 Correspondents Dinner, Obama continued his association with Hip-Hop and referenced southern rap artist Young Jeezy, who was associated with the notorious Black Mafia Family of gangsters in Atlanta, Georgia. Obama said, "In my first term, I sang Al Green. In my second term, I'm going with Young Jeezy."[10] While Obama was joking about the news that surrounded his singing of R&B singer Al Green's song "Let's Stay Together," he was also alluding to the underlying fear among right-wing voters of his ability to be more aggressive and powerful during his second term. Many feared the unbridled power Obama would wield if he were granted a second term (Gunter 2012). Some feared Obama would enslave Whites, take away guns, become a dictator, and instill martial law or even cut the defense budget rendering America powerless (Chapman 2012; Gunter 2012). Obama, like the rest of the American public, heard these fears, and he decided to play on them. Here, rap music and Young Jeezy represent the Black radical image that most people fear: that radical Black stereotype that is upset about the history of oppression Black people have endured and who only wants to punish White people and America for his injustices. Obama was playing on the fear that he was a real life "Spook" playing the system for the right time to unleash a race war, similar to the famous 1970s character from Sam Greenlee's book, *The Spook Who Sat by the Door*.

No one should have been surprised by Obama's use of rap imagery at this dinner, as he had used rap previously at Correspondents dinners and relating to other audiences (speaking to the NAACP and to young people). In this case, his choice of a rap artist was surprising. Obama may have referenced Young Jeezy because of his song "My President," which begins,

Yeah, be the realest shit I never wrote
I ain't write this shit by the way, nigga
Some real shit right here, nigga

In this prelude to the song Jeezy is suggesting that the topics he will rhyme about are fact not fiction. The song is a political rap song in which Young Jeezy discusess drug sales, disenfranchisement, war, prison, the election of Bush in 2000, Hurricane Katrina, and his admiration for Barack Obama. Jeezy ends his song by speaking directly to Obama.

It's June 3rd, haha, 2:08 a.m.
Nigga I won't say win, lose or draw man
Man we congratulate you already homie
See I motivate the thugs right
You motivate us homie

that's what it is
This a hands on policy,
Ya'll touchin' me right nigga
Yeah, first black president,
win, lose or draw nigga
Haha matter of fact, you know what it is, man
Shouts out to Jackie Robinson, Booker T Washington homie
Oh y'all ain't think I knew that shit?
Sidney Poitier, what d[th]ey do?
Haha, my president is black
I'm important too though

He congratulates Obama and acknowledges that Obama has motivated him and others in the rap community. He is moved by the symbolism of being able to witness the first viable Black candidate for president of the United States and also names other African American notables. Young Jeezy goes on to comment to MTV news that "I'm not endorsing the dude because he's black. . . . Listen to what he's saying: He's saying what I wanna hear, just like my favorite rapper. If [an MC] is saying what I wanna hear, I'mma go buy his album. If [a candidate] is saying what I wanna hear, I'mma go vote for him. I *can* vote, by the way. Watch me, I'm going to register to vote" (Reid 2008). The sentiments behind this song could have been one of the reasons Obama referenced it at the Correspondents Dinner, but I contend he also wanted to draw attention to Jeezy's known association with gangsters and thug imagery. This, of course, played directly into the stereotypes of Obama as the "spook" that would ruin the country (at least for Whites) after his reelection.

In May 2012, Michelle Obama invited Common to the White House Night of Poetry. This caused a wave of controversy because of Common's reference to George W. Bush in a poem: "burn a bush, cause for peace he no push no button."[11] Common was depicted as a "gangsta" rapper and the White House was criticized for inviting him to this poetry event. As mentioned above, many in the Hip-Hop community would have preferred that Obama avoid these kinds of associations. But Obama realized the important cultural influence of Hip-Hop and used it symbolically as well as overtly to demonstrate his connection with the genre, offering credibility to the Black community, and pulling in the youth vote.

The Democratic Party was not the only party that included the Hip-Hop community in its campaign. Others have attempted to capitalize on the popularity of Hip-Hop among youth including, Republican candidate John McCain, who shook hands on stage with rapper Young Jeezy. Similarly, previous Republican National Chairman Michael Steele publicly encouraged the Republican Party to figure out how to get the Hip-Hop vote and support (Reid 2008). Hip-Hop also figured prominently in the 2008 presidential bid of Green Party candidate Cynthia McKinney, who selected Hip-Hop activist Rosa Clemente as her running mate. These candidates championed a platform of minority, youth, and women's issues. Unfortunately, the viability of third parties in this country did not allow this party to amass much success electorally, but it did spark discussions of issues relevant to urban youth and gave them the opportunity to be included in political debates. Hip-Hop clearly has an influential relationship with electoral politics at the executive level, and it has been used extensively in lower-level campaigns as well.

Hip-Hop for Office

There have been several public efforts to encourage rap artists and other urban youth to run for political office and participate with local government. In New York, Conscious Hip-Hop Activism Necessary for Global Empowerment (CHHANGE) participated in voter registration and mobilization efforts as well as "challenging rappers to run for political office and get involved in politics at the local level" (Kitwana 2002: 177). Indeed, some rappers heard this challenge and embraced it. Chicago resident and rapper Che "Rhymefest" Smith ran for alderman of Chicago's 20th ward. Rhymefest is best known for co-writing the Grammy Award-winning song "Jesus Walks" with Kanye West. Rhymefest's campaign platform reflected many of the agenda items addressed by organizations such as HSAN and NHHPC, including inequality in the criminal justice system, high unemployment among minorities, and emphasis of entrepreneurship as a means of improving personal and community economic situations. The artist was helped by fellow Chicago rap artists Kanye West, who funded the field operation on Election Day, and rapper Lupe Fiasco, who donated turkeys for Rhymefest's Thanksgiving Day drive. But Rhymesfest's political bid was hampered when opponents brought up his criminal past.[12] After a run-off election, Rhymefest's (45.4 percent) bid to become the city's 20th ward alderman ended. He was defeated by a margin of 9.2 percentage points by incumbent Alderman Willie Cochran (54.6 percent).

Miami-based rapper and producer Luther "Luke" Campbell was well versed in dealing with controversy when he tossed his hat in the ring to become a candidate for mayor of Miami in 2011. Luke became famous for his raunchy and explicit music with the rap group 2 Live Crew. The rapper had his first experience with politics when he created a song to help Janet Reno secure her political seat as district attorney through his female rap group Anquette and by fighting for his first amendment rights as discussed previously. However, the Reno endorsement through song was the catalyst for Campbell's national immersion in American politics. This angered Reno's opponents and the governor of Florida, who targeted Luke and 2 Live Crew for indecency in their music and at their shows, banning the sales of their album, and charging those who were caught selling it. Luke responded by successfully fighting for his First Amendment rights in 1992 but was unsuccessful in his mayoral bid in 2011.

Similarly, after the devastating Haitian earthquake of 2010, Haitian American rapper Wyclef Jean mounted a high-profile bid for president of Haiti. His candidacy was cut short because he did not meet the residency requirements. Before the announcement about Jean's status, he had received support from many young Haitians and Haitian communities in the United States.

Not only do rappers lead by example through political action, they also provide important support to many programs and the Black community. Rap has a history of political contributions, including the creation of songs to support political candidates such as Melle Mel's song "Jesse" and Anquette and Uncle Luke's "Janet Reno." Rappers have also created songs to speak out against particular legislation, as is the case with Public Enemy's remake of the classic song "By the time I get to Arizona," and Talib Kweli's "Papers Please," both of which decry the discriminatory immigration policy created in Arizona and adopted in other southern states. And some rappers have even threw their hats in local political races.

Conclusion

Theories such as pluralism suggest that citizens who want to participate must have equal opportunity to participate and be heard in American politics. As Americans seeking our own versions of the American dream, we would like to believe that pluralism is an accurate description of how our country's political system works. However, it cannot be denied that certain groups are still systematically excluded from the political process. Oftentimes, relevant and highly significant issues in the Hip-Hop community may not be discussed in the larger Black community and are rarely identified in mainstream America.

Rappers have been politically engaged with grassroots organizations and with the creation of numerous foundations and programs in the Black community (Kitwana 2002). They have played and continue to play pivotal roles in political movements such as the Million Man March and the Million More Movement, often rallying participants for these movements and giving inspirational speeches at gatherings. What is unique about the political participation of many of the rap artists discussed in this chapter is that they are not typically categorized as message or conscious rappers. We do not expect Bow Wow, Busta Rhymes, or Ludacris to support and fight for political causes, but they have been vocal about their concerns and opinions. In fact, at a time when critics argue that rap is solely a commercial commodity devoid of cultural roots or political thoughts, these songs, events, and campaigns have turned that argument on its head.

Hip-Hop is a vast and varied genre whose songs and artists tend not to lend themselves to one-size-fits-all categorization. Hip-Hop can be political, sexist, nationalist, materialistic, violent, and self-serving, sometimes all in the same song. It is important, however, to understand that there are many subgenres that exist within Hip-Hop that have different impacts upon audience members. Even those artists who may produce a misogynistic, belligerent song can also produce a politically charged song that can enlighten listeners; songs coming from these unlikely sources can have even more impact. Finally, the efforts of Hip-Hop-based organizations and the political relevancy of rap music has clearly resulted in an increase in political awareness and voter participation. Therefore, we can contend that Hip-Hop represents, identifies, and establishes successful political organizations, political action, and political demands.

It's Still Bigger Than Hip-Hop: The Future of Rap and Politics

For Black and Latino youth who have been denied high-quality
education, school is no longer the place where they learn literacy and
politics. Rather, for many, mass media has become their classrooms.
  —Patricia Hill-Collins, *From Black Power to Hip-Hop*, 191

You've been shedding too much light, Lu (Dumb it down!)
You make'em wanna do right, Lu (Dumb it down!)
They're getting self-esteem, Lu (Dumb it down!)
These girls are trying to be queens, Lu (Dumb it down!)
They're trying to graduate from school, Lu (Dumb it down!)
They're starting to think that smart is cool, Lu (Dumb it down!)
They're trying to get up out the hood, Lu (Dumb it down!)
I'll tell you what you should do (Dumb it down!)
  —Lupe Fiasco featuring Gemini 2006, "Dumb it Down," *The Cool*

How do you rate music that thugs with nothing relate to it
  —Jay-Z and Eminem, "Renegade," *The Blueprint*

During the past thirty years, Hip-Hop culture has evolved from its foundation as an urban cultural form into an international phenomenon. There
are rappers in countries as diverse as New Zealand, Australia, Ghana, Ice-
land, Pakistan, Zimbabwe, Japan, Tunisia, Canada, China, France, Ger-
many, Norway, Egypt, and Cuba, among many others. Rap and Hip-Hop

as forms of resistance have spread across the world as one of America's greatest exports. Many cultures and nations utilize rap songs as a means of resistance, motivation, information and entertainment for marginalized movements and groups. In fact, rap songs aided the recent "Arab Spring," which saw the unraveling of regimes in Tunisia, Egypt, Yemen, and Libya in 2011. Tunisian artist El General, whose real name is Hamada Ben Amor, was listed as one of *Time*'s 2011 top hundred influential people. As a rap artist, he was arrested because officials believed his lyrics, specifically in the song "Head of State," which addresses then-President Zine El Abidine Ben Ali, encouraged youth uprisings. El General's music commented on the situation of many people in Tunisia with the lyrics:

> Mr. President, today I am speaking in name of myself and of all the
>   people
> who are suffering in 2011, there are still people dying of hunger
> who want to work to survive, but their voice was not heard
> get off into the street and see, people have become like animals
> see the police with batons, takatak they don't care
> since there is no one telling him to stop
> even the law of the constitution, put it in water and drink it.

These lyrics made direct appeals to President Ali. The song is reminiscent in tone of New York rapper Nas's song "I Want to Talk to You," included in his release of *I Am*. Not only did this song incite Tunisian youth to overthrow their government, but it was also embraced by revolutionaries in Egypt, Morocco, and Libya (Bohn 2011).

Artists such as Egyptians A-Rush and MC Deeb, Moroccan El Haqed, and Libyan rap group Music Masters also wrote revolutionary songs during the Arab Spring, and many were arrested or were charged due to the nature of their lyrics (Bohn 2011; Deghett 2012). Similarly, in France more than two hundred government officials signed a petition to request legal action against several French rappers who were accused of inciting violence in the 2005 uprisings through their rap lyrics (Muggs 2005). Without a doubt regimes and administrations recognize the power of rap music to change and influence public opinion and further to empower the disenchanted and oppressed people in their societies. Hip-Hop has expanded from its origination as a subculture of urban youth in America and has gone global, exciting, energizing, and motivating youths of various ethnicities and cultures.

Back home, the United States has embraced Hip-Hop as a cultural phenomenon by instituting cultural ambassadors to represent Hip-Hop internationally, including former ambassador poet Toni Blackman and activist George "Rithm" Martinez. And American Hip-Hop artists are also using their resources and influence beyond American borders. Rapper Immortal Technique was instrumental in the construction of orphanages in Afghanistan, where America has waged war on the Taliban and al Qaeda. Rapper Wyclef Jean raised money through his organization Yelé Haiti to donate after his native country, Haiti, was devastated by an earthquake in 2010. As Hip-Hop evolved from simply music, scholarship on the culture has also increased.

Hip-Hop Scholarship

Recently there has been an increase in discussions involving rap artists, songs, and politics. Similarly, the study of various aspects of Hip-Hop culture has also increased (Chang 2005; Condry 2006; George 2005; Forman and Neal 2004; Rose 1994, 2008; Ogbar 2008; Perry 2004; Cohen 2010; Spence 2011; Watkins 2005). While many aspects of rap are still seen as deviant there is an understanding that this cultural art form is also important to behavior and attitudes (Dawson 1999, 2001; Harris-Lacewell 2004; Spence 2011). This has led directly to Hip-Hop's use in political campaigns. However, this understanding is not a new concept. Many have commented on the political possibility of rap music as an oppositional culture (Martinez 1997).

Lester Spence (2011) in *Stare in the Darkness* explains that rap music can influence political attitudes and circulate political information. One could argue that all rap is political just by virtue of rebelling from society's views of conformity, but this would be overly simplistic. Instead, I contend that there is a specific subgenre I call political rap that directly impacts specific Black political ideologies, namely Black Nationalism and Black Feminism. As my study showed, we can directly observe and predict the attitude adoption of those that are exposed to political rap as compared to those exposed to rap in general.

Spence is able to draw some of his conclusions on rap as a broader genre based on experimentation that includes exposing subjects to rap videos. While videos are important, they may complicate the transmission of attitudes because individuals are able to associate images with words that may have a stronger, deeper impact than just hearing the lyrics. For instance, is political information transferred if you are passively listening only to the music while in your vehicle, walking, exercising, or working? How do the images in rap music videos enhance or distort the messages in the songs? This is particularly important for individuals who receive their rap music primarily from mainstream media stations that have the ability to censor or ban videos of their choosing. Observing the music and not the video can ensure that the music is influencing individuals, and not the images associated with the music.[1] Spence concludes that while the Hip-Hop community is attempting to create a new type of politics that includes the voices of urban youth, it is reproducing instead neoliberalist philosophies and tactics within the rap community (Spence 2011). While scholars have demonstrated the possible influence of rap on political attitudes, this work further expands that research by examining the impact of specific subgenres of rap music upon particular political ideologies, Black Nationalism and Black Feminism. Thus, I am not making an argument that all rap music is "bad" or "good" in terms of various measures but only that political rap influences the adoption of historical and established Black political ideologies. Therefore, this book is aligned with Spence's assertion that rap affects political attitudes, but expands on Spence's examination of rap in general by observing specific subgenres of rap and its impact on political attitudes.

In her book *Hip-Hop Wars*, Tricia Rose (2008) details the many discussions against and in favor of Hip-Hop culture. She discusses some of the major arguments that have existed over the years about the impact of rap music on sexist and violent behavior, the emphasis of Hip-Hop on antisocial attitudes, and the harm Hip-Hop may cause not only to American values but also to the Black community. She explains the contrasting views that Hip-Hop reflects life in impoverished neighborhoods and sexism as an American issue and the declaration by many artists that they are not role models. This book is a timely addition to the current discussions surrounding Hip-Hop culture. Rose concludes that rap artist Nas's assertion that Hip-Hop is dead is not totally true. She asserts that "Hip-Hop is not dead but it is gravely ill" (2008: ix). Rose argues that the commercialization of

Hip-Hop has eliminated some of its components as protest music and instead has only emphasized violent and deviant behavior. This is a popular contention within the discussion of Hip-Hop, but my book has demonstrated differently. The components Rose discusses do still exist and are influential in the genre, but they are not the only aspects of the music. Today, rap artists talk about myriad issues both political and nonpolitical, and individual rappers can't always be confined to one subgenre, although one may say that much of their music reflects one specific style such as political, gangster, or snap rap.[2] Even nonpolitical, popular, mainstream artists have been known to create politically conscious songs, as in the case of artists like Young Jeezy, Rick Ross, Jay-Z, T.I., and Lil Wayne.

Finally, filmmaker Byron Hurt also examines rap music and the impact that it has on society in his 2006 documentary film, *Hip-Hop: Beyond Beats and Rhymes*. Hurt explores hypermasculinity, homophobia, and sexism as traits pervasive in rap music. He interviews various aspiring artists in cities throughout the country and is appalled by the similarity of the lyrics regardless of region or age. He asserts that there is a popular theme of hypermasculinity presented in rap music. In one scene, Hurt asks aspiring rappers why is there an emphasis on killing and berating others in freestyle rap. They respond that they rap that way because that is what sells. They emphasize that positive, thought provoking rap does not sell as much as rap that emphasizes stereotypes and "ghetto culture." But why is there a difference and what do music executives know that other people do not know? Similarly, does "ghetto culture" sell because of the way it is marketed and emphasized through mainstream outlets? What would the genre look like if mainstream outlets allowed diversity in message or presentation, and music executives did not try to force artists to create a certain type of music? These questions will be further explored below.

I do agree with Rose (2008) and Hurt that some subgenres of rap are more pervasive than others within the mainstream media market. However, I assert that artists who are dominant in nonpolitical rap also produce records that display political attitudes and information. For instance, Jay-Z is one of the highest-grossing rap artists of all time and he often presents political issues in his songs. One of his more blatantly political rap songs is "99 Problems." In this song Jay-Z rhymes,

> "Son, do you know why I'm stopping you for?"
> Cause I'm young and I'm Black and my hat's real low

Or do I look like a mind reader sir? I don't know
Am I under arrest or should I guess some mo'?
"Well, you was doin fifty-five in the fifty-four;
license and registration and step out of the car—
are you carrying a weapon on you? I know a lot of you are"
I ain't stepping out of shit, all my papers legit
"Well, do you mind if I look around the car a little bit?"
Well my glove compartment is locked, so is the trunk in the back
And I know my rights, so you gon' need a warrant for that
"Aren't you sharp as a tack! You some type of
lawyer or somethin, somebody important or something?"
Child I ain't passed the bar, but I know a little bit
Enough that you won't illegally search my shit
"Well, we'll see how smart you are when the canine comes"
I got 99 problems, but a bitch ain't one—hit me!

In the song Jay-Z describes what he maintains is a true story about a time that he was pulled over in 1994 while he was still selling drugs. He not only discusses the issue of racial profiling, but also alludes to the Fourth Amendment protection against illegal search and seizure, detailing what he perceives are his inalienable rights as a citizen (Mason 2012).[3]

This is just one example of how a popular rap artist uses music to present political issues. While some argue that these messages may not be as dominant in mainstream Hip-Hop as they were in the past, they are still present and influence the political views of Hip-Hop audiences. Still, the question remains, what role do recording labels and mainstream media outlets have on the music that is produced, distributed, and popularized?

Controlling Your Voice and Technological Advances

Two examples demonstrate the roles of executives and mainstream media outlets on what type of music is produced and displayed. The first example involves Chicago rapper Lupe Fiasco, whose fans ultimately created an online petition and participated in demonstrations outside of Atlantic Records to demand a release date for his highly anticipated third album, *L.A.S.E.R.S.* One of Fiasco's problems with his label was that they wanted him to sign a 360 deal that would have required him to contribute a portion of all his earnings to the label, including shows and endorsement deals with other companies. The most controversial issue surrounding this album stemmed from a standoff in which Atlantic Records wanted more pop songs on the album while Fiasco pledged to stay genuine to his core audience by presenting socially and politically relevant songs. While Fiasco was able to include some of the music he wanted, he still argued that the album was influenced by the pressures of the label. In fact, Fiasco commented in his interview with the *Chicago Sun-Times*, "It's their record. My words, their music" (Conner 2011). He continues, "I was specifically told . . . [d]on't rap too deep on this record." Lupe Fiasco's album and release demonstrates some of the "negotiations" that occur between an artist and his record label, especially in relation to the commercial success and perceived unviability of political rap music.

The second example involves North Carolina based rap group Lil Brothers. A rumor that floated through many of the Hip-Hop sites was that BET refused to play Lil Brothers' first single "Loving It" because it was deemed too intelligent for BET's audience. While this rumor has yet to be confirmed, many Hip-Hop sites discussed the allegation (www.allhiphop .com; www.hiphopdx.com).[4] These two examples reveal the restraints some artists have to act under because of the power of record labels and television networks. However, many socially and politically conscious rappers have adapted and learned to use other means to get their music to their audiences. This is especially important because many young people are deciding to take their cues of what "good music" consists of not entirely from mainstream media outlets but also from alternative media.

For instance, with the increase and sophistication of technology, many artists become household names without having to go through major labels or media outlets such as radio stations and television networks. A perfect example of this is Kendrick Lamar: over ten thousand people purchased his independent album during its first week.[5] Lamar's album *Section.80* was released solely on iTunes, without using mainstream marketing or media sources. In fact, with the advent of iPods, MP3 players, and tablets, most people purchase portable files of their music instead of purchasing CDs. We saw this tactic used even more recently with resounding success with the release of R&B artist Beyonce's self-titled 2013 album, which remained number one for several weeks with no previous publicity. The first couple of weeks of album sales were exclusively through iTunes. Earlier in the summer of 2013, Beyonce's husband, rap superstar Jay-Z, gave away free copies of his album as an app for all Samsung users through a deal he brokered with Samsung. Similarly, with social networks like Facebook, Twitter, and Bandcamp artists are able to chat with their fans and market their music without the help of a label and marketing team. Mark Anthony Neal made a similar observation in a recent NPR interview in which he stated, "Suddenly, recording artists don't have to go the traditional routes to get out their messages, . . . They don't have to go through the traditional label structure. And if there's something they want to respond to in real time, they can do so via this new technology" (NPR 2008). One of the most significant and relevant developments is YouTube. Many artists create music and videos that appear on YouTube and have a large number of hits even if they never make it to mainstream outlets or charts.

This technology assists in diversifying the genre and allowing more politically relevant and politically explicit rap to be created because rap artists may not have to "dumb down" their music or do "what sells." They can instead depict and describe issues that they are interested in and that impacts their communities, whether that is local or national politics, what life is like in their community, male and female relationships, or simply a materialistic braggadocios album. The aforementioned Arab and African rappers were able to successfully disseminate messages through rap songs by taking advantage of technological advances such as MP3s, Facebook, YouTube, and various other websites. Thus, one can no longer make the argument that rap music is not as politically relevant today as it was previously. More and more, fans are using sources other than the big radio and television stations (e.g., BET, Clear Channel, Radio One) to learn about new artists.

This technology also allows artists to react to and comment on issues in real time via Twitter and YouTube videos, as in the cases of Trayvon Martin and Troy Davis. They can instantly post their thoughts on oppressive governmental regimes and disseminate information about natural disasters like the earthquake in Haiti, hurricane Katrina in New Orleans or share their views on governmental proceedings as during the 2013 government shutdown. This ability to share their opinions with fans immediately allows rap artists to influence significantly their followers' opinions. This effect is further influenced by the fact that celebrities are often viewed as experts by their fans. Zaller (1992) argues that only specialists possess ideology. He states, "ideology . . . is a mechanism by which ordinary citizens make contact with specialists who are knowledgeable on controversial issues and who share the citizen's predispositions" (237). Some would argue that rappers are now the elite or specialists that many youth turn to for political information—and to determine their own attitudes and ideology (Fernandes 2012).

Summary of Results

This book begins by establishing the importance of studying the effect of rap music on public opinions and attitudes. It establishes that marginalized communities will often embrace nonmainstream tactics to discuss their political issues and rights. One way to gauge the political issues and viewpoints of a community is to understand its political attitudes and the ideology that have been adopted. Chapter 1 discusses the importance of attitude formation to political ideology adoption. Political attitudes are established through a variety of information sources and use heuristics to form concise, coherent ideologies. Cultural forms such as rap music are one such source or heuristic. This chapter further establishes that different subgenres of rap exist and we must examine them separately to assess the impact this cultural form has on political attitudes and political behavior. Most important, Chapter 1 presents a concise definition of political rap, thereby differentiating it from other subgenres of rap music. This is essential because while many have discussed both the negative and positive impact of rap music, there has not been a succinct method to identify political rap songs, as opposed to grouping rap artists into categories. Political rap is any rap song that makes a political reference and also comments on social issues or provides some form of solution to social and political injustices described in the song.

Chapter 2 argues that rap is a conduit of political information and a form of resistance (Levine 2006; Martinez 1997). This chapter situates rap in the existing African American tradition of coded messages and Black culture as a form of resistance, detailing the longstanding history of music as an outlet to voice grievances in the American political and social arenas (Iton 2008; Southern 1997). More specifically, this chapter describes the history of rap music and shows that rap's direct lineage can be traced to the use of culture during the Black Arts Movement, particularly with poetry and oratory skills. One person from this era who used the style of rhyming and "playing the dozens" that rap artists use today was political activist H.

"Rap" Brown, commonly known today as Jamil Abdullah Al-Amin. Rap music is a cultural form that uses hidden transcripts to critique and analyze American institutions. Specifically, Chapter 2 examines some of the dominant themes in rap music and political issues that rap artists have tackled in their lyrics such as racism and disparities in drug laws and socioeconomic conditions.

Chapter 3 empirically examines the relationships between Black Nationalism and exposure to rap music and shows that positive relationships exist. However, the first data analysis is limiting because the survey was conducted in the early 1990s. These data over twenty years old and the type of rap argued to be popular during that period is different from the type popular today. It is difficult to know what type of rap was recalled when individuals were answering these survey questions. My argument is that this relationship partly existed because of the popularity of political rap during the time the survey was conducted. Because this study occurred toward the end of the golden era (late 1980s to early 1990s), it can also be argued that at the time of the survey "gangsta rap" was increasing in popularity and when respondents were asked their views on rap, "gangsta rap" may have been the type immediately recalled, thus not giving an accurate representation of rap music as a whole and possibly distorting answers. Therefore, an analysis that specifically observes the impact of political rap upon Black Nationalist attitudes is further examined in this chapter.

Here I was able to create conditions that measured various genres of music including pop, rap, and R&B.[6] Similarly, I was able to divide the genre of rap into the subgenres of nonpolitical rap (party music) and political rap. I hypothesized that listening to rap increases support of Black Nationalism compared to listening to pop music. I also hypothesized that those who listen to political rap are more accepting of Black Nationalism than those who are exposed to nonpolitical rap music or no music. I concluded through experimentation that among the Black sample, political rap significantly increases support of Black Nationalist ideology. These results were significantly different from those for subjects who listened to nonpolitical rap music and pop music and those who did not listen to any music, whose support of Black Nationalist ideology did not increase. However, I found no statistically significant difference between those who were exposed to pop and those exposed to nonpolitical rap. These were very important findings because they demonstrate that political rap is significant to the formation of Black political attitudes, and more specifically increases the listener's support for Black Nationalist ideology. Hence, compared to exposure to nonpolitical rap or no exposure to any music, political rap increases support of Black Nationalist ideology. This result alone provides significant arguments for the examination of the impact of political music on political attitudes formation. Therefore, political rap increases one's support of Black Nationalist ideology.

Building on the findings from Chapter 3, I posit in Chapter 4 that there will be no relationship between rap music in general and Black Feminism when observing results from the 1993–1994 NBPS. Rap's relationship with Black Nationalism complicates the possible relationship it has with Black Feminist ideology. These findings are supported by assertions of sexism and misogyny present in Black Nationalist ideology and in rap music (Adams and Fuller 2006; Alexander-Floyd 2007; Brown 1992; Hill-Collins 2006; Morgan 1999; Perkins 2000; Perry 2004; Pough 2004; Ransby and Matthews 1995; Simien 2006; White 1995). The results demonstrate that exposure to political rap makes one significantly more supportive of Black Feminist ideology than nonpolitical rap. Nonpolitical rap decreases support of Black Feminism more than any of the other conditions examined. This result supports the popular contention that some rap music is negative, misogynistic, and harmful to the attitudes and behavior toward Black women (Adams and Fuller 2006; Pough 2004; Carpentier, Dillman, and Zillman 2003; Johnson, Trawalter, and Dovidio 2000; Johnson, Jackson, and Gatto 1995). However, it should be pointed out that all rap is not negative toward Black women, as exposure to political rap led to an increase in the acceptance of Black Feminist attitudes. But nonpolitical rapm a specific subgenre is negative in relation to attitudes and behaviors toward Black women.

Chapter 5 describes the political participation of rappers and the Hip-Hop community through both electoral and nonelectoral forms of participation. Many may argue that the increased political participation of rap artists and the rap community, particularly during the 2008 election season, was a direct result of the possibility of having an African American president. It's true the Obama campaign was able to galvanize the youth population by getting them involved and out to vote, but it would not have succeeded without the help of Hip-Hop, including the use of symbolic cues from Obama to younger voters, endorsements of the candidate by major Hip-Hop stars, and voter mobilization efforts by Hip-Hop organizations and rappers. Many rappers as well as their communities supported Obama and liberals like him because he championed some of the same issues that

Hip-Hop organizations are involved in, including eliminating disparities in drug laws, ending the wars in Iraq and Afghanistan, and reforming health care. During his administration, Obama followed through on these issues by overseeing a reduction in the disparity between crack and powder cocaine, an end to the Iraq war, and the implementation of universal health care.

Conclusion

I have detailed here the existence of relationships between rap music and Black political attitudes. Specifically, I have demonstrated that there is a causal relationship between political rap and Black Nationalist attitudes and that nonpolitical rap music decreases one's Black Feminist sentiments when compared to political rap. These findings are very important because they prove the relevance of Black music, particularly political rap, in the formation of Black political attitudes. These results are especially interesting in comparison to the many studies that suggest that rap music influences deviant behavior and negative attitudes (Johnson, Jackson, and Gatto 1995; Johnson, Trawalter, and Dovidio 2000; Carpentier, Dillman, and Zillman 2003; Adams and Fuller 2006).

This research adds to the ongoing debate about public opinion and attitude formation. As Charles Henry (1990) concludes, culture is an important aspect of Black politics. My experimental results confirm the assertion that the study of Black politics, specifically public opinion, must begin with the oral tradition. These results also add to Harris-Lacewell's (2004) argument that looking towards other avenues can help us understand and assess Black political attitudes. Many scholars have asserted the political relevance of rap music (Decker 1993; Rose 1994; Allen 1996; Henderson 1996; Stapleton 1998; Dawson 1999, 2001; Neal 1999, 2004, 2006; Walton and Smith 2000; Kitwana 2002; Sullivan 2003; Harris-Lacewell, 2004; Lusane 2004; Perry 2004; Pough 2004; Miyakawa 2005; Hill-Collins 2006; Norfleet 2006; Spence 2011). My research provides empirical evidence that rap not only is important when studying Black politics but is an important source for public opinion formation. Political rap can now be included in the discussions about the formations of public opinions and possibly identified as a heuristic when assessing political attitudes.

This is just one attempt at recognizing the differences within the larger rap genre and understanding the impact that political rap has upon the adoption of Black political attitudes. This research must not stop here. Similar studies must be expanded to observe how political rap from different communities affects audience members. For instance, does listening to artists such as British native, Sri Lanka descendent, M.I.A. increase knowledge of the oppression of Tamil people? Similarly, how does exposure to political rap affect white listeners? Does listening to political rap cause whites to support "Black issues" or policies that have been characterized as race specific or to oppose legislation that disproportionately and negatively affects urban communities of color?

My research is not perfect and has numerous boundaries or limitations that are identified here. For instance, individuals who do listen to political rap may be those who already support Black Nationalist sentiment. However, I attempted to account for this problem by using experimental methods to uncover causal relationships between exposure to music and responses to political attitudinal questions.

These results were uncovered in controlled situations. Students were passively exposed to the music but it can be argued that simply informing them that they were participating in a study cued them to pay more attention to the song lyrics than they normally would. If this is true, is everyday exposure to rap music influencing Black political attitudes? Similarly, since political rap is rarely heard at celebrations, in night clubs, and in the car, should we expect to observe different results among the general population? If the political messages presented in rap songs are adopted, what does this mean for the future participation of younger adults? It is possible that the youth will incorporate other methods of seeking political knowledge?

Similarly, there may be a problem with my characterization of political rap that could either eliminate some songs that seem political or not be inclusive of political songs based on the criteria. I attempted to address all these issues when creating the characterization by observing how others have categorized similar music. One of the major critiques of this work, I expect, will be to question how popular political rap songs are. I have made a case for why political rap songs do not have to be "popular" or mainstream according to charts such as Billboard because of the use of new technology, including social media sites such as Twitter and Facebook and alternative media purchasing sites such as iTunes, Amazon, and Bandcamp.

This book was limited because I chose to focus almost exclusively on male artists so as not to risk further complicating the results in my experimental analysis. Future analyses should include female rappers as well and could compare political messages in songs from male rappers and female rappers to determine whether they have different messages or affect the listener differently. Female artists may emphasize different political attitudes than do male rap artists because of the marginalization they often experience within the genre. Do women discuss different issues in their songs? If so, do these issues impact Black political attitudes differently?

However, I must note that this may be a difficult task considering the limited number of female rappers. When female rappers do become popular, they often replicate the rap style, position, and language of male artists. For example, many refer to Nicki Minaj, a popular female rapper, as a female version of Lil Wayne. This characterization is problematic because what critics are referring to is her style as an artist, which is significantly influenced by the style of her mentor, Lil Wayne. She was Lil Wayne's protégé just as Lil Kim was The Notorious B.I.G.'s protégé. Both women adopt a style that glorifies power, respect, sexuality, and femininity while simultaneously asserting common perceptions of masculinity. This is most observable if we look at Nicki Minaj's popular song, "A Moment for Life." Minaj sings, "In this very moment I'm King," which is very telling about her thoughts on the implications of being male versus female. Most female artists would have referred to themselves as queen instead of king simply because of the gender of these monarchs. However, Nicki Minaj instead takes on the persona of the king who she believes, based on her lyric, has a more dominant role in the hierarchy and therefore is more powerful than the queen. This alludes to the disrespect she believes women receive in the genre unless they take on "male" characteristics. There should be a more thorough investigation of the way female artists contribute to hyper masculinity in this musical genre.

Similarly, future studies might consider how social and economic issues might affect the popularity of nonpolitical and political rap. Are there times when nonpolitical (party) rap is more dominant and popular than political rap or times when political rap increases in frequency on mainstream radio? Perhaps prosperous times and less social tension may result in an increase of party music consumed. On the other hand, the opposite relationship may be true. Perhaps nonpolitical (party) rap is more popular during an economic recession because this type of music can be more uplifting than seriously critical political rap. Society may be interested in hearing about having a good time and spending beyond one's means, allowing listeners to embrace this music as a method of escape.

Ultimately, one of the most important conclusions to gather from this text is that there are different subgenres of rap with observably different effects on listeners. It is easy to generalize about rap being wholly positive or negative, but there is much more to this genre of music. Understanding the effects of different subgenres allows for a more nuanced and accurate understanding of the ways rap and Hip-Hop are affecting the next generation of political participants.

Political Rap Songs

This list is not all-inclusive but provides examples of rap songs that are political according to my definition.

Artist: 2Pac
Album: Greatest Hits
Song: Change
Chart Positions: Single peaked at #32 on US Billboard's Hot 100 (1998);
    19 weeks on Billboard Charts
Issues: Poverty, Police Brutality, Racism, War

Artist: 2Pac
Album(s): Tupac Resurrection, 1 in 21: A Tupac Shakur Story, Sunset Blvd,
    A Decade of Silence
Song: Panther Power
Chart Positions: n/a
Issues: Social Inequality, Revolution, Slavery

Artist: Angel Haze
Album(s): Classick
Song: Cleaning Out My Closet
Chart Positions: n/a
Issues: Sexual Abuse

Artist: Big Boi
Album(s): Idlewild

Song: Mighty O
Chart Positions: Single peaked at #77 on the Hot 100 (2013); 2 weeks on
    Billboard Charts
Issues: Government Abuse

Artist: Big Boi Featuring Mary J. Blige
Album(s): Sumthin's Gotta Give
Song: Sumthin's Gotta Give
Chart Positions: n/a
Issues: Unemployment, Single-Mother Child Rearing, Poverty, Prison

Artist: Black Star
Album(s): Black Star
Song: K.O.S. (Determination)
Chart Positions: n/a
Issues: Black Empowerment, Poverty

Artist: Boogie Down Productions
Album(s): By Any Means Necessary
Song: Stop the Violence
Chart Positions: Single peaked at #76 on Top R&B/Hip Hop Tracks (1988)
Issues: Political and Media Corruption, War, Racism, Violence

Artist: Boogie Down Productions
Album(s): Edutainment
Song: The Racist
Chart Positions: Album peaked at #9 on R&B Albums (1990)
Issues: Racism, Slavery, Civil Rights

Artist: Body Count Featuring Ice T
Album: Body Count
Song: Cop Killer
Chart Positions: Album peaked at #26 on the Billboard 200 (1992); 20
    weeks on Billboard Charts
Issues: Racism, Police Brutality, Racial Profiling, Violence

Artist: Common
Album: Like Water for Chocolate

Song: A Song for Assata
Chart Positions: Album peaked at #5 on Top R&B/Hip Hop Albums
    (2000); 40 weeks on Billboard Charts
Issues: Oppression, Violence, Police Brutality, Corruption, Freedom

Artist: Dead Prez
Album: Let's Get Free
Song: They Schools
Chart positions: album peaked at #22 on Top R&B/Hip Hop Albums
    (2000); 20 weeks on Billboard Charts
Issues: Structural Racism, Slavery, Historical Eurocentrism, Educational
    Reform, Poverty, Police Brutality, Police Militarization

Artist: Dead Prez
Album: Turn Off the Radio The Mixtape Vol.2: Get Free or Die Tryin'
Song: Fuck the Law
Chart positions: album peaked at #32 on Top R&B/Hip Hop Albums
    (2003); 5 Weeks on Billboard Charts
Issues: Revolution

Artist: Dead Prez Featuring/ Stephen Marley, Ghetto Youths Crew
Album: Black and White soundtrack
Song: Dem Crazy
Chart Positions: n/a
Issues: White Patriarchy, Structural Discrimination, Wealth Inequality

Artist: Dead Prez
Album: Turn Off the Radio: The Mixtape, Vol.1
Song: Know Your Enemy
Chart Positions: album peaked at #78 on Top R&B/Hip Hop Albums
    (2002); 3 Weeks on Billboard Charts
Issues: Propaganda, Black Empowerment

Artist: Dead Prez
Album: Let's Get Free
Song: Propaganda
Chart positions: album peaked at #22 on Top R&B/Hip Hop Albums
    (2000); 20 Weeks on Billboard Charts

Issues: Education Reform, Poverty, Abuse Among Corporations, Government Agencies

Artist: Dead Prez
Album: Let's Get Free
Song: It's Bigger than Hip-Hop
Chart Positions: album peaked at #22 on Top R&B/Hip Hop Albums (2000); 20 Weeks on Billboard Charts
Issues: Revolution, Rap Culture

Artist: Dead Prez
Album: DJ-Drama Revolutionary But Gangsta Grillz Mixtape: Turn off The Radio Vol. 4
Song: Malcolm, Garvey, Huey
Chart Positions: n/a
Issues: Revolution

Artist: Digable Planets
Album: Reachin' (a New Refutation of TIme and Space)
Song: La Femme Fetal
Chart Positions: album peaked at #5 on Top R&B/Hip Hop Albums (1993); 32 weeks on Billboard Charts
Issues: Abortion & Associated Violence, War, Wealth Inequality

Artist: Doug E Fresh & the Get Fresh Crew
Album: Chuck D Presents: Louder Than a Bomb
Song: Abortion
Chart Positions: n/a
Issues: Abortion, Societal Dependence, Immorality

Artist: Dr. Dre
Album: The Chronic
Song: The day the Niggaz Took Over
Chart Positions: Album peaked at #3 on Top R&B/Hip-Hop Albums (1993); 105 weeks on Billboard Charts
Issues: Revolution, 1992 Los Angeles Riots, Violence

Artist: Eve
Album: Let There Be Eve . . . Ruff Ryders' First Lady

Song: Love Is Blind
Chart Positions: Single peaked at #34 on Hot 100 (2000); 16 weeks on
    Billboard Charts. Album peaked at #1 on Top R&B/Hip Hop Albums
    (1999); 42 weeks on Billboard Charts
Issues: Sexual Abuse

Artist: El General
Album(s): n/a
Song: Mr. President
Chart Positions: n/a
Issues: Authoritarianism, Arab Spring, Freedom of Speech, Political
    Legitimacy

Artist: Field Mob Featuring Slimm Calhoun
Album: From Tha Roota to Tha Toota
Song: Nothing 2 Lose
Chart Positions: Album peaked at #4 on Top R&B/Hip Hop Albums
    (2002); 35 weeks on Billboard Charts
Issues: Slavery, Poverty

Artist: Goodie Mob
Album: Soul Food
Song: Thought Process
Chart positions: Album peaked at #8 on Top R&B/Hip Hop Albums
    (1995); 47 weeks on Billboard Charts
Issues: Structural Discrimination, Poverty, Black Empowerment

Artist: Goodie Mob
Album: Soul Food
Song: Cell Therapy
Chart Positions: Single peaked at #39 on the Hot 100 (1995); 20 Weeks on
    Billboard Charts. Album peaked at #8 on Top R&B/Hip Hop Albums
    (1995); 47 weeks on Billboard Charts
Issues: Racial Warfare, Addiction, Drug Violence, Government Control

Artist: Grandmaster Flash and Melle Mel
Album: White Lines (Don't Do It)
Song: White Lines (Don't Do It)

Chart Positions: n/a
Issues: Drug Abuse, Corporate Abuse, Government Corruption, Wealth
    Inequality

Artist: Grandmaster Flash and the Furious Five
Album: The Message
Song: The Message
Chart Positions: Single peaked at #62 on Top R&B/Hip Hop Tracks (1982);
    7 weeks on the Billboard Charts
Issues: Poverty, Destitution, Drug Addiction, Wealth Inequality, Social
    Stagnation, Violence

Artist: Gucci Mane & Young Jeezy
Album: Trap House
Song: Icy
Chart Positions: Single peaked at #23 on Hop Rap Tracks (2005); 5 weeks
    on Billboard Charts.
Issues: Black Empowerment, Rap Culture

Artist: Ice Cube
Album: Death Certificate
Song: Us
Chart Positions: Album peaked at #1 on Top R&B/Hip Hop Albums
    (1991); 44 weeks on Billboard Charts
Issues: Black Empowerment, Poverty, Prejudice, Police Abuse, Structural
    Discrimination, Familial Abuse

Artist: Ice Cube
Album: The Predator
Song: We had to Tear This Mother Fucker Up
Chart Positions: Album peaked at #1 on the Billboard 200 (1992); 52 weeks
    on Billboard Charts
Issues: Mistrust of Police, Revolution, Violence, 1992 Los Angeles Riots

Artist: J. Cole
Album(s): Cole World: the Sideline Story
Song: Lost Ones

Chart Positions: Album peaked at #1 on The Billboard 200 (2013); 37
    weeks on Billboard Charts
Issues: Abortion, Poverty, Single-Parent Culture, Parental Abandonment

Artist: Jadakiss
Album(s): Kiss of Death
Song: Why
Chart Positions: Album peaked at #1 on Top R&B/Hip Hop Albums
    (2004); 38 weeks on Billboard Charts
Issues: Corporate Greed, Violence, Cultures of Violence, Structural
    Discrimination, Government Abuse, Racially Based Policies

Artist: Jasiri-X
Album: Trayvon
Song: Trayvon
Chart Positions: n/a
Issues: Racial Violence, Racial Stereotypes, Racial Inequality

Artist: Jasiri-X
Album: #TheWholeWorldIsWatching
Song: I am Troy Davis (T.R.O.Y.)
Chart Positions: n/a
Issues: Structural Discrimination in the Justice System, Prison, Racism

Artist: Jay-Z
Album(s): The Blueprint
Song: Renegade
Chart Positions: Album peaked at #1 on the Billboard 200 (2001); 35 weeks
    on Billboard Charts
Issues: Ghetto Culture, Drug Culture, Poverty, Media Culture

Artist: Jay-Z
Album(s): The Black Album
Song: 99 Problems
Chart Positions: Album peaked at #1 on the Billboard 200 (2004); 58 weeks
    on Billboard Charts
Issues: Socio-Economic Mobility, Poverty Culture, Rap Culture, Legal
    Inequality in Representation

Artist: Jay-Z
Album: Kingdom Come
Song: Minority Report
Chart Positions: Album peaked at #1 on the Billboard 200 (2006); 19 weeks
    on Billboard Charts
Issues: Racial Stereotypes, Poverty, Government Indifference

Artist: Jay Electronica
Album: What the F*ck is a Jay Electronica
Song: When the Levees Broke (Katrina)
Chart Positions: n/a
Issues: Government Indifference, Racial Discrimination, Slavery, Poverty

Artist: Jean Grae
Album(s): Jeanius
Song: My Story
Chart Positions: Album peaked at #71 on Top R&B/Hip Hop Albums
    (2008); 2 weeks on Billboard Charts
Issues: Sexual Abuse, Violence, Addiction, Poverty, Abortion

Artist: Kanye West
Album(s): The College Dropout
Song: All Falls Down
Chart Positions: Single peaked at #7 on the Billboard Hot 100 (2004); 20
    weeks on Billboard Charts.
Issues: Culture around Education, Poverty, "Keeping Up with the Jones,"
    Self-Hate, Police Dislike, Wealth Inequality

Artist: Kendrick Lamar
Album(s): Section.80
Song: Fuck Your Ethnicity
Chart Positions: Album peaked at #21 on Top R&B/Hip Hop Albums
    (2012); 52 weeks on Billboard Charts
Issues: Racism, Wealth Inequality, Revolution

Artist: Kendrick Lamar
Album(s): Section.80
Song: Hiii Power

Chart Positions: Album peaked at #21 on Top R&B/Hip Hop Albums
    (2012); 52 weeks on Billboard Charts
Issues: Civil Rights Activism, Revolution, Police Dislike, Black
    Empowerment

Artist: Lil Wayne Featuring Jay-Z
Album(s): Tha Carter III
Song: Mr. Carter
Chart Positions: Single peaked at #13 on Hot Rap Tracks (2008); 17 weeks
    on Billboard Charts
Issues: Violence, Revolution, Gang Culture

Artist: Lil Wayn Featuring Robin Thicke
Album(s): Tha Carter III
Song: Tie My Hands
Chart Positions: Album peaked at #1 on the Billboard 200 (2012); 147
    weeks on Billboard Charts
Issues: Hurricane Katrina, Socio-Economic Mobility, Structural Inequality,
    Government Indifference

Artist: Lil Wayne
Album(s): Dedication 2
Song: Georgia . . . Bush
Chart Positions: Album peaked at #69 on Top R&B/Hip Hop Albums
    (2007); 49 weeks on Billboard Charts
Issues: Political & Media Racism, Government Abuse, Drug Culture,
    Violence,

Artist: Lupe Fiasco
Album(s): Lasers
Song: Words I Never Said
Chart Positions: Single peaked at #89 on the Hot 100 (2011); 1 week on
    Billboard Charts
Issues: Government Conspiracy, Military-Industrial Complex, Education
    Quality, Racism, Revolution, Empowerment

Artist: Lupe Fiasco
Album(s): Lasers

Song: All Black Everything
Chart Positions: Album peaked at #1 on Top R&B/Hip Hop Albums
    (2011); 47 weeks on Billboard Charts
Issues: Slavery, Black Diaspora, Rap Culture, Racism, Empowerment

Artist: Lupe Fiasco
Album(s): The Cool
Song: Dumb It Down
Chart Positions: Album peaked at #14 on the Billboard 200 (2008); 25
    weeks on Billboard Charts
Issues: Educational Disparities, Corporate Influence, Rap Culture

Artist: LL Cool J
Album(s): Bigger and Deffer
Song: I'm Bad
Chart Positions: Single peaked at #4 on Hot R&B/Hip Hop Singles (1987);
    14 weeks on Billboard Charts
Issues: Rap culture, wealth, violence

Artist: Lord Jamar
Album(s): The 5% Album
Song: Supreme Mathematics
Chart Positions: Album peaked at #94 on Top R&B/Hip Hop Albums
    (2006);
Issues: Addiction, Black Empowerment, Islam (5 percent Ideology)

Artist: Ludacris
Album(s): Release Therapy
Song: Runaway Love
Chart Positions: Single peaked at #2 on the Billboard 200 (2006); 28 weeks
    on Billboard Chart
Issues: Abandonment, Addiction, Sexual and Physical Abuse, Alcoholism

Artist: Ludacris
Album(s): The Preview
Song: Politics as Usual
Chart Positions: n/a
Issues: Political Empowerment, Elections, the Presidency

Artist: Melle Mel
Album: Grandmaster Flash Vs. the Sugarhill Gang
Song: Jesse
Chart Positions: n/a
Issues: Political Representation, Poverty, Political Cynicism, Slavery,
    Systemic Discrimination

Artist: Mos Def
Album(s): Tru3 Magic
Song: Katrina Clap/ Dollar Day
Chart Positions: Album peaked at #25 on R&B Albums (2007); Weeks on
    Billboard Chart Unavailable
Issues: Government Discrimination, Racial Poverty, Mishandling of
    Katrina, Government Apathy

Artist: Nas
Album(s): I Am
Song: I Want to Talk to You
Chart Positions: Album peaked at #1 on the Billboard 200 (1999); Chart
    History unavailable
Issues: Racism, Government Conspiracy and Deception, Systemic
    Discrimination, Revolution

Artist: Nas Featuring Millenium Thug
Album(s): Stillmatic
Song: My Country
Chart positions: Album peaked at #2 on the Billboard 200 (2002); 42
    Weeks on Billboard Charts
Issues: Violence, Drugs, Ghetto Culture, Historical Racism, Revolution

Artist: Nas
Album(s): Stillmatic
Song: Rule
Chart positions: Single peaked #67 on the Hot R&B/Hip-Hop Songs
    (2002); 9 Weeks on Billboard Charts
Issues: Racism, Poverty, Pacifism, Violence, Ghetto Culture

Artist: Nas
Album(s): The Lost Tapes

Song: Doo Rags
Chart Positions: Album peaked at #3 on Top R&B/Hip Hop Album (2002); 13 weeks on Billboard Charts
Issues: Ghetto Culture, Government Abuse, Drugs, Police Violence, Black Empowerment

Artist: Nas
Album(s): The Lost Tapes
Song: Black Zombie
Chart Positions: Album peaked at #3 on Top R&B/Hip Hop Album (2002); 13 weeks on Billboard Charts
Issues: Drugs, Ghetto Culture, Single-Parent Poverty, Cultural Paralysis, Black Empowerment, Revolution

Artist: Nas
Album(s): Nastradamus
Song: Project Windows
Chart Positions: Album peaked at #2 on the Top R&B/Hip Hop Albums (1999); 33 weeks on Billboard Charts
Issues: Ghetto Culture, Addiction, Black Empowerment, Revolution, Police Abuse

Artist: Nas
Album: Nas
Song: My President
Chart Positions: n/a
Issues: Prison, Police Brutality, Political Cynicism, Modern Slavery, Racism

Artist: Nelly
Album(s): Sweatsuit
Song: Grillz
Chart Positions: Single peaked at #1 on the Billboard Hot 100 (2005); 28 weeks on Billboard Charts
Issues: Rap Culture, Criminality, Ghetto Culture

Artist: Nick Cannon
Album(s): Can I Live?
Song: Can I Live?

Chart Positions: n/a
Issues: Abortion, Single-Parent Poverty

Artist: Nick Cannon
Album: If I Die Young
Song: If I Die Young
Chart Positions: n/a
Issues: LGBT Discrimination, Social Isolation, Slut Shaming

Artist: Nicki Minaj
Album(s): Sucka Free
Song: Autobiography
Chart Positions: Album peaked at #95 Top R&B/Hip Hop Albums (2008);
    1 week on Billboard Charts
Issues: Addiction, Childhood Abandonment, Violence, Abortion

Artist: Organized Konfusion
Album(s): The Equinox
Song: Invetro
Chart Positions: Album peaked #29 on Top R&B/Hip Hop Albums (1997);
    5 weeks on Billboard Charts
Issues: Marital Abuse, Addiction, Abortion, Drugs

Artist: OutKast
Album(s): ATLiens
Song: Jazzy Belle
Chart Positions: Single peaked at #7 on Hot Rap Singles (1997); 27 weeks
    on Billboard Charts
Issues: Sex Culture, Drugs, Abandonment

Artist: OutKast Featuring Big Rube
Album(s): ATLiens
Song: 13th Floor/Growing Old
Chart Positions: Album peaked at #1 on Top R&B/Hip Hop Albums
    (1996); 40 weeks on Billboard Charts
Issues: Black Empowerment, Structural Discrimination, Self-Hate

Artist: OutKast Featuring Goodie Mob
Album(s): Southernplayalisticadillacmuzik

Song: Git Up, Git Out
Chart Positions: Single peaked at #13 on Hot Rap Singles (1994); 18 weeks
    on Billboard Charts
Issues: Black Empowerment, Drugs, Poverty, Social Inequality

Artist: Plies
Album(s): We Are Trayvon
Song: We Are Trayvon
Chart Positions: n/a
Issues: Racial Profiling, Racism, Systemic Discrimination, Social Justice

Artist: Public Enemy
Album(s): Apocalypse 91
Song: By the Time I get to Arizona
Chart Positions: Album peaked at #1 on R&B Albums (1991); 32 weeks on
    Billboard Charts
Issues: Political Marginalization, Poverty, Racism, Political Indifference,
    Revolution, Civil Rights Activism

Artist: Public Enemy
Album(s): Hell No (We Ain't Alright)
Song: Hell No (We Ain't Alright)
Chart Positions: n/a
Issues: Systemic Racism, Katrina, Government Indifference, Revolution,
    Violence, Racial Stereotypes

Artist: Screwball
Album(s): Y2K: The Album
Song: Who Shot Rudy
Chart Positions: Album peaked at #50 on Top R&B/Hip Hop Albums
    (2000); 3 weeks on Billboard Charts
Issues: Assassination, Ghetto Culture, Racial Profiling, Gang Violence,
    Drugs

Artist: Stop the Violence Movement
Album(s): Self Destruction
Song: Self Destruction
Chart Positions: n/a

Issues: Rap Culture, Violence, Perceptions of Rap, Racial Activism, Prison, Drugs

Artist: Trick Daddy
Album(s): Thug Holiday
Song: Thug Holiday
Chart Positions: Single peaked at #24 on Hot Rap Tracks (2003); 4 weeks on Billboard Charts
Issues: Jail, Ghetto Culture, Drugs, Education Reform,

Artist: Remy Ma
Album(s): There's Something About Remy: Based on a True Story
Song: What's Going On
Chart Positions: Album peaked at #7 on Top R&B/Hip Hop Albums; 29 weeks on Billboard Charts
Issues: Drugs, Abortion, Sex, Poverty

Artist: West Coast Rap All-Stars
Album(s): We're all in the Same Gang
Song: We're all in the Same Gang
Billboard Charts: Single peaked at #10 on Hot R&B/Hip-Hop Songs (1990); 16 weeks on Billboard Charts
Issues: Gang Violence, Poverty, Incentives for Criminality, Gang Culture, Systemic Discrimination

Artist: Wu-Tang Clan Featuring Isaac Hayes
Album(s): The W
Song: I Can't Go to Sleep
Chart Positions: Album peaked at #7 on on Top R&B/Hip Hop Albums (2006); 29 weeks on Billboard Charts
Issues: Government Abuse, Violence, Addiction, Drugs, Ghetto Culture, Black Empowerment, Structural Racism

Artist: Wu-Tang Clan Featuring Junior Reid
Album(s): The W
Song: Jah World
Chart Positions: Album peaked at #1 on Top R&B/Hip Hop Albums (2000); 19 weeks on Billboard Charts
Issues: Violence, Slavery, Sexual Abuse, Cultural Imperialism

Artist: Wyclef Jean
Album(s): n/a
Song: Justice (If You're 17)
Chart Positions: n/a
Issues: Racial Profiling, Racism, Black Empowerment

Artist: Yasiin Bey, Dead Prez, MikeFlo
Album(s): n/a
Song: Made You Die
Chart Positions: n/a
Issues: Trayvon Martin, Racial Stereotypes, "Stand Your Ground" Laws,
    Political Cynicism, Racial Profiling, Revolution

Artist: Young Jeezy
Album(s): TM:103: Hustlerz Ambition
Song: Trapped
Chart Positions: Album peaked at #1 on Top R&B/Hip-Hop Albums
    (2013); 77 weeks on Billboard Charts
Issues: Ghetto Culture, Violence, Structural Inequality, Racism, Prison
    System, Poverty

Artist: Young Jeezy
Album(s): The Recession
Song: My President
Chart Positions: Single peaked at #13 on Hot Rap Songs (2008); 12 weeks
    on Billboard Charts
Issues: Prison, Election Controversy, Poverty, Jim Crow Laws

HSAN and BPP Demands

What We Want—Demands from the Hip-Hop Summit Action Network

Retrieved from http://www.hiphoparchive.org/node/9067

1. We want freedom and the social, political and economic development and empowerment of our families and communities; and for all women, men and children throughout the world.
2. We want equal justice for all without discrimination based on race, color, ethnicity, nationality, gender, sexual orientation, age, creed or class.
3. We want the total elimination of poverty.
4. We want the highest quality public education equally for all.
5. We want the total elimination of racism and racial profiling, violence, hatred and bigotry.
6. We want universal access and delivery of the highest quality health care for all.
7. We want the total elimination of police brutality and the unjust incarceration of people of color and all others.
8. We want the end and repeal of all repressive legislations, laws, regulations and ordinances such as "three strikes" laws; federal and state mandatory minimum sentencing; trying and sentencing juveniles as adults; sentencing disparities between crack and powdered cocaine use; capital punishment; the Media Marketing Accountability Act; and hip-hop censorship fines by the FCC.
9. We want reparations to help repair the lingering vestiges; damages and suffering of African Americans as a result of the brutal enslavement of generations of Africans in America.

10. We want the progressive transformation of American society into a Nu America as a result of organizing and mobilizing the energy, activism and resources of the hip-hop community at the grassroots level throughout the United States.

11. We want greater unity, mutual dialogue, program development and a prioritizing of national issues for collective action within the hip-hop community through summits, conferences, workshops, issue task force and joint projects.

12. We want advocacy of public policies that are in the interests of hip-hop before Congress, state legislatures, municipal governments, the media, and the entertainment industry.

13. We want the recertification and restoration of voting rights for the 10 million persons who have lost their right to vote as a result of a felony conviction. Although these persons have served time in prison, their voting rights have not been restored in 40 states in the U.S.

14. We want to tremendously increase public awareness and education on the pandemic of HIV/AIDS.

15. We want a clean environment and an end to communities in which poor and minorities reside being deliberately targeted for toxic waste dumps, facilities, and other environmental hazards.

October 1966 Black Panther Party Platform and Program
What We Want, What We Believe

Retrieved from http://www.blackpanther.org/TenPoint.htm

1. *We want freedom. We want power to determine the destiny of our Black Community.*
> We believe that Black people will not be free until we are able to determine our destiny.
2. *We want full employment for our people.*
> We believe that the federal government is responsible and obligated to give every man employment or a guaranteed income. We believe that if the white American businessmen will not give full employment, then the means of production should be taken from the businessmen and placed in the community so that the people of

the community can organize and employ all of its people and give a high standard of living.

3. *We want an end to the robbery by the white man of our Black Community.*
    We believe that this racist government has robbed us and now we are demanding the overdue debt of forty acres and two mules. Forty acres and two mules was promised 100 years ago as restitution for slave labor and mass murder of Black people. We will accept the payment as currency which will be distributed to our many communities. The Germans are now aiding the Jews in Israel for the genocide of the Jewish people. The Germans murdered six million Jews. The American racist has taken part in the slaughter of over twenty million Black people; therefore, we feel that this is a modest demand that we make.

4. *We want decent housing, fit for shelter of human beings.*
    We believe that if the white landlords will not give decent housing to our Black community, then the housing and the land should be made into cooperatives so that our community, with government aid, can build and make decent housing for its people.

5. *We want education for our people that exposes the true nature of this decadent American society. We want education that teaches us our true history and our role in the present-day society.*
    We believe in an educational system that will give to our people a knowledge of self. If a man does not have knowledge of himself and his position in society and the world, then he has little chance to relate to anything else.

6. *We want all Black men to be exempt from military service.*
    We believe that Black people should not be forced to fight in the military service to defend a racist government that does not protect us. We will not fight and kill other people of color in the world who, like Black people, are being victimized by the white racist government of America. We will protect ourselves from the force and violence of the racist police and the racist military, by whatever means necessary.

7. *We want an immediate end to police brutality and murder of Black people.*
    We believe we can end police brutality in our Black community by organizing Black self-defense groups that are dedicated to defending our Black community from racist police oppression and brutality. The Second Amendment to the Constitution of the United States

gives a right to bear arms. We therefore believe that all Black people should arm themselves for self-defense.

8. *We want freedom for all Black men held in federal, state, county and city prisons and jails.*

We believe that all Black people should be released from the many jails and prisons because they have not received a fair and impartial trial.

9. *We want all Black people when brought to trial to be tried in court by a jury of their peer group or people from their Black communities, as defined by the Constitution of the United States.*

We believe that the courts should follow the United States Constitution so that Black people will receive fair trials. The 14th Amendment of the U.S. Constitution gives a man a right to be tried by his peer group. A peer is a person from a similar economic, social, religious, geographical, environmental, historical and racial background. To do this the court will be forced to select a jury from the Black community from which the Black defendant came. We have been, and are being tried by all-white juries that have no understanding of the "average reasoning man" of the Black community.

10. *We want land, bread, housing, education, clothing, justice and peace. And as our major political objective, a United Nations-supervised plebiscite to be held throughout the Black colony in which only Black colonial subjects will be allowed to participate for the purpose of determining the will of Black people as to their national destiny.*

When in the course of human events, it becomes necessary for one people to dissolve the political bands which have connected them with another, and to assume, among the powers of the earth, the separate and equal station to which the laws of nature and nature's God entitle them, a decent respect to the opinions of mankind requires that they should declare the causes which impel them to the separation.

We hold these truths to be self-evident, that all men are created equal; that they are endowed by their Creator with certain unalienable rights; that among these are life, liberty, and the pursuit of happiness. *That, to secure these rights, governments are instituted among men, deriving their just powers from the consent of the governed; that, whenever any form of government becomes destructive of these ends, it is the right of the people to alter or to abolish it, and to institute a new government, laying its foundation on such principles, and organizing its powers in such form, as to them shall seem most likely to effect their safety and happiness.* Prudence, indeed, will dictate that governments long established should not be changed for light and transient causes; and accordingly, all experience hath shown, that mankind are more disposed to suffer, while evils are sufferable, than to right themselves by abolishing the forms to which they are accustomed. *But, when a long train of abuses and usurpations, pursuing invariable the same object, evinces a design to reduce them under absolute despotism, it is their right, it is their duty, to throw off such government, and to provide new guards for their future security.*

Notes

Introduction. Watch for the Hook

1. In 2011 New York native rapper Mos Def changed his rap monicker to Yasiin Bey (Perpetua 2011); they are used interchangeably in the text.

2. Here the Hip-Hop community refers to those who practice some element of Hip-Hop, rapping, break dancing, djing, or doing graffiti art, as well as those who listen to Hip-Hop music and label executives.

3. Cathy Cohen (1999) describes marginal groups as "those who . . . exist politically, socially or economically 'outside' of dominant norms and institutions" (37). Specifically, marginalized groups are "those who still suffer from imposed, extralegal segregation, isolation and exclusion" (40). Marginalization is different from alienation, as marginalization describes those who do not have access to the resources and/ or skills needed for inclusion, whereas alienation describes attitudes of estrangement, separation, or seclusion from political and social agendas. Thus, those who are alienated have low if any political efficacy and are not even considered in most political or social policies, speeches, and agendas.

Chapter 1. Behind the Music: Black Political Attitudes and Rap Music

Epigraph: Lawrence W. Levine, "African American Music as Resistance," in *African American Music: An Introduction*, ed. Mellonee V. Burnim and Portia K. Maultsby (New York: Routledge, 2006), 587.

1. http://www.cbsnews.com/stories/2005/09/03/katrina/main814623.shtml.

2. However, Cathy Cohen's seminal research from the Black Youth Project and her book *Democracy Remixed* (2010) has provided scholars with more succinct data on issues and concerns of youth.

3. In 1990 George Will wrote a *Newsweek* article in which he connected the beating and rape of the Central Park Jogger to the music of rap group 2 Live Crew. Will's argument was that the convicted teens' admission that raping and beating a thirty-year-old woman fun resulted in the type of violence suggested through 2 Live Crew's lyrics. Will directly correlated rap music, specifically 2 Live Crew's lyrics, to the alleged

behavior of those men and their justification of the acts as acceptable. In 2009, the case was overturned due to DNA evidence and the admission of another incarcerated man.

4. Their next album *Banned in the USA* had many political songs, including songs that discussed their previous court case (as in the title track "Banned in the USA"). Songs celebrating the popularity of their music as a result of their political trial (in "Man, Not a Myth"), and the most explicit "Fuck Martinez," in which the chorus and the verses are call and response lyrics defaming then Florida governor Bob Martinez, Martinez's wife, and Broward County sheriff Nick Navarro (who were associated with bringing charges against the rappers and demanding that music stores not sell the album).

5. Renegade by Jay-Z featuring Eminem.

6. Wu Tang Clan is a Staten Island, New York, rap group of nine members that formed in 1993: Ghostface Killah (Dennis Coles), RZA (Robert Diggs), Raekwon (Corey Woods), GZA (Gary Grice) u-God (Lamont Hawkins), Ol' Dirty Bastard (Russell Jones), Method Man (Clifford Smith), Masta Killa (Elgin Turner), and Inspectah Deck (Jason Hunt). All nine had individual commercial success as rappers while in the group and after leaving it.

7. Centre for Political Song, http://www.gcal.ac.uk/politicalsong.

8. Robert Walker (1976: 7) states in his dissertation on Black music and society that message songs "symbolized solidarity by relating in a specific way" to one or more solidarity dimensions.

9. Luther Campbell is a popular artist and creator of rap group 2 Live Crew. He is often criticized for his lewd language but widely credited for bass music, a popular party music in the American South. Lyrics in this type of music emphasize sexual content and are noted for strong bass beats.

10. This classification is indicated by his album titles *Book of Thugs* and *Thug Holiday* and his popular song "I'm a Thug."

Chapter 2. Music and Political Resistance: The Cultural Foundation of Black Politics

Epigraphs: Angela Davis, *Women, Culture, and Politics* (New York: Vintage, 1990), 201; Langston Hughes, "Minstrel Man," *Crisis* (December 1925): 66–67.

1. "Hip-Hop Artist Nas Protests Fox Coverage of Obama," *USA Today*, 28 July 2008.

2. Hughes was one of the most popular names associated with the Harlem Renaissance, an important cultural era in Black history. It was a time when cultural forms were embraced by people both within and outside the Black community, allowing African American cultural artists a platform outside the Black community.

3. Meeropol was also the adoptive parent of Ethel and Julius Rosenberg's two sons, Robert and Michael Meeropol. The sons changed their last name following the

conviction and death of their parents, who were charged with conspiracy and espionage for their involvement in attempting to provide atomic secrets to the USSR (Blair 2012).

4. "This Is My Country" was a single from the album of the same title released in 1968 by the rhythm and blues group the Impressions. This song specifically discussed African Americans' right to claim America as their country. The artists detail the history of slavery and murder and the deaths of Blacks, particularly Black activists. This album was released the same year that Martin Luther King, Jr., was assassinated.

5. Poverty has long been associated with Blackness; however, Wilson popularized this equation with the discussion of the underclass in his work (Wilson 1978, 1987).

6. The popularity of these caricatures of Blacks and women flourished during various eras of American history. Examples can be found throughout popular culture and literature, including D. W. Griffith's *Birth of a Nation*, which presented African American men as a threat to the purity and chastity of White women, and Harriet Jacobs's *Life in the Incident of a Slave Girl*, in which she explains that, even when they are raped, Black women are viewed as promiscuous and manipulative.

7. Other notable figures of this era were Haki Madhabuti (Don Lee), Amiri Baraka (Leroi Jones), and Sonia Sanchez.

8. Gullah is a creole or hybrid language that combines English with other languages from western and central Africa. This language was created by enslaved Africans who needed a way to communicate because they were from different groups, regions, and countries. Though some Gullah is understandable to English-speaking Americans, many of the words and phrases are incomprehensible, and it has been used as a code language to plan rebellions and escapes.

9. "Thirty Years of America's Drug Wars: A Chronology," *Frontline*, August 2014, http://www.pbs.org/wgbh/pages/frontline/shows/drugs/cron/.

10. Recently there has been a decrease in the disparity between the amount of powder and crack cocaine possessed and the sentence given.

11. This image of undeserving government cheats is still promulgated by many Republicans, and as recently as the 2012 Republican presidential primaries, when candidates Rick Santorum, Mitt Romney, and Newt Gingrich all invoked this attitude. Santorum stated, "I don't want to make black people's lives better by giving them somebody else's money" in reference to welfare programs and distribution of government terms (Blake 2012). What is unique about this statement is that he specifically singled out Black recipients and not all those who receive government assistance. He implicitly invoked latent attitudes that Blacks are the only citizens receiving governmental assistance because of inherent laziness and deception. Mitt Romney was a little more covert by referring to benefit programs as entitlement programs, which have invoked negative connotations over the years (Blake 2012; Williams 2003). The most blatant and overt use of the "welfare queen" imagery and racial fears was Newt Gingrich's labeling of President Obama as a food stamps president (Blake 2012). This title could have multiple meanings, but they all invoke racial sentiments. But in his

defense, Gingrich stated he gave President Obama this title because of the number of people receiving food stamps since President Obama was in office. All these presidential candidates stated that their comments were in reference to the poor economic condition the United States was then enduring. They were using a covert economic frame instead of an overt race frame.

12. Recently, Jay-Z has become more prominent in American society, not only because of his position as a mogul but also because of his relationship with President Obama. Jay-Z and President Obama's relationship is so close that Obama gave Jay-Z parenting advice after the birth of his daughter, and Jay-Z performed the closing concert at Obama's last campaign stop in 2012 in the swing state of Ohio.

Chapter 3. It's Bigger Than Hip-Hop: Rap Music and Black Nationalism

Epigraphs: Patricia Hill-Collins, *From Black Power to Hip-Hop* (Philadelphia" Temple University Press, 2006), 13.

1. Although controversial, this conspiracy theory was believed by a number of Americans, a trend that culminated in documentaries about the subject.

2. Schwarzenegger was not the first actor elected governor of California; previously Ronald Reagan went from actor to governor of California to president of the United States.

3. Some would argue that richer Blacks should align themselves with the Republican Party because of its emphasis on tax cuts for members of the upper class. But Dawson concludes that even when economic situations change, African Americans align with political parties that discuss more issues relevant to them and their extended families, who may have not achieved the same economic success.

4. Separatism has never been a highly supported aspect of Black Nationalism. However, it is one of the most discussed principles of Black Nationalism because of its radical nature.

5. These lyrics are detailed in Chapter 1.

6. Jay Z was recently named number one emcee of all time by MTV.com and has been identified by *Forbes* magazine as one of the wealthiest Hip-Hop artists because of his commercial and entrepreneurial success. According to RIAA.com, all Jay-Z's albums have reached gold and platinum status based on record sales, ultimately beating out Elvis Presley for the record of number one albums. Similarly, Jay Z has won 17 Grammy awards throughout his career. According to Billboard, in 2012 Drake topped Jay Z by having the most number one records on the R&B/Hip Hop Billboard charts in the history of its existence.

7. The Black Liberation Army (BLA) is an armed Black Nationalist underground movement comprising mainly BPP members and ex-BPP members. While it is noted by Umoja (1999) that BLA had been in existence as an underground movement since the beginning of the BPP, it did not appear on the federal government radar until 1971 during the elimination of the BPP by the FBI COINTELPRO (counter-intelligence

program). In her autobiography Assata Shakur describes the BLA as "various organizations and collectives working together and simultaneously independent of each other" with no centrally organized group or leadership (Shakur 1987: 241, cited in Umoja 1999).

8. This controversy is discussed in greater detail in Chapter 6.

9. For more on illuminati as discussed in rap music, see Tupac Shakur's "They Don't Give a Fuck About Us" and lectures by Professor Griff, former member of rap group Public Enemy.

10. NBPS was sponsored by the University of Chicago and conducted by SSI, a private company. The survey was designed "to provide information on attitudes and opinions regarding a number of issues of importance to Black Americans" (Dawson et al. 1993: 2). Data were collected through random telephone calls to 1,206 participants. The subjects were selected randomly and represented a sample of 65 percent of all Black households in the United States in 1993–1994.

11. Bakari Kitwana (2002) defines the Hip-Hop generation as those born between 1965 and 1984. However, the NBPS latest recorded year of birth is 1975, because an individual must be at least eighteen to participate. Thus these percentages reflect only 274 individuals, those born between 1965 and 1975, as part of the Hip Hop Generation for these statistics.

12. All the "don't know" or "refused" responses were coded as system missing.

13. My interests are specifically about the effects of political rap music on Black political attitudes. Therefore, an all-Black sample was necessary to examine these questions. Benedict College was founded in 1870 by Bathsheba Benedict as part of the 80-acre Benedict plantation that comprised the Benedict Institute. The founder's goal was to educate newly emancipated Blacks and transform them into productive, aware, responsive citizens. The college currently offers approximately thirty majors and degrees.

14. Note that Dead Prez has been recognized as a political rap group (although I do not prefer to label artists), because their songs all demonstrate political elements and references.

15. Self-criticism has been a popular conservative political tactic throughout Black history. We have seen examples of self-criticism followed by reform tactics from the Black Women's Club Movement, Booker T. Washington, and more recently Bill Cosby (Cohen 2010; Spence 2011).

16. The ten Black Nationalist strategies listed earlier in the chapter were computed into an additive index that measures support of Black Nationalism, with higher numbers equaling higher support. This Black Nationalist scale has a reliability score of .73.

Chapter 4. Beyond the Music: Black Feminism and Rap Music

Epigraph: Melissa Harris-Lacewell, *Barbershops, Bibles, and BET* (Princeton, N.J.: Princeton University Press, 2004), 1.

1. While rap music is often used as a scapegoat for discussions about misogyny and sexism, it is not the only musical form that espouses these views. Many have argued that the misogyny in rap music is only a reflection of the misogyny in the rest of society (Burns 2008; Chang and Zirin 2007; Dyson 2007; hooks 1994; Johnson 1996). In fact, bell hooks states, "It is much easier to attack gangsta rap than to confront the culture that produces that need" (1994).

2. This song does use political references by explicitly shouting the name of Florida governor Martinez and Broward County sheriff Navarro and is considered a political song because it advocates a response to the freedom of speech court case through the use of explicit language. Sometimes political songs are also misogynistic and sexist.

3. Harris-Lacewell (2004: 101) found that rap does not "generate less attachment to women." Spence (2011) did not find any significant relationship between rap exposure and Black Feminist ideology.

4. Lauryn Hill was one of the first female rappers to win multiple Grammy awards.

5. Eve is the first and only woman signed to Ruff Ryders Entertainment, which managed rappers such as DMX and L.O.X.

6. Sara Baartman, popularly known as the Hottentot Venus, was kidnapped from southern Africa and displayed in various European nations as a circus attraction because of her anatomical shape, specifically the size of her buttocks (Crais and Scully 2008; Fausto-Sterling 1995; Gilman 1985).

7. Some may wonder how this song is a considered a political rap song while "Beautiful Skin" by Goodie Mob, which also discusses love and beauty of Black women, is not. This is a very good question and precisely why we need some formal categorization to differentiate between subgenres of songs. "Beautiful Skin" is not political because it lacks political references, while "Brown Skin Lady" does.

8. Evelyn Simien (2006) discusses the issues of conflating feminism with Black Feminism. Because of frequent incorrect interpretations, many Black women embraced the term womanism as first presented by Alice Walker.

9. Using rap videos instead of songs might have complicated the analysis and results because it would be impossible to determine whether it was the music or the combination of music and images that activated or created specific political attitudes.

10. According to my definition, political rap must display political references in the lyrics. It can make a reference to a social issue or problem or advocate for a solution to injustices and problems in society.

11. Lauryn Hill was an advocate of women's rights. Many of her ideals and thoughts recently have been more conservative, which she suggests are actually more liberating because they fall outside the strict "boxes" of mainstream media. She refers to herself as a more traditional woman, sometimes conforming to society's ideals of woman and motherhood, and ignores those who oppose her lifestyle and choices. She eventually chose to be a more devout Christian and gave up listening to music, doing

interviews, and watching television. I am interested not in Hill's title, or classification as a Black Feminist per se, but in the lyrics of particular songs she produced.

Chapter 5. The Future of Politics: The Implications of Rap Music
and Political Attitudes

1. Not only have news articles been written about these task forces, but documentaries have been created that detail the extent of the task force, including one that focuses on a real "Hip-Hop Cop," entitled *Black and Blue: Legends of the Hip-Hop Cop*.

2. All these leaders have criticized members of the Hip-Hop community directly, blaming them for their poor living conditions, high prison rates, broken families, and increasingly high murder rates. Bill Cosby and Barack Obama were the latest critics of this community, citing the music as contributing to these issues instead of seeing it as a reflection of the conditions which brought it about.

3. Both platforms can be found in Appendix 2.

4. See HHC website, www.hiphopcaucus.org.

5. Proposition 21, "Juvenile Crime. Initiative Statute," passed in California in 2000, lowers the age to be tried as an adult to fourteen for murder or certain sex offenses. The law also increases the punishment for gang-related crimes, increasing gang-related murder to the death penalty and mandating life sentences for gang-related crimes of home invasion, witness intimidation, rape, looting, kidnapping, and drive-by shootings. This legislation also eliminates the possibility of probation for those fourteen or older who commit certain crimes. This information was retrieved from http://primary2000.sos.ca.gov/VoterGuide/Propositions/21text.htm and http://www.smartvoter.org/2000/03/07/ca/state/prop/21/.

6. See Ella Baker website, http://ellabakercenter.org/about/about-us.

7. http://www.mtv.com/videos/news/332902/a-look-back-diddy-interviews-obama.jhtml.

8. See http://cantstopwontstop.com/reader/its-obama-time-the-vibe-cover-story/.

9. Obama was a supporter of southern rap artist Ludacris despite the condemnation Ludacris suffered at the hands of Bill O'Reilly. As a part of his Talking Points Memo segment on his television show, Bill O'Reilly challenged Pepsi for allowing Ludacris to be featured in a commercial for them, claiming his lyrics were vile and antisocial.

10. Young Jeezy, who voted for the first time in his life in the 2008 election, also wrote a song called "My President," an unofficial ode to Obama. The chorus goes: "My president's Black / my lambo's blue."

11. See, e.g., Foxnews, "White House Invite of Political Rapper Stirs Controversy," 10 May 2011, http://www.foxnews.com/politics/2011/05/10/white-house-invite-political-rapper-stirs-controversy/.

12. Rhymefest's criminal past includes a 2001 domestic violence conviction and a 2005 firearm possession charge.

Conclusion. It's Still Bigger Than Hip-Hop: The Future of Rap and Politics

Epigraph: Patricia Hill-Collins, *From Black Power to Hip-Hop* (Philadelphia: Temple University Press, 2006), 191.

1. Some may also be interested in the relationship between the lyrics and the beats of the music. One argument could be that words followed by specific beats can enhance listeners' perception of specific words. On the other hand, not having any music associated with lyrics and allowing subjects to simply read the lyrics may have a different impact as well, depending on the type of learning style an individual uses. Reading the lyrics allows for less ambiguity about what the words are in the song and a different kind of internalization. For the purposes of this study, I had subjects listen to the songs the way they were produced, as lyrics over beats.

2. Snap rap is a Southern style of rap that often incorporates snapping fingers in the dances and beats.

3. I say "what he perceives are his rights" because law professor Caleb Mason has argued that the lyrics are not an accurate representation of an individual's Fourth Amendment rights in the situation Jay-Z describes in this song (Mason 2012).

4. For example, http://rapmusic.com/threads/bet-banns-little-brothers-lovin-it-video-its-not-relevant-to-their-target-market.1004435/.

5. Kendrick Lamar has since signed with Interscope Records.

6. To account for any temporal deceptions I chose songs that represented a ten-year period, a follow up to the rap popular during the 1993–1994 NBPS.

Bibliography

Adams, Terri M., and Douglas B. Fuller. 2006. "The Words Have Changed, but the Ideology Remains the Same: Misogynistic Lyrics in Rap Music." *Journal of Black Studies* 36: 938–57.

Adorno, Theodor, Else Frenkel-Brunswick, Daniel J. Levison, and R. Nevitt Sanford. 1950. *The Authoritarian Personality*. New York: Harper.

Alexander-Floyd, Nikol G. 2007. *Gender, Race and, Nationalism in Contemporary Black Politics*. New York: Palgrave Macmillan.

Allen, Ernest, Jr. 1996. "Making the Strong Survive: The Contours and Contradictions of Message Rap." In William E. Perkins, ed., Droppin' Science: Critical Essays on Rap Music and Hip Hop Culture. Philadelphia: Temple University Press.

Allen, Richard L., Michael C. Dawson, and Ronald E. Brown. 1989. "A Schema-Based Approach to Modeling an African American Belief System." *American Political Science Review* 83: 421–42.

Ards, Angela. 2004. "Organizing the Hip-Hop Generation." In Murray Forman and Mark Anthony Neal, eds., *That's the Joint: The Hip-Hop Studies Reader*. New York: Routledge.

Axelrod, Robert. 1973. "Schema Theory: An Information Processing Model of Perception and Cognition." *American Political Science Review* 67, 4: 1248–166.

Bachrach, Peter, and Morton S. Baratz. 1962. "Two Faces of Power." *American Political Science Review* 56, 4: 947–52.

Berry, Bruce, ed. 1989. *Malcolm X: The Last Speeches*. New York: Pathfinder.

Berinsky, Adam. 1999. "Two Faces of Public Opinion." *American Journal of Political Science* 43, 4: 1209–30.

Black, M. C. et al. (2011). The National Intimate Partner and Sexual Violence Survey (NISVS): 2010 Summary Report. Atlanta: National Center for Injury Prevention and Control, Centers for Disease Control and Prevention.

Black Feminist Working Group. 2011. "What Sistas Want, What Sistas Believe: Black Feminist Twelve Point Plan."

Blair, Elizabeth. 2012. "The Strange Story of the Man Behind 'Strange Fruit'." NPR, 5 September.

Blake, John. 2012. "Return of the 'Welfare Queen'." CNN Online, 21 January.

Blassingame, John. 1972. *The Slave Community: Plantation Life in the Antebellum South*. New York: Oxford University Press.

Bohn, Lauren E. 2011. "Rapping the Revolution." *Foreign Policy*, 22 July, Middle East Channel.

Boyd, Todd. 2003. *The New H.N.I.C.: The Death of Civil Rights and the Reign of Hip Hop*. New York: New York University Press.

———. 2004. "Check Yo Self Before You Wreck Yo Self: The Death of Politics in Rap Music and Popular Culture." In Murray Forman and Mark Anthony Neal, eds., *That's the Joint: The Hip-Hop Studies Reader*. New York: Routledge

Bracey, John H., August Meier, and Rudwick Elliot. 1970. *Black Nationalism in America*. Indianapolis: Bobbs-Merrill.

Brown, Elaine. 1992. *A Taste of Power: A Black Woman's Story*. New York: Doubleday.

Brown, Robert, and Todd Shaw. 2002. "Separate Nations: Two Attitudinal Dimensions of Black Nationalism." *Journal of Politics* 16, 1: 22–44.

Browning, Rufus, Dale Marshall, and David Tabb. 2003. *Racial Politics in American Cities*. New York: Addison Wesley.

Burns, Kate. 2008. *Rap Music and Culture*. Detroit: Greenhaven Press.

Carpentier, Fracesca Dillman, Silva Knohbloch and Dolf Zillman. 2003. "Rock, Rap and Rebellion: Comparisons of Traits Predicting Selective Exposure to Defiant Music." *Personality and Individual Differences* 35: 1643–55

Chan Y. M., Peter W. H. Lee, T. Y. Ng, H. Y. Ngan, and L. C. Wong. 2003. "The Use of Music to Reduce Anxiety for Patients Undergoing Colposcopy: A Randomized Trial." *Gynecologic Oncology* 92, 1: 213–17.

Chang, Jeff. 2005. *Can't Stop, Won't Stop: A History of the Hip-Hop Generation*. New York: Macmillan.

Chang, Jeff, and David Zirin. 2007. "Not All Hip-Hop Is Misogynistic, Violent." *Los Angeles Times*, 29 April.

Chapman, Steve. 2012. "The Right's Fraudulent Fears: Obama's Second Term Wouldn't Mean Radical Change." *Chicago Tribune*, 1 April.

Chung, Jen. 2008. "Nas Protests Fox News over Racist Coverage." *gothamist*, 24 July.

Cohen, Cathy. 1999. *Boundaries of Blackness: AIDS and the Breakdown of Black Politics*. Chicago: University of Chicago Press.

———. 2007. "Black Youth Project." Chicago: University of Chicago/Center for the Study of Race, Politics, and Culture.

———. 2010. *Democracy Remixed: Black Youth and the Future of American Politics*. New York: Oxford University Press.

Combahee River Collective. 2000. "Combahee River Collective Statement" In Barbara Smith, ed., *Home Girls: A Black Feminist Anthology*. New Brunswick. N.J.: Rutgers University Press

Condry, Ian. 2006. *Rap and the Paths of Cultural Globalization: Hip Hop Japan*. Durham, N.C.: Duke University Press.

Conner, Thomas. 2011. "Lupe Fiasco's Battles with Atlantic Dampens Long-Awaited 'Lasers'." *Chicago Sun-Times*, 4 March.

Conover, Pamela Johnston. 1988. "Feminists and the Gender Gap." *Journal of Politics* 50, 4: 985–1010.

Cook, Elizabeth A. 1989. "Measuring Feminist Consciousness." *Women and Politics* 9, 3: 71 88.

Cooper, Anna Julia. 1988. [1892] *A Voice from the South*. New York: Oxford University Press.

Crais, Clifton and Pamela Scully. 2008. *Sara Baartman and the Hottentot Venus: A Ghost Story and a Biography*. Princeton, N.J.: Princeton University Press.

Crenshaw, Kimberle. 1991a. "Mapping the Margins: Intersectionality, Identity Politics, and Violence Against Women of Color." *Stanford Law Review* 43: 1241–99

———. 1991b. "Beyond Racism and Misogyny: Black Feminism and 2 Live Crew." *Boston Review* 16: 6. 6–32.

Dahl, Robert. 1961. *Who Governs*. New Haven, Conn.: Yale University Press.

Davis, Angela. 1983. *Women, Race, and Class*. New York: Vintage.

———. 1989. *Women, Culture, and Politics*. New York: Random House.

———. 1990. "Black Women and Music: A Historical Legacy of Struggle." In Joanne M. Braxton and Andree Nicola McLaughlin, eds., *Wild Women in the Whirlwind: Afro-American Culture and the Contemporary Literary Renaissance*. New Brunswick, N.J.: Rutgers University Press.

Davis, Darren. 1997. "The Direction of Race of Interviewer Effects Among African Americans: Donning the Black Mask." *American Journal of Political Science* 42: 309–22.

Davis, Darren W. and Ronald E. Brown. 2002. "The Antipathy of Black Nationalism: Behavioral and Attitudinal Implications of an African American Ideology." *American Journal of Political Science* 46, 2: 239–53.

Davis, Darren W., and Christian Davenport. 1997. "The Political and Social Relevancy of Malcolm X: The Stability of African American Political Attitudes." *Journal of Politics* 59, 2: 550–64.

Dawson, Michael, Ronald Brown, and James S. Jackson. 1993. "National Black Politics Study." [Computer file]. ICPSR version. Chicago: University of Chicago/Detroit: Wayne State University/Ann Arbor: University of Michigan.

Dawson, Michael C. 1994. *Behind the Mule: Race and Class in African-American Politics*. Princeton, N.J.: Princeton University Press.

———. 1999. "Dis Beat Disrupts." In Michele Lamont, ed., *The Cultural Territories of Race: Black and White Boundaries*. Chicago: University of Chicago Press.

———. 2001. *Black Visions*. Chicago: University of Chicago Press.

Decker, Jeffrey Louis. 1993. "The State of Rap: Time and Place in Hip Hop Nationalism." *Social Text* 34: 53–84.

Deflem, Mathieu. 1993. "Rap, Rock, and Censorship: Popular Culture and the Technologies of Justice." Paper presented at annual meeting of the Law and Society Association, Chicago, May 27–30. www.mathieudeflem.net.

DeGhett, Torie Rose. 2012. "El Haqed, Morocco's Hip Hop Revolutionary." *The Guardian*, 17 April.

Devine, Patricia G. 1989. Stereotypes and Prejudice: Their Automatic and Controlled Components. *Journal of Personality and Social Psychology* 56: 5–18.

Dunbar, Paul Lawrence. 1896. "We Wear the Mask." In Dunbar, *Lyrics of Lowly Life*. New York: Dodd, Mead.

Durham, Aisha. 2007. "Using [Living Hip-Hop] Feminism: Redefining an Answer (to) Rap." In Aisha Durham, Gwendolyn Pough, Rachel Raimist and Elaine Richardson, eds., *Home Girls Make Some Noise: A Hip Hop Feminist Anthology*, Mira Loma Calif.: Parker Publishing.

Dyson, Michael E. 2007. *Know What I Mean?: Reflections on Hip-Hop*. New York: Basic Civitas.

Fausto-Sterling, Anne 1995. "Gender, Race, and Nation: The Comparative Anatomy of 'Hottentot' Women in Europe, 1815–1817." In Jennifer Terry and Jacqueline Urla, eds., *Deviant Bodies: Critical Perspectives on Difference in Science and Popular Culture*. Bloomington: Indiana University Press.

Fernandes, Sujatha. 2012. "The Mixtape of the Revolution." *New York Times*, 30 January, A23.

Finkel Steven E., Thomas M. Guterbock, and Marian J. Borg. 1991. "Race of Interviewer Effects in a Pre-Election Poll: Virginia 1989." *Public Opinion Quarterly* 55, 3: 313–30.

Fontaine, Smokey. "A Hip-Hop Victory: The End of the Rockefeller Drug Laws." *NewsOne*, March 27, 2009. Retrieved from http://newsone.com/140151/a-hip-hop-victory-the-end-of-the-rockerfeller-drug-laws/.

Forman, Murray, and Mark A. Neal, eds. 2004. *That's the Joint: The Hip-Hop Studies Reader*. New York: Routledge.

Fox, William S., and James D. Williams. 1974. "Political Orientation and Music Preferences Among College Students." *Public Opinion Quarterly* 18: 352–71.

Franklin, John H. 1967. *From Slavery to Freedom*. New York: Knopf.

Frederickson, George M. 1997. *The Comparative Imagination: On the History of Racism, Nationalism, and Social Movements*. Berkeley: University of California Press.

Gates, Henry L., Jr., and Nellie Y. McKay, eds. 1997. *The Norton Anthology of African American Literature*. New York: Norton.

Gay, Claudine, and Katherine Tate. 1998. "Doubly Bound: The Impact of Gender and Race on the Politics of Black Women." *Political Psychology* 19: 169–83.

Gaertner, Samuel L., and John F. Dovidio, 1986. "The Aversive Form of Racism." In John F. Dovidio and Samuel L. Gaertner, eds., *Prejudice, Discrimination, and Racism*. New York: Academic Press.

Garofalo, Reebee. 1992. "Popular Music and the Civil Rights Movement." In Reebee Garofalo, ed., *Rockin' the Boat: Mass Music and Mass Movements*. Cambridge, Mass.: South End Press.

George, Nelson. 2005. *Hip Hop America*. New York: Penguin.

Gray, Madison. 2009. "A Brief History of New York's Rockefeller Drug Laws." *Time*, 2 April.

Gilman, Sander L. 1985. "Black Bodies, White Bodies: Toward an Iconography of Female Sexuality in Late Nineteenth-Century Art, Medicine, and Literature." In Henry Gates, ed., *Race, Writing, and Difference*. Chicago: University of Chicago Press.

Gold Christian, Hans Petter Solli, Viggo Krueger, and Stein Alte Lie. 2009. "Dose Response Relationship in Music Therapy for People with Serious Mental Disorders: Systematic Review and Meta-Analysis." *Child Psychology Review* 19, 3: 193–207.

Gunter, Booth. 2012. "Six Most Paranoid Fears for Obama's Second Term." *Salon*, 2 November.

Hancock, Ange-Marie. 2004. *The Politics of Disgust: The Public Identity of the Welfare Queen*. New York: New York University Press.

Harding, Vincent. 1981. *There Is A River: The Black Struggle for Freedom in America*. New York: Harcourt Brace Jovanovich

Hardt, Michael, and Antonio Negri. 2011. "The Fight for 'Real Democracy' at the Heart of Occupy Wall Street: The Encampment in Lower Manhattan Speaks to a Failure of Representation." *Foreign Affairs*, October 11.

Harris-Lacewell, Melissa. 2004. *Barbershops, Bibles, and BET*. Princeton, N.J.: Princeton University Press.

Hastie, Reid, and Bernadette Park. 1986. "The Relationship Between Memory and Judgment Depends on Whether the Task Is Memory-Based or On-Line." *Psychological Review* 93: 258–68.

Hechter, Michael. 1975. *Internal Colonialism: Celtic Fringe in British National Development, 1536–1966*. Berkeley: University of California Press.

Heim, Joe. 2004. "Rapper Ups the Ante on Bush and 9/11." *Washington Post*, 17 July, C01.

Henderson, Errol. 1996. "Black Nationalism and Rap Music." *Journal of Black Studies* 26, 3: 308–39.

Henry, Charles. 1990. *Culture and African American Politics*. Bloomington: Indiana University Press.

Hess, Mickey. 2007. *Icons of Hip Hop: An Encyclopedia of the Movement, Music, and Culture*, Vol. 1. Westport, Conn.: Greenwood.

Hill-Collins, Patricia. 1990. *Black Feminist Thought*. New York: Routledge.

———. 2006. *From Black Power to Hip Hop*. Philadelphia: Temple University Press.

Hip Hop Summit Action Network (HSAN). 2001. www.hiphopsummitactionnetwork.org.

hooks, bell. 1994. "Sexism and Misogyny: Who Takes the Rap? Misogyny, Gangsta Rap, and Piano." *Z Magazine*, February 1994.

Hughes, Langston. (1961). 1990. *The Best of Simple*. New York: Farrar, Strauss and Giroux.

Hurwitz, Jonathan, and Mark Peffley. 1987. "How Are Foreign Policy Attitudes Structured? A Hierarchical Model." *American Political Science Review* 81: 1099–1120

Iton, Richard. 2008. *In Search of the Black Fantastic: Politics and Popular Culture in the Post-Civil Rights Era.* Oxford: Oxford University Press.

Iyengar, Shanto, and Donald R. Kinder. 1987. *News That Matters: Television and American Opinion.* Chicago: University of Chicago Press.

Jacks, Brian. 2011. "Rhymefest Explains How Hip-Hop Career Helps Him in Politics: Kanye West Protégé Made It to a Run-Off Election for Chicago City Council." *MTV News*, 25 February.

Johnson, James D., Lee Anderson Jackson, and Leslie Gatto. 1995. "Violent Attitudes and Deferred Academic Aspirations: Deleterious Effects of Exposure to Rap Music." *Basic and Applied Social Psychology* 16: 27–41

Johnson, James D., Sophie Trawalter, and John F. Dovidio. 2000. "Converging Interracial Consequences of Exposure to Violent Rap Music on Stereotypical Attributions of Blacks." *Journal of Experimental Social Psychology* 36: 233–51.

Johnson, Leola 1996. "Rap, Misogyny and Racism." *Radical America* 26, 3: 7–19.

Jordan-Zachery, Julia. 2008. *Black Women, Cultural Images, and Social Policy.* New York: Routledge.

Karenga, Maulana. 2002. *Introduction to Black Studies.* Los Angeles: University of Sankore Press.

Key, V. O., Jr. 1961. *Public Opinion and American Democracy.* New York: Knopf.

Keyes, Cheryl L. 2004. "Empowering Self, Making Choices, Creating Spaces: Black Female Identity via Rap Music Performance." In Murray Forman and Mark Anthony Neal, eds., *That's the Joint: The Hip-Hop Studies Reader.* New York: Routledge

Kinder, Donald R. 1983. "Diversity and Complexity in American Public Opinion." In Ada W. Finifter, ed., *Political Science: The State of the Discipline.* Washington, D.C.: American Political Science Association.

Kinder, Donald R. and L. Sanders. 1996. *Divided by Color: Racial Politics and Democratic Ideals.* Chicago: University of Chicago Press

King, Martin Luther, Jr. 1964. *Why We Can't Wait.* New York: Penguin.

Kitwana, Bakari. 2002. *The Hip Hop Generation.* New York: BasicCivitas.

Kofsky, Frank. 1970. *Black Nationalism and the Revolution in Music.* New York. Pathfinder.

Kozol, Jonathan. 1991. *Savage Inequalities: Children in American Schools.* New York: Crown.

Kuklinski, James H., Robert C. Luskin, and John Bolland. 1991. "Where Is the Schema? Going Beyond the 'S' Word in Political Psychology." *American Political Science Review* 85: 1341–56.

Lang, Derrick J. 2007. "VH-1's 'Salt-N-Pepa Show' Tackles Jena 6." *Associated Press*, 26 November.

Lelinwalla, Mark. 2011."Hip-Hop Reacts to Planned Troy Davis Execution." *XXL*, 21 September.

Levine, Lawrence W. 2006. "African American Music as Resistance." In Mellonee V. Burnim and Portia K. Maultsby, eds., *African American Music: An Introduction*. New York: Routledge.

Lodge, Milton, Kathleen M. McGraw, and Patrick Stroh. 1989. "An Impression-Driven Model of Candidate Evaluation." *American Political Science Review* 83, 2: 399–419.

Lodge, Milton, and Marco Steenbergen, with Shawn Brau. 1995. "The Responsive Voter: Campaign Information and the Dynamics of Candidate Evaluation." *American Political Science Review* 89: 309–26.

Lorde, Audre. 1984. *Sister Outsider: Essays and Speeches*. Berkeley, Calif.: Crossing Press.

Lowenstein, Karl. 1953. "The Role of Ideologies in Political Change." *International Social Science Bulletin* 5, 1: 51–74.

Lupia, Arthur. 1994. "Shortcuts Versus Encyclopedias: Information and Voting Behavior in California Insurance Reform Elections." *American Political Science Review* 88 (March): 63–76.

Lusane, Clarence. 2004. "Rap, Race, and Politics." In Murray Forman and Mark Anthony Neal, eds., *That's the Joint: The Hip-Hop Studies Reader*. New York: Routledge.

Lucas, Greg. 2000. "Proposition 21, Huge Changes Proposed for Juvenile Justice. Teenagers Would Face Adult Courts." *San Francisco Chronicle*, 14 February.

Martinez, Theresa A. 1997. "Popular Culture as Oppositional Culture: Rap as Resistance." *Sociological Perspectives* 30, 2: 265–86.

McAdams, Doug. 1982. *Political Process and the Development of Insurgency, 1930–1970*. Chicago: University of Chicago Press.

McGuire, William. 1985. "Attitudes and Attitude Change." In Gardner Lindzey and Elliott Aronson, eds., The Handbook of Social Psychology. 3rd ed. New York: Random House.

Mendelberg, Tali. 2001. *The Race Card: Campaign Strategy, Implicit Messages, and the Norm of Equality*. Princeton, N.J.: Princeton University Press.

Mink, Gwendolyn. 1998. *Welfare's End*. Ithaca, N.Y. Cornell University Press.

Mitchell, Bonnie L., and Joe R. Feagin. 1995. "America's Racial-Ethnic Cultures: Opposition Within a Mythical Melting Pot." In Benjamin P. Bowser, Terry Jones, and Gale Auletta Young, eds., *Toward the Multicultural University*. Westport, Conn.: Praeger.

Miyakawa, Felicia M. 2005. *Five Percenter Rap: God Hop's Music, Message and Black Muslim Mission*. Indianapolis: Indiana University Press.

Mollenkopf, John. 2003. "New York: Still the Great Anomaly." In Rufus Browning, Dale R. Rogers and David H Tabb, eds., *Racial Politics in American Cities*. 3rd ed. New York: Addison Wesley.

Morgan, Joan. 1999. *When Chickenheads Come Home to Roost: A Hip-Hop Feminist Breaks it Down.* New York: Touchstone.

Morris, Aldon. 1984. *The Origins of the Civil Rights Movement: Black Communities Organizing for Change.* New York: Free Press.

Moynihan, Daniel P. "A Family Policy for the Nation." *America* 113 (1965): 280–83.

Muggs, Joe. 2005. "Should Hip Hop Take the Rap for Rioting?" *The Telegraph*, 8 December 2005.

Neal, Mark Anthony. 1999. *What the Music Said: Black Popular Music and Black Public Culture.* New York: Routledge.

———. 2004a. "I'll be Nina Simone, Defecating on your Microphone: Hip Hop and Gender." In Murray Forman and Mark Anthony Neal, eds., *That's the Joint: The Hip-Hop Studies Reader.* New York: Routledge.

———. 2004b. "Postindustrial Soul: Black Popular Music at the Crossroads." In Murray Forman and Mark Anthony Neal, eds., *That's the Joint: The Hip-Hop Studies Reader.* New York: Routledge

———. 2006. "Post-Civil Rights Period." In Mellonee V. Burnim and Portia K. Maultsby, eds., *African American Music: An Introduction.* New York: Routledge.

Nelson, David, and Robert Weathers. 1998. "Necessary Angels: Music and Healing in Psychotherapy. *Journal of Humanistic Psychology* 38, 1: 101–8.

Nelson, Thomas E., & Donald R. Kinder. 1996. "Issue Framing And Group-Centrism In American Public Opinion." *Journal of Politics* 58, 4: 1055–78.

Nelson, William, Jr. 2000. *Black Atlantic Politics: Dilemmas of Political Empowerment in Boston and Liverpool.* Albany: State University of New York Press.

Newsweek. 2000. "Beyond Ghetto Fabulous: Faces of a Hip-Hop Nation." 13 September.

Nicholson, Jan M., Donna Betherelsen, Vicky Abad, Kate Williams, and Julie Bradley. 2008. "Impact of Therapy to Promote Positive Parenting and Child Development." *Journal of Health Psychology* 13, 2: 226–38.

Nielson Erick. 2012. "How Hop-Hop Fell Out of Love with Obama." *The Guardian*, 23 August.

Norfleet, Dawn M. 2006. "Hip Hop and Rap." In Mellonee V. Burnim and Portia K. Maultsby, eds., *African American Music: An Introduction.* New York: Routledge.

National Public Radio (NPR). 2010. "Strange Fruit: Anniversary of a Lynching." 6 August.

———. 2008. "Obama Hip-Hop: From Mixtapes to Mainstream." 7 November.

———. 2002. "Present at the Creation: Lift Every Voice and Sing." 4 February.

Ogbar, Jeffrey O. G. 2007. *Hip Hop Revolution: The Culture and Politics of Rap.* Lawrence: University of Kansas Press.

Omi, Michael, and Howard Winant. 1994. *Racial Formation in the United States: From the 1960s to the 1990s.* New York: Routledge.

Oskamp, Stuart, and P. Wesley Schultz. 2005. *Attitudes and Opinions.* 3rd ed. Mahwah, N.J.: Lawrence Erlbaum.

Paine, Jake. 2012. "Willie D Talks Reuniting with Scarface for Trayvon Martin, Remembers "Fuck Rodney King" *HipHopDX*, 26 April. http://www.hiphopdx.-com/index/interviews/id.1881/title.willie-d-talks-reunitingwithscarface-for-trayvon-martin-remembers-fuck-rodney-king.

Perkins, Margo V. 2000. *Autobiography as Activism: Three Black Women of the Sixties.* Jackson: University Press of Mississippi.

Peralta, Eyder. 2013. "Rapper Lupe Fiasco Booted Off Inaugural Party Stage After Criticizing Obama." NPR, 21 January.

Perpetua, Matthew. 2011. "Mos Def to Retire the Name 'Mos Def'." *RollingStone*, 7 September.

Perry, Imani. 2004. *Prophets of the Hood: Politics and Poetics in Hip Hop.* Durham, N.C.: Duke University Press.

Pough, Gwendolyn D. 2004a. *Check It While I Wreck It: Black Womanhood, Hip-Hop Culture, and the Public Sphere.* Boston: Northeastern University Press.

———. 2004b. "Seeds and Legacies: Tapping the Potential in Hip Hop." In Murray Forman and Mark Anthony Neal, eds., *That's the Joint: The Hip-Hop Studies Reader.* New York: Routledge.

Powell, Catherine Tabb. 1991. "Rap Music: An Education with a Beat from the Street." *Journal of Negro Education* 60, 3: 245–54.

Price, Melanye. 2009. *Dreaming Blackness: Black Nationalism and African American Public Opinion.* New York: New York University Press.

Price, Kimala. (2007). "Hip Hop Feminists at the Political Crossroads: Organizing for Reproductive Justice and Beyond." In Aisha S. Durham Gwendolyn Pough, Elaine Richardson, and Rachel Raimist, eds., *Home Girls Make Some Noise: A Hip Hop Feminist Anthology*, Mira Loma, Calif.: Parker.

Radford-Hill, Sheila. 2000. *Further to Fly: Black Women and the Politics of Empowerment.* Minneapolis: University of Minnesota Press.

Ransby, Barbara. 2005. *Ella Baker and the Black Freedom Movement: A Radical Democratic Vision.* Chapel Hill: University of North Carolina Press.

Ransby, Barbara, and Tracye Matthews. 1995. "Black Popular Culture and the Transcendence of Patriarchal Illusions." In Beverly Guy-Sheftall, ed., *Words of Fire: An Anthology of African-American Feminist Thought.* New York: New Press.

Raze, Steve, and Black Magic. 2012. "Exclusive Video: Waka Flocka Launches Anti-Bully Campaign in Atlanta." *All Hip-Hop.Com.*

Reid, Shaheem. 2008. "Barack Obama and Hip-Hop: Does the Support of Jay-Z, Nas, T.I. Hurt His Chances?: '[Rappers] need to be super quiet on Barack,' Scarface Says, or Critics Will 'smash on him because of what somebody else said'." *www.MTV.com.*

Reid-Brinkley, Shanrah R. 2008. "The Essence of Res(ex)pectability: Black Women's Negotiation of Black Femininity in Rap Music and Music Video." *Meridians* 8, 1: 236–60.

Rich, Wilbur C. 1996. *The Politics of Minority Coalitions.* Westport: Conn.: Praeger.

Roberts, Dorothy. 1997. *Killing the Black Body: Race, Reproduction, and the Meaning of Liberty.* New York: Vintage.

Robinson, Dean. 2001. *Black Nationalism in American Politics and Thought.* New York: Cambridge University Press.

Rose, Tricia. 1994. *Black Noise: Rap Music and Black Culture in Contemporary America.* Hanover, N.H.: Wesleyan University Press.

————. 2004. "Never Trust a Big Butt and a Smile." In Murray Forman and Mark Anthony Neal, eds., *That's the Joint: The Hip-Hop Studies Reader.* New York: Routledge

————. 2008. *Hip-Hop Wars: What We Talk About When We Talk About Hip Hop and Why It Matters.* New York: Perseus.

Royster, Jacqueline Jones, ed. 1997. *Southern Horrors and Other Writings.* Boston: Bedford/St. Martin's.

Rubin, Allen M., Daniel West, and Wendy S. Mitchell. 2001. "Differences in Aggression, Attitudes Toward Women, and Distrust as Reflected in Popular Music Preferences." *Media Psychology* 3: 25–42.

Sapiro, Virginia. 1994. "Political Socialization During Adulthood: Clarifying the Political Time of Our Lives." In Michael X. Delli Carpini, Leonie Huddy, and Robert Y. Shapiro, eds., *Research in Micropolitics,* vol. 4, 197–223. Greenwich, Conn.: JAI Press.

Schlozman, Kay L., Nancy Burns, and Sidney Verba. 1994. "Gender and the Pathways to Participation: The Role of Resources." *Journal of Politics* 56: 963–90.

Scott, James C. 1990. *Domination and the Arts of Resistance: Hidden Transcripts.* New Haven, Conn.: Yale University Press.

Scott, Sam. 2005. "Officials Wish This Snowman Would Melt." Wilmington, N.C., *Star News,* A1, 3. November 20.

Schattschneider, Elmer E. 1960. *The Semisovereign People: A Realist's View of Democracy in America.* New York: Holt, Rinehart, and Winston.

Shakur, Assata. 1987. *Assata: An Autobiography.* Chicago: Lawrence Hill.

Shoup, John. 1997. "Pop Music and Resistance in Apartheid South Africa." *Alif: Journal of Comparative Poetics* 17: 73–92

Simien, Evelyn M. 2006. *Black Feminist Voices in Politics.* Albany: State University of New York Press.

Sims, Melanie. 2007. "Hip Hop Stars Rally for Jena 6." *USA TODAY,* 4 October.

Sniderman, Paul, and Thomas Piazza. 1993. *The Scar of Race.* Cambridge, Mass.: Harvard University Press

Sniderman, Paul M., Thomas Piazza, Phillip E. Tetlock, and Ann Kendrick. 1991. "The New Racism." *American Journal of Political Science* 35, 2: 423–47.

Sonneck, Oscar, and George Theodore. 1972. *Report on the Star-Spangled Banner, Hail Columbia, America, Yankee Doodle.* New York: Dover.

Southern, Eileen. 1997. *The Music of Black Americans: A History.* 3rd ed. New York: Norton.

Spence, Lester 2011. *Stare in the Darkness: The Limits of Hip-Hop and Black Politics*. Minneapolis: University of Minnesota Press.

Springer, Anthony. 2007. "Mos Def and Others Sponsor School Walk Out for Jena 6." *hiphodx.com*.

Stapleton, Katina R. 1998. "From the Margins to Mainstream: The Political Power of Hip Hop." *Media, Culture and Psychology* 20: 219–34.

Stone, Clarence. 1989. *Regime Politics: Governing Atlanta, 1946–1988*. Wichita: University Press of Kansas.

Sullivan, Rachel E. 2003. "Rap and Race: It's Got a Nice Beat, But What About the Message?" *Journal of Black Studies* 33, 5: 605–22.

Tansik, David A., and Robert Routhieaux. 1999. "Customer Stress-Relaxation: The Impact of Music in a Hospital Waiting Room." *International Journal of Service Industry Management*. 10, 1: 68–81.

Tareen, Sophia. 2011. Associated Press. "Rhymefest Could Be on Chicago's City Council: Supports Swells for Rapper in 20th Ward." *Huffington Post Online*, 18 February.

Tate, Katherine. 1994. *From Protest to Politics: The New Black Voters in American Elections*. Enl. ed. Cambridge, Mass.: Harvard University Press.

Tyson, Edgar H. 2006. "Rap-Music Attitude and Perception Scale: A Validation Study." *Research on Social Work Practice* 16: 211–23.

Umoja, Akinyele. 1999. "Repression Breeds Resistance: The Black Liberation Army and the Radical Legacy of the Black Panther Party." *New Political Science* 21, 2: 131–55.

Updike Paul. 1990. "Music Therapy Results for ICU Patients." *Dimensions of Critical Care Nursing* 9, 1: 39–45.

Verba, Sidney. Kay L. Schlozman, and Henry E. Brady, 1995. *Voice and Equality: Civic Voluntarism in American Politics*. Cambridge, Mass.: Harvard University Press

Verba, Sidney, Kay L. Schlozman, Henry Brady, and Norman Nie. 1993. "Race, Ethnicity and Political Resources: Participation in the United States." *British Journal of Political Science* 23: 453–97

Walker, Robert G. 1975. "Society and Soul." Ph.D. dissertation, Stanford University.

Wallace, Michele. 1994. Black Macho and the Myth of the Superwoman. New York: Verso.

Walton, Hanes, Jr. 1985. *Invisible Politics: Black Political Behavior*. Albany: State University of New York Press.

Walton, Hanes, and Robert Smith. 2000. *American Politics and the African American Quest for Universal Freedom*. New York. Addison-Wesley.

Watkins, Craig, S. 2005. *Hip Hop Matters: Politics, Pop Culture and the Struggle for the Soul of a Movement*. Boston: Beacon Press.

Weiner, Rachel. 2013. "Lupe Fiasco Escorted Off Stage After Anti-Obama Comments." *Washington Post*, 21 January.

White, Frances E. 1995. "Africa on My Mind: Gender, Counterdiscourse, and African American Nationalism." In Beverly Guy-Sheftall, ed., *Words of Fire: An Anthology of African American Feminist Thought.* New York: New Press.

Whitford, Andrew B., and Jeff. Yates. 2009. *Presidential Rhetoric and the Public Agenda: Constructing the War on Drugs.* Baltimore: Johns Hopkins University Press.

Williams, Linda F. 2003. *The Constraint of Race: Legacies of White Skin Privilege in America.* University Park: Pennsylvania State University Press.

Wilson, William Julius. 1987. *The Truly Disadvantaged: The Inner City, the Underclass, and Public Policy.* Chicago: University of Chicago Press.

———. 1978. *The Declining Significance of Race.* Chicago: University of Chicago Press.

Welch, Susan, and Philip Secret. 1981. "Sex, Race and Political Participation." *Western Political Quarterly* 34: 5–16.

Woldu, Gail H. 2003. "Bring the Noise: The Roots of Rap and Hip Hop." In Jared Green, ed., *Rap and Hip Hop: Examining Popular Culture.* San Diego, Calif.: Greenhaven.

Woodard, Komozi. 1999. *Nation Within a Nation: Amiri Baraka (Leroi Jones) and Black Power Politics.* Chapel Hill: University of North Carolina Press

X, Malcolm. 1964a. *The Autobiography of Malcolm X, as told to Alex Haley.* New York: Ballantine.

———. 1964b. "The Ballot or the Bullet." Speech, 3 April, Cory Methodist Church, Cleveland. americanrhetoric.com/speeches/malcolmxballot.htm.

Zaller, John. 1992. *The Nature and Origins of Mass Opinion.* New York: Cambridge University Press.

Zillman Dolf, et al. 1995. "Radical Rap: Does It Further Ethnic Division?" *Basic and Applied Social Psychology* 16: 1–25.

Discography

The majority of the copyright information comes from http://cocatalog.loc.gov/cgi -bin/Pwebrecon.cgi?DB = local&PAGE = first, and then itunes.com. If I couldn't find it there I looked up the album to see the back of the cd to get copyright information. Many of the singles were released as free downloads or youtube videos and did not have copyright available or were a part of a mixtape where the information could not be found.

Introduction

Big Boi. 2003. "War" *Speakerboxx* (album). Lyrics Copyright 2007. Chrysalis Music Publishing, LLC, Wedontplayevenwhenwereplayin', Mosquito Puss, Chysalis Music Broup, Organized Noize Music & Divad Sniboor Music. Rap lyrics retrieved from http://rapgenius.com/Outkast-war-lyrics

Chapter 1

2 Live Crew. 1990. "Man, Not a Myth." *Banned in the USA* (album). Lyrics Copyright 2001 Lil' Joe Records Inc.

————. 1990. "Fuck Martinez." *Banned in the USA* (album). Lyrics Copyright 1998 Lil' Joe Records Inc.

Billie Holiday. 1939. "Strange Fruit" (single). Lyrics Copyright 1979 CBS, Inc. and 2003 The Verve Music Group, a Division of UMG Recordings, Inc.

Chamillionaire. 2006. "Ridin' Dirty." *The Sound of Revenge* (album). Lyrics Copyright 2005 Universal Records a division of UMG Recordings Inc.

Dead Prez. 2000. "It's Bigger than Hip-Hop." *Let's Get Free* (album). Lyrics Copyright 2001 Loud Records LLC. Rap lyrics retrieved from http://rapgenius.com/Dead -prez-its-bigger-than-hip-hop-lyrics

GoodieMob. 1998. "Beautiful Skin." *Still Standing* (album). Lyrics Copyright 1998 Goodie Mo'-B Music, Inc., C' Amore Music, and 1998 LaFace Records LLC. Rap lyrics retrieved from http://rapgenius.com/Goodie-mob-beautiful-skin-lyrics

Ice T. 1992 "Cop Killer." *Body Count* (album). Lyrics Copyright 1992 Warner Bros. Records. Marketed by Rhino Entertainment, a Warner Music Group Company

Jay-Z. 2003. "99 Problems." *The Black Album* (album). Lyrics Copyright 2004 BMG Songs, Inc., Careers-BMG Music Publishing, Inc., Spirit Two Music, Inc.

Jay-Z featuring Eminem. 2001. "Renegade." *The Blueprint* (album). Lyrics Copyright 2007 Roc A-Fella Records, LLC

Lauryn Hill. 1998. "Superstar." *The Mis-Education of Lauryn Hill* (album). Lyrics Copyright 1998 Ruffhouse Records. Rap lyrics retrieved from http://rapgenius .com/Lauryn-hill-superstar-lyrics

Lil Wayne. 2006. "Georgia . . . Bush." *Dedication 2: Gangsta Grillz* (album). Lyrics Copyright 2012 Firefly Entertainment.

———. 2008. "Tie My Hands." *Tha Carter III* (album). Lyrics Copyright Young Money Publishing, Inc. and Warner-Tamerlane Publishing Corp., and I like 'Em Thicke and Da' Gass Co.

Nas. 1999. "I Want to Talk to you." *I Am.* (album). Lyrics Copyright 1999 Sony Music Entertainment Inc. Rap lyrics retrieved from http://rapgenius.com/Nas-i-want-to -talk-to-you-lyrics

N.W.A. 1989. "Fuck tha Police." *Straight Outta Compton* (album). Lyrics Copyright 2002 Priority Records, LLC

Plies. 2009. "Becky." *Goon Affiliated.* (album). Lyrics Copyright 2009 Sony/ATV Music Publishing LLC, Jonathan Rotem Music, and 2010 Slip-N-Slide Records, Inc. licensed to Atlantic Recording Corporation for the United States and WEA Inter- national Inc. for the world outside the United States

———. 2010. "Why You Hate." *You Need People Like Me* (album). Lyrics Copyright 2014 Slip-N-Slide Records

Sam Cooke. 1964. "A Change Is Gonna Come" (single). Lyrics Copyright 2003 ABKCO Music & Records, Inc.

Trick Daddy. 2000. "America." *Book of Thugs: Chapter AK verse 47* (album). Lyrics Copyright 2000 Slip-N-Slide Records, Inc. and 2000 Atlantic Recording Corporation

———. 2001. "I'm a Thug" *Thugs Are Us* (album). Lyrics Copyright 2001 Slip-N- Slide Records, Inc. and licensed to Atlantic Recording Corporation for the United States and WEA International Inc. for the world outside of the United States

———. 2002. "Thug Holiday." *Thug Holiday* (album). Lyrics Copyright 2002 Slip-N- Slide Records, Inc. and licensed to Atlantic Recording Corporation for the United States and WEA International Inc. for the world outside of the United States

Wu-Tang Clan and Isaac Hayes. 2000. "I Can't Go to Sleep." *The W.* (album). Lyrics Copyright 2000 New Hidden Valley Music, Casa David Music, Irving Music, Inc., Careers-BMG Music Publishing, Inc. & Wu-Tang Publishing, Inc. & Loud Records LLC. Rap lyrics retrieved from http://rapgenius.com/Wu-tang-clan-i-cant-go -to-sleep-lyrics

Chapter 2

Aretha Franklin. 1967. "Respect." Written by Otis Redding. *I Never Loved a Man the Way that I Love You.* (album). Lyrics Copyright 1967 Atlantic Recording Corp.

Billie Holiday. 1939. "Strange Fruit" (single). Lyrics Copyright 1979 CBS, Inc. and 2003 The Verve Music Group, a Division of UMG Recordings, Inc. Song lyrics retrieved from http://www.lyricsfreak.com/b/billie + holiday/strange + fruit_2001 7859.html

Bob Dylan. 1975. "Hurricane." *Desire* (album). Lyrics Copyright 1976 Columbia Records

Bob Marley. 1973. "400 Years." *Soul Rebels* (album). Lyrics Copyright 2013 Universal Island Records

———. 1975. "Get Up, Stand Up." *Burnin'* (album). Lyrics Copyright 2001 Universal Island Records Ltd.

———. 1980. "Redemption Song." *Uprising* (album). Lyrics Copyright 1980 Bob Marley Music, LTD and 2001 The Island Def Jam Music Group

Curtis Mayfield. 1964. "Keep on Pushing." *Gospel Greats* (album). Lyrics Copyright 2000 Geffen Records

———. 1990. "We People Who Are Darker Than Blue." *New World Order* (album). Lyrics Copyright 1996 Warner Bros.

Dead Prez. 2000. "Propaganda." *Let's Get Out* (album). Lyrics Copyright 2000 Loud Records LLC

George Cohan. 1906. "You're a Grand Old Flag." (single). Lyrics Copyright 2012 Classique Perfecto

Goodie Mob. 1995. "Thought Process." *Soul Food* (album). Lyrics Copyright 1995 LaFace Records LLC. Rap lyrics retrieved from http://rapgenius.com/Goodie-mob -thought-process-lyrics

Grandmaster Flash and Melle Mel. 1983. "White Lines (Don't Do It)" (single). Lyrics Copyright 2009 X-Ray Records. Rap lyrics retrieved from http://rapgenius.com/ Grandmaster-flash-and-the-furious-five-white-lines-dont-do-it lyrics

Grandmaster Flash and the Furious Five. 1982. "The Message." *The Message* (album). Lyrics Copyright 1982 Sugar Hill Records, LTD and 2009 X-Ray Records. Rap lyrics retrieved from http://rapgenius.com/Grandmaster-flash-and-the-furious -five-the-message-lyrics.

The Impressions. 1968. "This Is My Country." *This Is My Country* (album). Lyrics Copyright 1968 Rhino Entertainment

James Brown. 1968. "Say It Loud: I'm Black and I'm Proud." *A Soulful Christmas* (album). Lyrics Copyright 1969 Universal Records

James Weldon. 1900. "Lift Every Voice and Sing" (single). Lyrics Copyright 1990 Childrens Press, Inc. and 2014 Star Spangled Music Foundation.

Jay-Z featuring Eminem. 2001. "Renegade." *The Blueprint* (album). Lyrics Copyright 2007 Roc- A-Fella Records, LLC

Johnny Clegg and Savuka 1987. "Asimbonanga." *Third World Child* (album). Lyrics Copyright 1987 HRBV Music and EMI Music Catalogue Marketing

Julia Ward Howe. 1862. "Battle Hymn of the Republic" (single). Lyrics Copyright 2011 Altissimo! Recordings

Kendrick Lamar. 2011. "Fuck Your Ethnicity". *Section.80* (album). Lyrics copyright 2011 Top Dawg Entertainment / Section.80. Rap lyrics retrieved from http://rap genius.com/Kendrick-lamar-fuck-your-ethnicity-lyrics

Marvin Gaye. 1971. "What's Going On." *What's Going On* (album). Lyrics copyright 2012 Motown Records Lyrics retrieved from http://www.azlyrics.com/lyrics/ marvingaye/whatsgoingon.html

———. 1971. "Inner City Blues." *What's Going On* (album). Lyrics copyright 2012 Motown Records

Nas. 1999. "Project Windows." Nastradamus (album). Lyrics copyright 1999 Sony BMG Music Entertainment. Rap lyrics retrieved from http://rapgenius.com/Nas -project-window-lyrics

———. 2002. Doo Rags." *The Lost Tapes* (album). Lyrics Copyright 1999, 2001, 2002 Sony Music Entertainment Inc. Rap lyrics retrieved from http://rapgenius.com/ Nas-doo-rags-lyrics

———. 2006. "Hip Hop is Dead" Hip Hop is Dead (album). Lyrics copyright 2006 The Island Def Jam Music Group and Columbia Records. Rap lyrics retrieved from http://rap.genius.com/Nas-hip-hop-is-dead-lyrics

———. 2008 "Sly Fox." *Untitled* (album). Lyrics copyright 2008 The Island Def Jam Music Group and Columbia Records. Rap lyrics retrieved from http://rapgenius .com/Nas-sly-fox-lyrics

Outkast. 2006. "Mighty O." *Idlewild* (album). Lyrics copyright 2006 LaFace Records LLC. Rap lyrics retrieved from http://rapgenius.com/Outkast-mighty-o-lyrics

Pete Seeger. 1962. "If I Had a Hammer" (single). Lyrics copyright 1998 Smithsonian Folkways

Queen Latifah 1989. "Evil That Men Do." *All Hail the Queen.* (album). Lyrics Copyright 2004 Warner Strategic Marketing. http://rapgenius.com/Queen-latifah-evil -that-men-do-lyrics

Sam Cooke. 1964. "A Change is Gonna Come" (single). Lyrics Copyright ABKCO Music & Records, Inc.

Sarafina. 1992. "Safa Seph'isizwe." *Sarafina! The Sound of Freedom* (soundtrack). Lyrics Copyright 1994 Sony Music Entertainment

Sly and the Family Stone. 1968. "Everyday People." *Stand!* (album). Lyrics Copyright 1969 Sony BMG Music Entertainment

Stevie Wonder. 1970. "Heaven Help Us All." *Signed, Sealed, and Delivered* (album). Lyrics Copyright 1970 The Motown Record Company LP

Sugarhill Gang. 1979. "Rapper's Delight." *Sugarhill Gang* (album). Lyrics Copyright 2005 Warner Strategic Marketing. Rap lyrics retrieved from http://rapgenius .com/Sugar-hill-gang-rappers-delight-lyrics

Temptations. 1970. "Ball of Confusion (That's What the World is Today)." *Greatest Hits II* (album). Lyrics Copyright 2007 Motown Records.

Too $hort. 1990. "The Ghetto." *Short Dog's in the House* (album). Lyrics Copyright 1990 Zomba Recording LLC. Rap lyrics retrieved from http://rapgenius.com/Too -short-the-ghetto-lyrics

Tupac Shakur. 1989/2000 "Panther Power." *The Lost Tapes* (album) Lyrics Copyright 2000 ZYX Music. Rap lyrics retrieved from http://rapgenius.com/2pac-panther -power-lyrics

———. 1992. "Changes." *Greatest Hits* (album). Lyrics Copyright 1998 Death Row Records/Interscope Record. Rap lyrics retrieved from http://rapgenius.com/2pac -changes-lyrics

Woody Guthrie. 1940. "This Land Is Your Land." Lyrics Copyright 1999 Smithsonian Folkways Recordings

Young Jeezy. 2011. "Trapped." *TM:103 Hustlerz Ambition* (album). Lyrics Copyright 2011 The Island Def Jam Music Group. Rap lyrics retrieved from http://rapgen ius.com/Jeezy-trapped-lyrics

Chapter 3

50 Cent. 2003. "In Da Club." *Get Rich or Die Trying* (album). Lyrics Copyright 2003 Shady Records/Aftermath Records/Interscope Records and 2003 Curtis James Jackson, WB Music Corporation, Ain't Nothing But Funkin' Music, Music of Windwept, Blotter Music, Elvis Mambo Music

Common featuring Cee-lo. 2000. "A Song for Assata." *Like Water for Chocolate* (album). Lyrics Copyright 2000 Songs of Universal, Inc., Senseless Music, Inc., Universal PolyGram International Publishing, Inc., EPHCY Publishing, Jajapo Music, Inc. and 2000 Geffen Records

Dead Prez. 2000. "Police State." *Let's Get Free* (album). Lyrics Copyright 2000 Loud Records LLC. Rap lyrics retrieved from http://rapgenius.com/Dead-prez-police -state-lyrics

———. 2000. "Hip-Hop." *Let's Get Free* (album). Lyrics Copyright 2000 Loud Records LLC

———. 2000. "Mind Sex". *Let's Get Free* (album). Lyrics Copyright 2000 Loud Records LLC

———. 2010. "Malcolm, Garvey, Huey." *Turn Off the Radio: The Mixtape Vol.4: Revolutionary but Gangsta Grills* (album).

Dj Unk. 2006. "Walk It Out." *Beat'n Down Yo Block* (album). Lyrics Copyright 2006 Koch Records

Drake. 2009. "Forever." *Relapse: Refill* (album). Lyrics Copyright 2009 Interscope Records. Rap lyrics retrieved from http://rapgenius.com/Drake-forever-lyrics

Ice Cube. 1991. "Us." *Death Certificate* (album). Lyrics Copyright 2010 Priority Records LLC.

Jadakiss. 2004. "Why." *Kiss of Death* (album). Lyrics Copyright EMI April Music, Inc., Justin Combs Publishing Company, Inc., Jae'won's Publishing, EMI Virgin Music, Ltd., Universal Music Publishing, Juvenile Hell Music and 2004 Ruff Ryders

Kendrick Lamar. 2011. "Hiii power." *Section.80* (album). Lyrics Copyright 2011 Top Dawg Entertainment. Rap Lyrics retrieved from http://rapgenius.com/Kendrick -lamar-hiiipower-lyrics

Lil Wayne. 2006. "Georgia . . . Bush." *Dedication 2: Gangsta Grillz* (album). Lyrics Copyright 2012 Firefly Entertainment

———. 2008. "Mr. Carter." *Tha Carter III* (album). Lyrics Copyright 2008 Cash Money Records Inc. Rap lyrics retrieved from http://rapgenius.com/Lil-wayne -mr-carter-lyrics

LL Cool J. 1987. "I'm Bad." *Bigger and Deffer* (album). Lyrics Copyright 1987 Def Jam Recordings

———. 1987. "I Need Love." *Bigger and Deffer* (album). Lyrics Copyright 1987 Def Jam Recordings

Linkin' Park. 2007. "What I've Done." *Minutes to Midnight* (album). Lyrics Copyright 2007 Warner Bros Records, Inc.

Lupe Fiasco. 2011. "All Black Everything." *L.A.S.E.R.S.* (album) Lyrics Copyright 2011 Atlantic Recording Corporation. Rap lyrics retrieved from http://rapgenius.com/ Lupe-fiasco-all-black-everything-lyrics

———. 2011. "Words I Never Said." *L.A.S.E.R.S.* (album) Lyrics Copyright 2011 Atlantic Recording Corporation. Rap lyrics retrieved from http://rapgenius.com/ Lupe-fiasco-words-i-never-said-lyrics

Maroon 5. 2002. "This Love." *Songs About Jane* (album). Lyrics Copyright Careers-BMG Music Publishing, Inc., February Twenty Second Music, BMG Songs, Inc. and 2007 A&M/Octone Records

Montell Jordan. 1995. "This Is How We Do It." *This Is How We Do It* (album). Lyrics Copyright 1995 Rush Associated Labels Inc.

Nas. 2001. "My Country." *Stillmatic* (album). Lyrics Copyright 2001 Sony Music Entertainment Inc.

———. 2001. "You're Da Man." *Stillmatic* (album). Lyrics Copyright 2001 Sony Music Entertainment Inc. Rap lyrics retrieved from http://rapgenius.com/Nas -youre-da-man-lyrics

———. 2001. "What Goes Around." *Stillmatic* (album). Lyrics Copyright 2001 Sony Music Entertainment Inc.

———. 2002. "Black Zombie." *The Lost Tapes* (album). Lyrics Copyright 1999, 2001, 2002 Sony Music Entertainment Inc. Rap lyrics retrieved from http://rapgenius .com/Nas-black-zombie-lyrics

Screwball. 2000. "Who Shot Rudy?" *Y2K* (album). Lyrics Copyright 2007, All Hoodz Musik. Rap lyrics retrieved from http://rapgenius.com/Screwball-who-shot -rudy-lyrics

Snoop Dogg. 1993. "Gin and Juice." *Doggystyle* (album). Lyrics Copyright 1\
Row Records

Too $hort. 1990. "The Ghetto." *Short Dog's in the House* (album). Lyrics Copy.
1990 Zomba Recording LLC. Rap lyrics retrieved from http://rapgenius.com/1\
-short-the-ghetto-lyrics

Trick Daddy. 2002. "Thug Holiday." Thug Holiday (album). Lyrics Copyright 2002
Slip-N-Slide Records, Inc. and licensed to Atlantic Recording Corporation for the
United States and WEA International Inc. for the world outside of the United
States. Rap lyrics retrieved from http://www.azlyrics.com/lyrics/trickdaddy/thug
holiday.html

Tupac Shakur. 2002. "They Don't Give a Fuck About Us." *Better Dayz* (album). Lyrics
Copyright 2002 Amaru Entertainment, Inc. under exclusive licence to Interscope
Records.

Usher. 2004. "Let It Burn" (single). Lyrics copyright 2004, EMI April Music, Inc., UR-
IV Music, Shaniah Cymone Music, Baby Boys Little Publishing Company

Vanilla Ice. 1990. "Ice Ice Baby." *Hooked* (album). Lyrics Copyright 1990, QPM Music,
Inc., Fern Hill Publishing, Ice Baby Music, Aftershock Music, Sony/ATV Songs,
LLC, Queen Music, Ltd., EMI Music Publishing, Ltd., Tintoretto Music

Wu-Tang Clan and Isaac Hayes. 2000. "I Can't Go to Sleep." *The W.* (album). Lyrics
Copyright 2000 Loud Records, Careers-BMG Music Publishing, Inc., Wu-Tang
Publishing, Isaac Hayes Publishing, Warner Chappell Music. Rap lyrics retrieved
from http://rapgenius.com/Wu-tang-clan-i-cant-go-to-sleep-lyrics

Chapter 4

2 Live Crew. 1996. "We Want Some Pussy." *2 Live Crew Is What We Are* (album).
Lyrics copyright 1996 Lil' Joe Wein Records. Rap lyrics retrieved from http://www
.azlyrics.com/lyrics/2livecrew/wewantsomepussy.html

———. 1990. "Fuck Martinez." *Banned in the USA* (album). Lyrics Copyright 1990
Lil' Joe Wein Records Inc.

———. 1997. "Face Down, Ass Up." *Banned in the USA* (album). Lyrics copyright
1997 Lil' Joe Wein Records. Rap lyrics retrieved from http://rapgenius.com/2-live
-crew-face-down-ass-up-lyrics

Angel Haze. 2012. "Cleaning Out My Closet." *Classick* (album). Rap lyrics retrieved
from http://rapgenius.com/Angel-haze-cleaning-out-my-closet-lyrics

Black Star. 1998. "Brown Skin Lady." *Black Star* (album). Lyrics copyright 2000 TVT
Music, Inc. Rap lyrics retrieved from http://ohhla.com/anonymous/blackstr/black
str/brwnskin.blk.txt

Common.1997. "Retrospect for Life." One Day It'll All Make Sense (album). Lyrics
copyright 1997 Relativity Records.

Digable Planets. 1993. "La Femme Fatale." *Reaching: A New Refutation of Time and
Space* (album). Lyrics copyright 1993 Pendulum Records. Rap lyrics retrieved from
http://rap.genius.com/Digable-planets-la-femme-fetal-lyrics.

Doug E Fresh and the Get Fresh Crew. 1999 "Abortion." *Chuck D Presents: Louder Than a Bomb* (album). Lyrics copyright 1999 Rhino Entertainment Company.

Eve. 1999. "Love Is Blind." *Let There Be Eve . . . Ruff Ryder's First Lady* (album). Lyrics copyright 1999 Dead Game Publishing, Solideas Songs, Songs of Windswept, Universal Music Corporation, Blondie Rockwell, Swizz Beats Rap lyrics retrieved from http://ohhla.com/anonymous/eve/firstldy/is_blind.eve.txt.

Flypside. 2005. "Happy Birthday." *We the People* (album). Lyrics copyright 2005 Interscope Records.

Geto Boys. 1992. "The Unseen." *Uncut Dope* (album). Lyrics copyright 1992 N-the Water Publishing, Inc.

Goodie Mob. 1998. "Beautiful Skin." *Still Standing* (album). Lyrics Copyright 1998 Goodie Mo'-B Music, Inc., C' Amore Music, and 1998 LaFace Records LLC. Rap lyrics

J. Cole. "Lost Ones." *Cole World: the Sideline Story* (album). Lyrics copyright 2012 Jermaine A. Cole.

Jean Grae. 2008. "My Story." *Jeanius* (album). Lyrics copyright 2008 Blacksmith Music Corporation.

Kendrick Lamar. 2011. "Keisha's Song." *Section.80* (album). Lyrics copyright 2011 Top Dawg Music, Hard Working Black Folks Inc., WB Music Corp Rap lyrics retrieved from http://ohhla.com/anonymous/kenlamar/section8/keishas.ken.txt

Lauryn Hill. 1998. "To Zion." *The Miseducation of Lauryn Hill* (album). Lyrics copyright 1998 Irving Music, Inc., Jenelle Rene Music, Sony/ATV Tunes, LLC & Obverse Creation Music

Lil Kim. 1996. "Big Momma Thang." *Hardcore* (album). Lyrics copyright 1998 EMI Blackwood Music, Inc., Lil Lulu Publishing, Sequins at Noon Music, Undeas Music, Inc., Warner Chappell, Reed Richards Music. Rap lyrics retrieved from http://ohhla.com/anonymous/lil_kim/hardcore/bigmomma.kim.txt

Lord Jamar. 2006. "Supreme Mathematics." *The 5% Album* (album). Lyrics copyright 2006 Babygrade Records, Inc. Rap lyrics retrieved from http://rap.genius.com/Lord-jamar-supreme-mathematics-knowledge-mix-lyrics

Ludacris. 2006. "Runaway Love." *Release Therapy* (album). Lyrics copyright 2006 Universal Music Corporation, Ludacris Universal Publ., Keriokey Music, songs of Universal, Inc., Slick Rick Music Corporation, Entertaining Music

———. 2008. "Politics as Usual." The Preview. (album). Lyrics copyright 2008 Aphilliates Music Group.

Lupe Fiasco. 2012. "Bitch Bad." *Food & Liquor II: The Great American Rap Album Pt. 1* (album). Lyrics copyright 2012 Atlantic Recording Corporation. Rap lyrics retrieved from http://ohhla.com/anonymous/l_fiasco/fliquor2/bitchbad.lup.txt

Nelly. 2003. "Tip Drill." *Da Derrty Versions—The Reinvention* (album). Lyrics copyright 2003 Universal Records, a division of UMG Recordings, Inc.

Nick Cannon. 2005. "Can I Live?" (single). Lyrics copyright 2005 Jive Records.

Nicki Minaj. 2008. "Autobiography." *Sucka Free* (album).

Organized Konfusion. 1997. "Invetro." *Equinox* (album). Lyrics copyright 1997 BMG Songs, Inc., Still Diggin Music Inc, Ombifarious Music.

Public Enemy. 1988. "She Watch Channel Zero?!" *It Takes a Nation of Millions to Hold Us Back* (album). Lyrics copyright 1988 Def American Songs, Inc. Rap lyrics retrieved from http://ohhla.com/anonymous/pb_enemy/nation/shewatch.pbe.txt

Queen Latifah. 1993. "U.N.I.T.Y." Black Reign (album). Lyrics copyright 1993 Motown Record Company. Rap lyrics retrieved from http://rap.genius.com/ Queen-latifah-unity-lyrics

Remy Ma. 2006. "What's Going On." *There's Something About Remy: Based on a True Story* (album). Lyrics copyright 2006 Universal Records, a Division of UMG Recordings, Inc. Rap lyrics retrieved from http://rapgenius.com/Remy-ma-whats -going-on-lyrics

Tech N9ne. 2001. "Real Killer." *Anghellic* (album). Lyrics copyright 2001 Alex Marlowe, Music of Windswept, QDIII Soundlab, E.G.N. Arts Musick All City Music.

Tiye Pheonix. 2009. "Half Woman, Half Amazin'." *Half Woman, Half Amazin'* (album). Lyrics copyright 2009 Babygrande Records Inc.

Tupac Shakur. 1991. "Brenda's Got a Baby." *2Pacalypse* (album). Lyrics copyright 1999 Zomba Songs, Inc., GLG Two Music (division of TNT Records, Inc.), Ghetto Gospel Music.

————. 1993. "Keep Ya Head Up." *Strictly for My N.I.G.G.A.Z.* (album). Lyrics copyright 1993 Warner-Tamerlane Publishing, Ghetto Gospel Music, Interscope Pearl Music, EMI Unart Music, Inc., Kama Sutra Music, Inc., Frantino Music, Rubberband Music & GLG Two Music. Rap lyrics retrieved from http://ohhla.com/anony mous/2_pac/str_4_my/keep_ya.2pc.txt.

Chapter 5

5th Ward Weebie. 2005. "Fuck Katrina (Katrina Song)" (single). Anquette. 1988. "Janet Reno." *Respect* (album). Lyrics copyright 1990 Global Satellite.

Big Boi. 2008. "Sumthin's Gotta Give (featuring. Mary J. Blige)" (single). Lyrics copyright 2008 Laface Records. Rap lyrics retrieved from http://www.azlyrics.com/ lyrics/bigboi/sumthinsgottagive.html

Dr. Dre. 1992. "The Day the Niggaz Took Over." *The Chronic* (Album). Lyrics copyright 1992 Interscope Records.

GdotO. "Trayvon Martin—Skittles & Arizona Iced Tea" (single).

Grandmaster Melle Mel. 1984. "Jesse." (single). Lyrics copyright 1984 Sugar Hill Records LTD.

Ice Cube. 1992. "We Had to Tear This Motherfucker Up." *The Predator* (album). Lyrics copyright 1992 Priority Records, Inc.

Ice T. 1992 "Cop Killer." *Body Count* (album). Lyrics copyright 1992 Polygram International Publishing, Inc., Ernkneesea Music & Rhyme Syndicate Music

Jasiri X. 2012. "I am Troy Davis (T.R.O.Y.)." *#TheWholeWorldIsWatching* (album).

————. 2012. "Trayvon" (single). Jay Electronica. 2009. "When the Levees Broke (Katrina)." *What the F*ck Is A Jay Electronica* (album). Lyrics copyright 2011 WeDoItRight.

Jay-Z. 2003. "99 Problems." *The Black Album* (album). Lyrics Copyright 2004 BMG Songs, Inc., Careers-BMG Music Publishing, Inc., Spirit Two Music, Inc. Rap lyrics retrieved from http://ohhla.com/anonymous/jigga/theblack/99_probs.jyz.txt

————. 2006. "Minority Report." *Kingdom Come* (album). Lyrics copyright 2006 Carter Boys Publishing, Ain't Nuthin' Goin' On But Fu-kin', Bat Future Music, Super Saying Publishing.

Lil Wayne. 2008. "Tie My Hands." *Tha Carter III* (album). Lyrics copyright 2008 Young Money Publishing, Inc. & Warner-Tamerlane Publishing Corp., I Like 'Em Thicke Music, Da' Gass Co.

Low Key. 2010. "Obama Nation." *Soundtrack to the Struggle* (album). Lyrics Copyright 2011 Mesopotamia Music.

————. 2011. "Obama Nation (Part 2)." *Soundtrack to the Struggle* (album). Lyrics Copyright 2011 Mesopotamia Music.

Ludacris. 2001. "Area Codes." *Word of Mouf* (album). Lyrics copyright 2001 EMI April Music, Inc., Ludacris Music Publishing, Inc., Nate Dogg Music, Bridgeport Music, Inc., Phalon Alexander. Rap lyrics retrieved from http://ohhla.com/anony mous/ludacris/wordmouf/areacode.crs.txt

————. 2008. "Politics as Usual." *The Preview* (album). Rap lyrics retrieved from http://rap.genius.com/Ludacris-politics-obama-is-here-lyrics

Lupe Fiasco. 2011. "Words I Never Said." *L.A.S.E.R.S.* (album) Lyrics copyright 2011 Atlantic Recording Corporation for the United States and WEA International Inc. for the world outside of the United States. Rap lyrics retrieved from http://www.ohhla.com/anonymous/l_fiasco/lasers/words_i.lup.txt

Mistah Fab. 2012. "God Don't Love Me (RIP Trayvon Martin)" (single)

Mos Def. 2006. "Dollar Day" *True Magic* (album). Lyrics copyright 2006 Geffen Records. Rap lyrics retrieved from http://ohhla.com/anonymous/mos_def/magic/dollar.mos.txt

Nas. 2001. "My Country." *Stillmatic* (album). Lyrics copyright 2001 Sony Music Entertainment Inc. Rap lyrics retrieved from http://ohhla.com/anonymous/nas/still/country.nas.txt

————. 2002. "Made You Look." *God's Son* (album). Lyrics copyright 2002 EMI April Music, Inc., Salaam Remi Music, Inc., Ill Will, Inc., Regent Music Corporation.

————. 2008. "Black President." *Nas* (album). Lyrics copyright 2008 R2M Music, Songs Of Universal, Inc, Lawhouse Music, Ruffnix B Here Music, Universal Music-Z Tunes, EMI-Blackwood Music, Damn Self Music / HRH Music, and Songs of Lastrada, Sony Music Entertainment.

Nick Cannon. 2012. "Die Young" (single). NCredible Music.

Ol' Dirty Bastard. 1995. "Shimmy Shimmy Ya." *Return to the 36 Chambers: the Dirty Version* (album). Lyrics copyright 1995 Careers-BMG Music Publishing, Inc. Ramecca Publishing and Russell Jones.

Outkast. 1994. "Git Up, Git Out." *Southernplayalisticadillacmuzik* (album). Lyrics copyright 1994. Chrysalis Music, Gnat Booty Music, Goddie Mo-B Music, Organized Noize Music, Stiff Shirt Music, Inc. Rap lyrics retrieved from http://ohhla.com/anonymous/outkast/southern/git_up.otk.txt

Pete Rock and CL Smooth.1992. "They Reminisce over You (T.R.O.Y.)." *Mecca and the Soul Brother* (album). Lyrics copyright 1992 Reach Global, Inc. Pete Rock Publishing, Smooth Flowing Publishing.

Plies. 2012. "We Are Trayvon" (single). Lyrics copyright 2012 Slip-N-Slide Records, Inc. exclusively licensed to Atlantic Recording Corporation for the United States and WEA International Inc. for the world outside of the United States.

Public Enemy. 2005 "Hell No (We Ain't Alright)." *Rebirth of a Nation* (album). 2006 Guerrilla Funk Recordings.

———. 1991. "By the Time I get to Arizona." *Apocalypse 91* (album). Lyrics copyright 1991 Sony Music Entertainment, Inc.

Razah featuring Papoose. "Mother Nature (Tribute to Hurricane Katrina Victims)." *The New R in R&B* (album). Lyrics Copyright Toy's Factory Records.

Reef the Lost Cauze. 2012. "They Prey (For Trayvon & my Son)" (single).

STV. 1989. "Self Destruction" (single). Lyrics copyright 1989 Jive Records.

Talib Kweli. 2010. "Papers Please" (single). Lyrics copyright 2012 Ontrak Entertainment. West Coast Rap All-Stars. 1990. "We're All in the Same Gang" (single). Lyrics copyright 1990 Warner Bros. Records.

Will.I.Am.2008. "Yes We Can" (single). Lyrics copyright 2008 Hidden Beach Records.

Wyclef Jean. 2012. "Justice (if You're 17)" (single).

Yasiin Bey, Dead Prez, MikeFlo. 2013. "Made You Die" (single). Rap lyrics retrieved from http://rapgenius.com/Dead-prez-made-you-die-trayvon-martin-tribute-lyrics

Young Jeezy. 2008. "My President" *The Recession* (album). Lyrics copyright 2008 The Island Def Jam Music Group, A Div. of UMG Recordings, Inc. Rap lyrics retrieved from http://ohhla.com/anonymous/yngjeezy/recess/my_pres.jzy.txt

Conclusion

El General. 2011. "Head of State" (single). Rap lyrics retrieved from http://hiphopdiplomacy.org/2011/01/31/the-rap-that-sparked-a-revolution-el-general-tunisia/

Jay-Z. 2003. "99 Problems." *The Black Album* (album). Lyrics Copyright 2004 BMG Songs, Inc., Careers-BMG Music Publishing, Inc., Spirit Two Music, Inc. Rap lyrics retrieved from http://ohhla.com/anonymous/jigga/theblack/99_probs.jyz.txt

Jay-Z featuring Eminem. 2001. "Renegade." *The Blueprint* (album). Lyrics copyright 2001 Roc-A-Fella Records, LLC. Rap lyrics retrieved from http://rapgenius.com/Jay-z-renegade-lyrics

Lil Brothers. 2005. "Lovin' it." *The Ministrel Show* (album). Lyrics copright Atlantic Records Inc. for the United States and WEA International Inc. for the world outside of the United States.

Lupe Fiasco. 2006. "Dumb it Down." *The Cool* (album). Lyrics Copyright 2006 Atlantic Recordd Inc for the United States and WEA International Inc. for the world outside the United States. Rap lyrics retrieved from http://rap.genius .com/Lupe-fiasco-dumb-it-down-lyrics

Nas. 1999. "I Want to Talk to You." *I Am* (album). Lyrics copyright 1999 Zomba Enterprises Inc., Ill Will Music, Inc., Alvin West & Mawkeen's Music, Inc.

Nicki Minaj. 2010. "A Moment 4 Life." *Pink Friday* (album). Lyrics copyright 2010 Cash Money Records. Inc.

Index

"La Femme Fetal" (Digable Planets), 86–87

Fiasco, Lupe, 60, 63–64, 93–94, 133, 137, 140, 145–46

Five Percenters, 56, 60, 95–96; numerology, 96. *See also* Nation of Gods and Earths (NOG&E)

Flavor Flav, 97–98. *See also* Public Enemy

Flypside, 86

"Forever" (Drake), 60

Fox News, 31, 51

Fuentes, Julio, 120

gangster rap, 22; "gangsta" rap, 23, 120–21, 149

Garvey, Marcus, 18–19, 51, 55, 60–64. *See also* Universal Negro Improvement Association (UNIA)

"Georgia . . . Bush" (Lil Wayne), 24, 69–70

Geto Boyz, 86, 120

"Get Up, Get Out" (Outkast), 128

"The Ghetto" (Too $hort), 43–44, 58–59

Goodie Mob, 27, 45, 61, 182n7

Grae, Jean, 80, 86–88

Grandmaster Flash, 39, 41–42; and Furious Five, 43–44. *See also* Sugarhill Gang

Grant, Oscar, 111, 117

Giuliani, Rudy, 57

H. "Rap" Brown, 39, 148–49. *See also* Al-Amin, Jamil Abdullah

Haitian earthquake, 138–42, 147

Harris-Lacewell, Melissa, 1, 4–5, 13–14, 20–22, 67, 74, 75, 88, 99–100, 151, 182n3. *See also* Harris-Perry, Melissa

Harris-Perry, Melissa, 88. *See also* Harris-Lacewell, Melissa

Haze, Angel, 84–85

"Hiii Power" (Kendrick Lamar), 64

Hill-Collins, Patricia, 51, 79, 90, 140

Hill, Lauryn, 1, 6, 80, 101, 182n11

Hip-Hop Caucus (HHC), 112, 117–18, 119, 128

"Hip-Hop cops," 106, 183n1. *See also* COINTELPRO

Hip-Hop Feminism, 81–82. *See also* Durham, Aisha; Morgan, Joan

Hip-Hop generation, 7–11, 66, 113–16, 119, 130, 181n11

"Hip Hop Is Dead" (Nas), 48–49

Hip-Hop Summit Action Network (HSAN), 112–17, 118–19, 137, What We Want statement, 171–72

Holiday, Billie, 7, 34

Hottentot Venus (Sartjie Baartman, Sara Baartman), 89, 182n6

Hoover, J. Edgar, 106. *See also* COINTELPRO

Hughes, Langston, 30, 33–34, 178n2

Hurricane Katrina, 6–8, 24, 69, 104–5, 111, 117, 135–36, 147. *See also* New Orleans

hypermasculinity, 76–77, 85, 95, 144

"I Can't Go to Sleep" (Wu-Tang Clan), 17, 59–60

Ice Cube, 71, 97–98, 120, 122, 131–32

Ice T, 11

Immortal Technique, 111, 133, 142

Imus, Don, 75

"I Want to Talk to You" (Nas), 26, 141

J. Cole, 86

Jackson, Jesse, 18–19, 39, 65, 138

Jacobs, Harriet, 83, 179n6

Jadakiss, 51–52

Jasiri X, 124, 127

Jay Electronica, 105

Jay-Z, 15–16, 49–50, 60, 61, 105, 114, 122, 128, 129, 131–34, 140, 144–46, 180nn12, 6, 184n3

"Jena 6," 111, 122–23

Jezebel, 38, 79, 83, 88, 115

Jim Crow, 36, 106–7

"Keep Ya Head Up" (Tupac), 92

Kennedy, John F. (JFK), 18–19. *See also* civil rights

Acknowledgments

This book is the result of a lot of hard work and research and many revisions. I discussed it with anyone who would listen, often staying up late to share my views and visions. Lorenzo Bailey, I am truly grateful to you for supporting me through the writing of this book. You debated with me on ideas and analysis, you encouraged me when I just wanted to quit, and you loved me throughout. I would also like to thank my daughters, Jahzari and Imani. I know sometimes it felt like mommy's computer was attached to her hands. I apologize for the times this project took me away from you. I love you and I am so grateful for your love, your smiles, your hugs and your eyes.

Of course, absolutely none of this would have been possible without the love and support of my family. Thank you for being there for me and always supporting me. I have the best family in the world! Thank you mom, Frances Bonnette, for everything! Mother, you are my best friend in the entire world. I love you with all my heart. You are the strong, caring, sophisticated, intelligent, mother, friend and woman I strive to be. Thank you for listening and talking to me. You provided a shoulder at times when crying was necessary, shelter when I was without one, will-power, encouragement, and motivation. I love you mommy! Thanks for everything. To my dear sister, girl, you kept me laughing! Thank you! Thanks for keeping me updated with music and for the late night conversations when no one else was up. I am glad that you always have my front and my back. I value your opinion, insight and knowledge. You are very special. I love you Tiffany Wallington! Barney Allen, thank you for all that you have done for me over the years. Anytime I need you, you are there. I also would like to thank Terence Wallington for his (silent) support (lol).

There were a number of colleagues who helped by providing comments, reading various versions of this book, supporting my research and ideas and encouraging me to continue pursuing this career. Many of you fall into various categories so I will list you here in no particular order. Thank you, William E. Nelson, Jr., Harwood McClerking, Thomas E. Nelson, Randy Burnside, Angela Lewis, Julia Jordan-Zachery, Niambi Carter, Melanye Price, Ravi Perry, Andrea Simpson, Byron D'Andra Orey, Nikol Floyd-Alexander, Chryl Laird, and Nadia Brown. To the late William E. Nelson, thank you for all the encouragement, editing, and sheer belief in me, you do not know how grateful I am to have met you and worked with you. You will definitely be missed, Dr. Nelson! You are a great scholar and mentor. Wendy G. Smooth, thank you for listening and talking about everything from life, scholarship, and the profession. You are a great mentor and friend. My tenure at the Ohio State University would have not been successful without your help, motivation, dedication, and encouragement. Harwood McClerking, thank you for taking the time to mentor us and making sure we understood how to survive. Thanks for being supportive and informative! I really appreciate all your hard work and time, never forget that.

Adolphus Belk, thank you for your support and encouragement. You believed in me from the time I met you and it was really needed. Thank you for being my friend all these years and for checking up on me and reading my work and inviting me to share my work. It is very rare to meet sincere people and I am glad that I met you. You are very much appreciated! Karen Kedrowski, Michael Lipscomb and Jennifer Disney, my Winthrop family, none of this would have been possible without your belief and encouragement. You transformed a student interested in becoming a medical doctor to an analytical scholar interested in understanding the inner workings of the political system. You supported me, not only through undergraduate and graduate school but also through my employment process and still to this day. You three introduced me to politics and made me fall in love with the subject. Thank you for inviting me to discuss my research and believing that I had something to say. I thank you for continuing to support me and think so highly of me. You have no idea how much it matters. Thank you.

Similarly, I would like to thank Benedict College for allowing me to conduct an experiment on their campus. Thank you to Ralph Bunche Summer Institute (RBSI) and Paula McClain for giving me the opportunity to start my venture as a political scientist. The RBSI is one of the best opportunities in the discipline. I would also like to thank my institution, Georgia

State University family for your support of my research and teaching. Particularly, thank you to Kim Reimann for your mentorship and to Sarah Gershon, Jeffrey Lazarus and Dan Franklin for reading various versions of this book and my articles. Thank you, Akinyele Umoja, Charles Jones, Jonathan Gayles and Sarita Davis, for your support, encouragement and inclusion. You have definitely made GSU home! To my research assistants, Tiffani Ellison, Ishmael Abdus-Saboor, Lael Abdus-Saboor, James McLawhorn, Alexandra Pauley, Stefan Martinez, Jeffrey Glas and Craig Pitts, thanks for your efforts and time assisting me! Chryl Laird, your support was insurmountable. Thank you very much!

I cannot forget my outside family who held me down throughout my career. To the lovely ladies of the Xi Beta Chapter of Delta Sigma Theta and particularly those undeniably Chosen 43, thank you sorors for all you have done and continue to do! Oo-oop! Thank you Safiya Tate, Leslie Evans, Titilayo Dillard, Eunika Simons and Kristen Dawson. Ish Abdus-Saboor and James Prince thank you for editing my papers on short notice, listening to my thoughts, dreams and ideas. I am so glad that you are in my life and I would not know what to do without you.

Finally, a special shout-out to Melissa Harris-Perry, Mark Anthony Neal, Richard Iton, Charles Henry, Lester Spence, Michael Dawson, Tricia Rose, Imani Perry, Gwendolyn Pough and Cathy Cohen for paving the way in researching important topics related to the Black experience and focusing on culture, rap music youth, ideology and political attitudes. I would like to thank all of those scholars who paved the way to allow me write and study political science. If I left anyone out I apologize. I have been blessed to have supportive people in my life. I hope I have done justice to the topic addressed in this book.

9 780812 224283